Best Rail Trails
PACIFIC NORTHWEST

MORE THAN 60 RAIL TRAILS IN WASHINGTON, OREGON, AND IDAHO

NATALIE L. BARTLEY

FALCONGUIDES ®

GUILFORD, CONNECTICUT
HELENA, MONTANA
AN IMPRINT OF THE GLOBE PEQUOT PRESS

FALCONGUIDES®

Copyright © 2001, 2009 by Morris Book Publishing, LLC

Photos: Mia Angela Barbera except where noted

Text design: Sheryl P. Kober
Maps: Tim Kissel/Trailhead Graphics, Inc. © Morris Book Publishing, LLC

Library of Congress Cataloging-in-Publication Data
Bartley, Natalie L.
  Best rail trails. Pacific Northwest : more than 60 rail trails in Washington, Oregon,
    and Idaho / Natalie L. Bartley.
    p. cm.
  ISBN 978-0-7627-4607-1
  1. Rail-trails—Northwest, Pacific—Guidebooks. 2. Outdoor recreation—Northwest, Pacific—
    Guidebooks. 3. Northwest, Pacific—Guidebooks. I. Title. II. Title: Pacific Northwest.

  GV191.42.N75B37 2008082
  917.97--dc22
                              2008031358

Printed in the United States of America
10 9 8 7 6 5 4 3 2 1

CONTENTS

ACKNOWLEDGMENTS

Hundreds of heartfelt thanks go to dozens of people who willingly gave their time to bring this book to reality. Trail managers in all three states unselfishly agreed to discuss and review details regarding their trails, putting aside their own deadlines to do so. Bicycle shop owners, nonprofit trail support organizers, and chambers of commerce also expanded on local details. Family, friends, and my editors were incredibly understanding and supportive in the process.

A special thanks goes to Leo Hennessy, nonmotorized trail coordinator for the Idaho Department of Parks and Recreation; Mike Beiser, Steve Mims, and Nick Fuller of the University of Idaho Outdoor Program; John Kolbe, co-owner of Pedal Pushers Bike Rental & Repair; Shirley and John Atteberry of the Friends of the Weiser River Trail; my friends and family Katja and Mark Casson, Erin Ferguson, Dave Lindsay, and Nora Bartley; and my editors Bill Schneider and Russ Schneider.

Lastly, kudos to Mia Barbera, the author of the first Pacific Northwest rail trails edition about Washington and Oregon trails. It was a pleasure to retrace her prior work, making minor changes to the information about the emerging network of rail trails in the Pacific Northwest as I followed her lead while adding the Idaho trails.

INTRODUCTION

The rail trails of Washington, Oregon, and Idaho provide scenic refuge, education, history, play, and body-beating adventure. Pick your trails and enjoy the surrounding cities, towns, and landscapes.

The trails described in these pages range from a 12-foot-wide paved path to a narrow, rugged, dirt single-track. You'll look out over an unobstructed view of the Columbia River, up to surrounding desert canyon walls, ahead through dense evergreen forest, or down upon neighborhood homes. Skaters, cyclists, equestrians, anglers, walkers, runners, skiers, snowshoers, and strollers join together to get fit, get relaxed, get together, or get to work in these linear parks. The trails skirt wineries, dams, cultural centers, waterfalls, old mines, rivers, lakes, fine dining, breweries, and the ocean.

McClellan Butte forms a scenic backdrop for cyclists on the John Wayne Pioneer Trail.

A Bit of Pacific Northwest Rail History

The Pacific Northwest is separated east from west by the Cascade Mountains. Agriculture built the east, where you'll find distinct seasons and striking rock formations. Logging dominated the temperate western side, which features lush forests and interesting urban centers.

Before the railroad reached them, Washington, Oregon, and Idaho were islands, their geographic isolation restricting trade. The story of how the railroad got here fills volumes. Territorial and financial politics, bankruptcy, buyouts, personal glory, personal breakdown, and financial maneuvering paint as chaotic and colorful a picture as you'll find in any chunk of history.

Simply getting to the mountain passes in winter to scope out a railroad route left engineers fighting for their lives. Even after the tracks were built, traveling over passes, below rock cliffs, above rivers, and through tunnels put rail passengers at risk of smoke asphyxiation and avalanches of snow and rock. In fact, the worst disaster in railroad history played out on Stevens Pass in 1910. A heavy snowstorm stopped one train on the tracks. After the frightened passengers watched rockslides and collapsing trees for eight days, an avalanche shoved the railcars off the track into the valley below. Ninety-six people lost their lives.

In 1850 railroads were experimental; few lines in the country were more than 150 miles long. In 1851 the first tracks were set down in the Pacific Northwest—a crude 6-mile portage line built alongside the Cascades Rapids on the Washington side of the Columbia River. The train was not powered by an engine; instead, the flatcars were hauled by mules. The first steam train arrived in 1862. By 1863, 19 miles of track had been laid in Oregon and 6 in Washington, all beside the Columbia River. Because the rapids were impassable by steamboats on this important inland water route, railroad portages picked up each load and dropped it off at a ship on the other side of the turbulent waters. The next set of tracks was built over the next decade to serve the agricultural Willamette Valley in Oregon.

Meanwhile, in Idaho railroad service first arrived in 1874 in the southeastern part of the state. Another boost to service in the Pacific Northwest was the completion of the Oregon Short Line across southern Idaho in 1884. Known as an outlet for the Union Pacific Railroad, it went through the Snake River Valley in Idaho and on to Portland, Oregon.

The Umatilla County Lewis and Clark Commemorative Trail follows the rugged banks of the Columbia River in Oregon.

In 1883 the first tracks reached the Pacific Northwest from the East; the dream of reaching the Pacific Coast had started decades earlier, however. In 1864 the U.S. Congress authorized the largest land grant in American history: A 60-million-acre swath the size of New England, extending from Lake Superior to the Pacific Ocean, was given to the Northern Pacific Railway. Even when you subtract the land that the company forfeited by failing to meet deadlines, Northern Pacific netted 39 million acres from this deal—twice the size of any other railroad grant. As a result, when many railroads consolidated into the Burlington Northern Railroad in 1970, this company became one of the largest private landholders in the country.

Northern Pacific's land grant provided it with timber to build tracks and cash from land sales. Land sales adjacent to the railroad path served another purpose. While eastern railroads were built between existing towns and transportation centers, this line would—in the words of one cynic—"have to generate passengers and freight revenue by running from nowhere in particular to nowhere at all, through thousands of miles of rugged and lightly populated country." The railroads of the West, in other words, would have to foster development. The area had no investors or capital; only the federal government could finance this project. The railroad would have to build the need for trains.

Due to financial problems, the Oregon Railway and Navigation Company (ORN) reached Portland from the East before the Northern Pacific route to Tacoma became a reality. In 1883 the owner of the ORN, Henry Villard, purchased the Northern Pacific to extend the ORN tracks east from the Columbia Gorge. He consolidated the two railroad companies to build the first railroad to connect the Midwest with the Pacific Northwest. Northern Pacific tracks had reached Tacoma from Portland years before, completing a route to Washington State. Only when threatened by a Seattle businessman's plan to build a line to the lucrative agricultural valleys of the Palouse and Walla Walla did Henry Villard extend his railroad up through the Yakima Valley, over Stampede Pass and into Tacoma. In 1893 the Northern Pacific went bankrupt, and in January of that year the next transcontinental line reached over Stevens Pass and into Seattle.

The railroad did build the need for trains. Wherever a depot sprouted, so did a post office and a population. Between 1887 and 1889, 95,000 newcomers arrived in Washington, a number of people equal to the residents of the territory in 1880. Seattle's population grew from 3,533 in 1880 to 42,837 in 1890. Tacoma went from 1,098 to 36,006. Many towns along the railroad line in rural Washington had a larger population than they have today.

In northern Idaho, mining and timber communities benefited from the full-scale effort ultimately known as the Milwaukee Road. About 2,300 miles of railroad went through five significant mountain ranges, including Idaho's Bitterroot Range and the Pacific Northwest's Cascade Range. The rails were built in an unusually rapid time span—just three years. Construction began in 1906, with the route open for passenger service the entire way to Seattle by 1909.

The Milwaukee Road, known in 1909 as the Chicago, Milwaukee & St. Paul Railway, was the third set of tracks to hit Seattle. It did not make instant railroad history when it arrived in the Pacific Northwest, as the first two lines had. A more significant event came in 1917, however, when the Milwaukee Road became the first electrified transcontinental railroad and the nation's longest electrified train. Travel became easier, faster, cheaper, and safer. Not only did the electrical system help clear smoke from railway tunnels, but trains braking while heading downhill regenerated power back into the overhead catenary wires—thereby powering the uphill trains. The electric railroad was so well designed that it operated from 1917 into the 1970s with few problems.

Trains of the Pacific Northwest carried passengers to a weekend at the shore, or on an elegant ride from town to town. The Union Pacific Railroad established the Sun Valley Resort in Idaho in 1936, creating the first ski lift–assisted resort in the world that still serves as a famous, internationally known full-season resort. Trains carried skiers from California to Idaho for ski holidays. Trains laden with logs climbed switchbacks to reach the mills or ships departing for the Orient. Coal cars ran to the bunkers on Puget Sound to ship their load to San Francisco. Produce from the fertile soils of the Palouse, Walla Walla, and Willamette Valleys, as well as southeastern King County, rolled through farmland to warehouses and on to the cities.

Today these same railbeds allow you to journey for days through neighborhoods and on isolated pathways, resting at hotels, bed-and-breakfasts, or campsites. You'll see the farmland, the mines, and the trees that built the Pacific Northwest once the rail lines freed the area from geographic isolation. The trails now free us to see our communities, our industries, and our neighbors' way of life—traveling from town to town, desert to mountains, city to sea; beside huge rivers, forest streams, urban lakes, Puget Sound, and the Pacific Ocean. Stay the weekend or spend a week on these trails, enjoying the culture and beauty of the Pacific Northwest.

Benefits of Rail Trails

Railbeds are an ideal location for trails. They come in all sizes, surfaces, and steepnesses. The paths of main lines are quite flat with wide, rounded turns, allowing them to safely accommodate equestrians, beginner skaters and cyclists, cross-country skiers, snowshoers, and families. Main lines rarely exceed a 2 percent grade, even on mountain switchbacks. Logging lines occasionally offer steeper grades for a challenging mountain bike ride or a great workout on foot.

Rail trails provide an ideal transportation corridor for commuters. Many lie in the path of local industry or run from rural areas to city centers. They often link to bus routes and highways. Get creative. Take a bus

Biking the Big Brother and Little Brother trestles of the King County Interurban Trail.

halfway to work and ride or walk the rest of the route, or bus to work and bicycle home. Try a rail trail on the Cascade Bicycle Club's Seattle Bike to Work Day and get free snacks and souvenirs as a bonus.

Much like the logging roads of the Pacific Northwest, however, rail trails also frequently abandon streets and highways for a more remote experience. They're parks that go somewhere. They expose us to our neighbors, to diverse lifestyles and commercial areas, to rural diners and waterfront restaurants, and, of course, past many espresso stands. They bring our communities closer together and provide the best of tourist opportunities.

Locals along the rail trails of Washington, Oregon, and Idaho claim that they became more active after the trails were built. One lovely young woman from Algona, Washington, reported, "I lost weight after my baby was born by walking this trail every day." Her friend added, enthusiastically, "Did you know this used to be a railroad line?" Such conversations with strangers rarely happen on the streets. They're common on the trails.

One of the great joys of train travel lies in the route—one moment you're in the middle of the city, and the next you're in a remote region of beauty. That we can now enjoy such experiences on a rail trail is noth-

This waterfall can be seen near the Red Town Trailhead on the Coal Creek Park Trail.

ing less than a gift from the railroad companies and our cities, counties, states, the federal government, community advocates, and Rails-to-Trails Conservancy.

The History of Rails-to-Trails Conservancy

As road construction and increased reliance on cars forced railroads to the sidelines, the question arose: What to do with all the abandoned tracks that crisscrossed the states?

Enter Rails-to-Trails Conservancy, an environmental group that since 1986 has campaigned to convert the railroad tracks to nature paths.

The beauty of Rails-to-Trails Conservancy (RTC) is that by converting the railroad rights-of-way to public use, it has not only preserved a part of our nation's history, but allows a variety of outdoor enthusiasts to enjoy the paths and trails.

Bicyclists, in-line skaters, nature lovers, hikers, equestrians, and cross-country skiers can enjoy rail trails, as can railroad history buffs. There is truly something for everyone on these trails, many of which are also wheelchair accessible.

The concept of preserving these valuable corridors and converting them into multiuse public trails began in the Midwest, where railroad abandonments were most widespread. Once the tracks came out, people started using the corridors for walking and hiking while exploring the railroad relics that were left along the railbeds, including train stations, mills, trestles, bridges, and tunnels.

Although it was easy to convince people that the rails-to-trails concept was worthwhile, the reality of actually converting abandoned railroad corridors into public trails proved a great challenge. From the late 1960s until the early 1980s, many rail trail efforts failed as corridors were lost to development, sold to the highest bidder, or broken into many pieces.

In 1983 Congress enacted an amendment to the National Trails System Act directing the Interstate Commerce Commission to allow about-to-be-abandoned railroad lines to be "railbanked," or set aside for future transportation use while being used as trails in the interim. In essence this law preempts rail corridor abandonment, keeping the corridors intact as trails or for other transportation uses into the future.

This powerful new piece of legislation made it easier for public and private agencies and organizations to acquire rail corridors for trails, but many projects still failed because of short deadlines, lack of information, and local opposition.

In 1986 Rails-to-Trails Conservancy was formed to provide a national voice for the creation of rail trails. RTC quickly developed a strategy that was designed to preserve the largest amount of rail corridor in the shortest period of time. A national advocacy program was formed to defend the new railbanking law in the courts and in Congress; this was coupled with a direct project-assistance program to help public agencies and local rail trail groups overcome the challenges of converting a rail into a trail.

The strategy is working. In 1986 Rails-to-Trails Conservancy knew of only seventy-five rail trails in the United States and ninety projects in the works. Today there are more than 1,100 rail trails on the ground and many more projects under way. The RTC vision of creating an interconnected network of trails across the country is becoming a reality.

The thriving rails-to-trails movement has created more than 11,000 miles of public trails for a wide range of users. People across the country are now realizing the incredible benefits of the rail trails.

How to Get Involved

If you really enjoy rail trails, there are opportunities to join the movement to save abandoned rail corridors and to create more trails. Donating even a small amount of your time can help get more trails up and going. Here are some ways you can help the effort:

- Write a letter to your city, county, or state elected official in favor of pro-trail legislation. You can also write a letter to the editor of your local newspaper highlighting a trail or trail project.

- Attend a public hearing to voice support for a local trail.

- Volunteer to plant flowers or trees along an existing trail or to spend several hours helping a cleanup crew on a nearby rail trail project.

- Lead a hike along an abandoned corridor with your friends or a community group.

- Become an active member of Rails-to-Trails Conservancy and a trail effort in your area. Many groups host trail events, undertake fundraising campaigns, publish brochures and newsletters, and carry out other activities to promote a trail or project. Virtually all of these efforts are organized and staffed by volunteers, and there is always room for another helping hand.

Whatever your time allows, get involved. The success of a community's rail trail depends on the level of citizen participation. Rails-to-Trails Conservancy enjoys local and national support. By joining RTC, you will get discounts on all of its publications and merchandise while supporting the largest national trails organization in the United States.

How to Use Rail Trails

By design, rail trails accommodate a variety of trail users. While this is generally one of the many benefits of rail trails, it also can lead to occasional conflicts among trail users. Everyone should take responsibility to ensure trail safety by following a few simple trail etiquette guidelines.

One of the most basic etiquette rules is "Wheels yield to heels." The figure below indicates the correct protocol for yielding right-of-way.

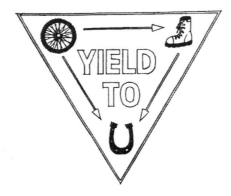

Bicyclists (and in-line skaters) yield to other users; pedestrians yield to equestrians.

Generally this means that you need to warn the users to whom you are yielding of your presence. If, as a bicyclist, you fail to warn a walker that you are about to pass, the walker could step in front of you, causing an accident that easily could have been prevented. Similarly, it is best to slow down and warn an equestrian of your presence. A horse can be startled by a bicycle, so make verbal contact with the rider and be sure it is safe to pass.

Here are some other guidelines you should follow to promote trail safety:

- Obey all trail rules posted at trailheads.

- Stay to the right except when passing.

- Pass slower traffic on the left; yield to oncoming traffic when passing.

- Give a clear warning signal when passing.

- Always look ahead and behind when passing.

- Travel at a responsible speed.

- Keep pets on a leash.

- Do not trespass on private property.

- Move off the trail surface when stopped to allow other users to pass.

The Morse Creek Trestle of the Olympic Discovery Trail.

- Yield to other trail users when entering and crossing the trail.

- Do not disturb the wildlife.

- Do not swim in areas not designated for swimming.

- Watch out for traffic when crossing the street.

- Obey all traffic signals.

How to Use This Book

For this book Washington, Oregon, and Idaho's top rail trails were chosen based on their length, historical or aesthetic features, access, and location. We also found that some trails benefit from a more detailed description; shorter trails are listed under More Rail Trails, because a brief summary is all you need to locate and enjoy them.

At the beginning of each chapter, you will find a map showing the location of the rail trails within that region. The main rail trails featured in this book include basic maps for your convenience. It is recommended, however, that street maps, topographic maps such as USGS quads, or a state atlas be used to supplement the maps in this book. The text description of every trail begins with the following information:

- **Trail name:** The official name of the rail trail.

- **Activities:** A list of icons tells you what kinds of activities are appropriate for each trail.

- **Location:** The areas through which the trail passes.

- **Length:** The length of the trail, including how many miles are currently open.

- **Surface:** The materials that make up the rail trail vary from trail to trail. This section describes each trail's surface. Materials range from asphalt and crushed stone to the significantly more rugged original railroad ballast.

- **Wheelchair access:** Some of the rail trails are wheelchair accessible. This allows physically challenged individuals the opportunity to explore the rail trails with family and friends.

- **Difficulty:** The rail trails range from very easy to hard, depending on the grade of the trail and the general condition of the trail.

- **Food:** The book will indicate the names of the towns near the rail trails in which restaurants and fast-food shops are located.

- **Restrooms:** If a restroom is available near the trail, the book will provide you with its location.

- **Seasons:** Most of these trails are open year-round, but special circumstances, such as severe winter rains or localized flooding, may preclude the use of certain routes during some seasons.

- **Access and parking:** The book will provide you with directions to the rail trails and describe parking availability.

- **Rentals:** Some of the rail trails have bicycle shops or other trail-related outdoor gear stores nearby. This will help you locate rentals, or a shop in which you can have repairs made if you have problems with your equipment.

Legend

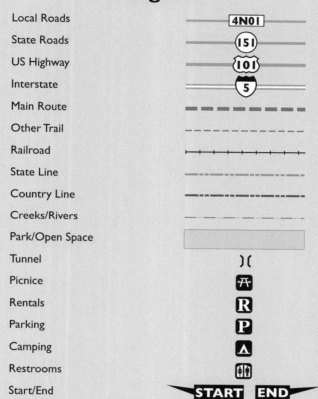

Local Roads	4N01
State Roads	151
US Highway	101
Interstate	5
Main Route	
Other Trail	
Railroad	
State Line	
Country Line	
Creeks/Rivers	
Park/Open Space	
Tunnel	)(
Picnice	
Rentals	R
Parking	P
Camping	
Restrooms	
Start/End	START END
Scale	0 1 2 Miles

Key to Activities Icons

 Backpacking

 Bird-Watching

 Camping

 Cross Country Sking

 Fishings

 Historic Sites

 Backpacking

 In-line Skating

 Mountain Biking

 Paddlesports

 Road Bicycling

 Running

 Swimming

 Walking/Day Hiking

 Wildlife Viewing

 Snowshoeing

Crown Point Trail attracts dogsledders during the winter months. (Courtesy Natalie Bartley)

- **Contact:** The name and contact information for each trail manager is listed here. The selected contacts are generally responsible for managing the trail and can provide information about the trail and its condition. Additional information sources are also listed.

- **Bus route:** Bus routes listed provide an alternate return route for individuals traveling the trails one way. Some extend the entire length of the trail; others cover only a portion. Contact carriers directly for more detailed and up-to-date information.

- **Description:** The major rail trails include an overview of the trail and its history, followed by a mile-by-mile description, allowing you the chance to anticipate the experience of the trail.

Information in this book was confirmed and is correct to the author's knowledge at press time. Given that rails trails are often in a state of change, trail users may want to call the local contacts prior to a visit to obtain the current information. Also, rockslides, flooding, and heavy snowpacks in the mountains can close trails, increase the difficulty of accessing them, or make trail use difficult. Be sure to check for an update on trail conditions before you start on a trail. If you discover changes along a trail, or that a store or restaurant has gone out of business, please contact us so that corrections can be made in future editions.

Rail Trails
WASHINGTON

OVERVIEW

Washington State boasts more than forty rail trails. The state, its cities, towns, and citizen groups deserve mountains of praise for their hard work in overcoming the financial, political, and social obstacles in their way as they developed these paths to fitness, sensible transportation, and joy.

The trails of Puget Sound run on main lines that once carried timber, coal, and passengers, logging lines that headed into the hills, and elegant interurban trolleys. The Burke-Gilman Trail receives the heaviest use. Commuters, cyclists, skaters, children, and walkers have all discovered that there's no better route for exploring the north-side neighborhoods of Seattle. Take yourself to breakfast, lunch, and dinner on this route. Sip cappuccino on the ship canal; watch floatplanes land while you enjoy happy hour beside Lake Washington; watch kites soar over Lake Union; ride, walk, or skate through the U-district at the University of Washington; and finish with an outdoor movie or the Sunday market in Fremont. Daniel Burke and Judge Thomas Gilman, founding fathers of Seattle, built the Seattle, Lakeshore & Eastern Railroad on this route.

The Elliot Bay Trail and the Seattle Waterfront Pathway carve a corridor through the downtown waterfront and through parks, ending at Smith Cove Park and Marina, former site of coal bunkers.

The King County Interurban Trail heads through the industrial regions and neighborhoods of South King County, past the racetrack and a huge mall to the tiny towns of Algona and Pacific. Commute, shop, have a day at the races, tour the cities along the way, or just enjoy a great workout while on this wide, paved trail. Urban trails also head north from Lynnwood to Everett along the old trolley line.

The trails east of Seattle offer some screaming mountain bike rides in Tiger Mountain State Forest, a ravine built from coal tailings, a great commuter trail along the Cedar River, and a 36-mile trail through the Snoqualmie Valley. The Cedar River Trail starts in the city of Renton on Lake Washington and ends on a wooded riverside pathway, enjoyed by equestrians. The Snoqualmie Valley Trail traverses the rolling terrain of a rural area showing the signs of development. Local antiques shops and eateries remain while Starbucks, grocery chains, and fast foods encroach. This is a pretty valley that takes you near Snoqualmie Falls with the luxurious Salish Lodge at its lip. The nearby Snoqualmie Centennial Trail begins at the Northwest Railroad Museum and continues alongside the old tracks, crowded with engines from the past. The Snoqualmie Valley Trail presently connects to the John Wayne Pioneer Trail. The gentle beauty of the Snoqualmie and Snohomish Valleys will be even more accessible when the Snoqualmie Valley Trail connects to the Snohomish Centennial Trail in northwestern Washington, creating an exceptional, continuous regional trail system.

Rail trails in northwestern Washington pass by farms, through forests, beside waterfalls, through the college town of Bellingham, and out to the Olympic Peninsula. Enjoy the calm waters of Lake Crescent and the views of distant peaks from the Spruce Railroad Trail. Enjoy the oceanfront city of Port Angeles and the forest bouquets of wildflowers on the two completed sections of the Olympic Discovery Trail. The Wallace Falls Railway Trail climbs through the forest for a good look at a logging route ascended by the "steam donkey" trains, along with some dramatic waterfalls. The Iron Goat Trail to Stevens Pass is an impressive interpretive hiking trail that transports you back to the difficulties and disasters that the Great Northern Railway experienced as it made its way through this rugged territory.

Southwestern Washington offers several rural rail trails. To the east you'll find the Foothills Trail, in the shadow of Mount Rainier; to the west is the Willapa Hills Trail on the Willapa River. Follow the trail to Raymond from South Bend, discovering this Oyster Capital of the World. There's also an easily accessible refuge just off Interstate 5 near the state capital of Olympia (Chehalis Western Trail) and rugged dirt trails in Lake Sylvia State Park.

Head to eastern Washington to find sunshine and hot, dry desert. East of the Cascades you'll discover Yakima wine country, the pretty Cowiche Canyon, and a trail through the city of Spokane to the Idaho border. Turbulent dams, museums, a century-old merry-go-round, and an equestrian area accent the 37-mile Spokane River Centennial Trail. Follow 113 miles of the path of the *Olympian-Hiawatha* passenger train that once rolled from Seattle to Chicago on the Milwaukee Road. Travel through changes in terrain, climate, and scenery, along rivers, through towns, past a unique espresso shop and cafe, and to the edge of the Columbia River on the John Wayne Pioneer Trail. A 2.25-mile tunnel through a mountain pass is dark

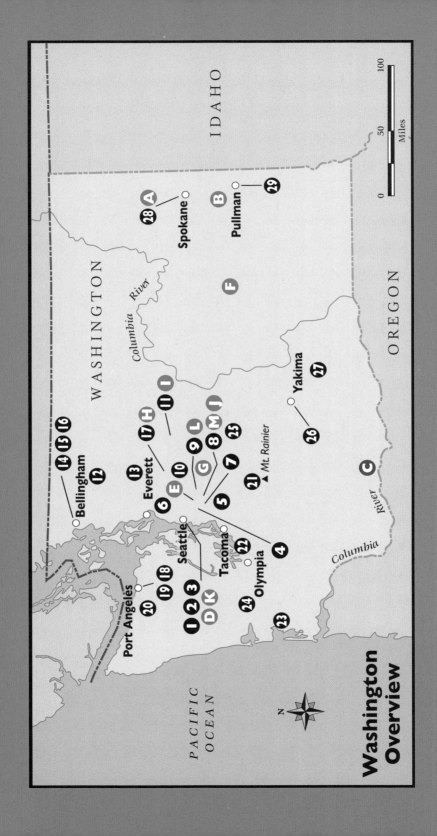

Washington Overview

PACIFIC OCEAN

N

IDAHO

WASHINGTON

OREGON

Columbia River

Columbia River

Mt. Rainier ▲

Port Angeles

Bellingham

Everett

Seattle

Tacoma

Olympia

Yakima

Spokane

Pullman

100

50

0

Miles

Washington
Puget Sound

1. Burke-Gilman Trail
2. Seattle Waterfront Pathway
3. Elliott Bay Trail
4. Coal Creek Park Trail
5. King County Interurban Trail
6. Snohomish County Interurban Trail
7. Cedar River Trail and Cedar to Green River Trail
8. Tiger Mountain State Forest
9. Preston-Snoqualmie Trail
10. Snoqualmie Valley Trail

Northwestern Washington

11. Iron Goat Trail
12. Cascade Trail
13. Snohomish County Centennial Trail
14. Whatcom County and Bellingham Interurban Trail
15. South Bay Trail
16. Railroad Trail
17. Wallace Falls Railway Trail
18. Olympic Discovery Trail: Deer Park Scenic Gateway
19. Olympic Discovery Trail: Port Angeles Waterfront Center to Sequim
20. Spruce Railroad Trail

Southwestern Washington

21. Foothills Trail
22. Chehalis Western Trail
23. Willapa Hills (Raymond to South Bend Riverfront Trail)
24. Lake Sylvia State Park

Eastern Washington

25. John Wayne Pioneer Trail (West)
26. Cowiche Canyon Trail
27. Lower Yakima Valley Pathway
28. Spokane River Centennial Trail
29. Bill Chipman Palouse Trail – Pullman, Washington

More Washington Rail Trails

A. Ben Burr Trail
B. Colfax Trail
C. Dry Creek Trail
D. Duwamish Bikeway
E. Issaquah-Preston Trail
F. John Wayne Pioneer Trail—Milwaukee Road Corridor
G. Middle Fork Trail
H. Necklace Valley Trail
I. Pacific Crest National Scenic Trail: Stevens Pass Right-of-Way Section
J. Rainier Multiuse Trail
K. Ship Canal Trail
L. Snoqualmie Centennial Trail
M. West Tiger Railroad Grade

and eerie and fun to explore. Adventurous travelers can continue east to the border of Idaho on the undeveloped portion of the trail.

Seattle and many surrounding areas have a serious traffic problem: The problem is us. Commuting on a rail trail is just as sensible as was commuting on the trains that ran these routes—and just as pleasant. Hop a bus one way or for part of your route and take your bike, skates, or your feet the rest of the way. Get fit and lean, meet people, protect the environment, and live longer. Men and women in their eighties and nineties haul groceries on primitive bikes in countries like Italy, Denmark, and China. We can likewise mount our modern bikes and ride to work in comfort as we age healthy and feisty. The Cascade Bicycle Club honors one such commuter each month and can help you get started. Check the bus schedules, talk to your coworkers, and make a plan. And join the Cascade Bicycle Club's Bike to Work Day this summer. (See Appendix B for contact information.)

Wherever or however you start your tour, don't miss the chance to see, play, study, commute, or simply wander Washington's wonderful rail trails.

1 BURKE-GILMAN TRAIL

Seattle's popular Burke-Gilman Trail invites you on a tour of funky Fremont, Lake Union and the ship canal, the University District, Lake Washington, and north-end neighborhoods. You'll pass above the old Sand Point naval base and along the busy, commercial Lake City Way as well as by a cornucopia of tempting eateries.

Activities:

Location: North Seattle to Lake Forest Park, King County

Length: 14 miles

Surface: Paved

Wheelchair access: The entire trail is wheelchair accessible.

Difficulty: Easy

Food: In the town of Fremont and along Lake City Way, you'll find everything from breweries and grocery stores to fast food and gourmet dining.

Restrooms: You'll find restroom facilities at Gas Works Park, Burke-Gilman Place Park, Mathews Beach Park, and Tracy Owen Station, as well as at various commercial establishments near the trail. There are also water fountains along the way.

Seasons: The trail can be used year-round.

Access and parking: You can access the trail from many points. The southern end of the trail sits at Eighth Avenue Northwest and Northwest 43rd Street just off Leary Way. Park on the street and hop on the trail at Hales Brewery. Gas Works Park, which offers parking and picnic facilities, is on North Northlake Way, just south of Fremont. Mathews Beach Park (with parking, picnicking, and swimming) is 7 miles north. To get there, take Sand Point Way Northeast to Northeast 93rd Street, then turn east, toward Lake Washington.

Tracy Owen Station is the trail's northern terminus and offers parking, picnicking, and fishing. It's found on 61st Avenue Northeast and Northeast Bothell Way in Kenmore. The trail continues 15 miles to Marymoor Park in Redmond as the Sammamish River Trail.

You can also park along the road in many areas, including Fremont Canal Park, found at Phinney Avenue North and Leary Way Northwest.

Rentals: You can rent bicycles at The Bicycle Center at 4529 Sand Point Way NE; (206) 523–8300.

Contact: Bicycle Alliance of Washington, (206) 224–9252, www.bicycle alliance.org.

Bus routes: #372, #312, or #306. For more information, call Metro Transit at (206) 553–3000. Or visit the Web site at transit.metrokc.gov.

||||||||||||||||||||||||||||||||||||||||||||||||||||||||||||||||||||||||||||||||

What a train ride this must have been! In 1885 Judge Thomas Burke and Daniel Gilman, two of Seattle's city fathers, set out to establish the Seattle, Lakeshore & Eastern Railroad. Originally planned to connect with the Canadian Transcontinental at Sumas, the rail line made it only to Arlington. Still, it became a major regional line serving Puget Sound logging areas. Northern Pacific purchased the line in 1913, used it heavily until 1963, and finally abandoned it in 1971. A cooperative effort by King County, Seattle, and the University of Washington then led to the right-of-way's development as a trail, dedicated in 1978.

Now a heavily used recreation and commuter pathway, the Burke-Gilman Trail takes you past boats, bridges, and breweries. You can stop at cafes, parks, and bookstores while marveling at the 72,500 seats of Husky Stadium, the Gothic architecture of the University of Washington, and the shiny, square buildings that have been added in recent years.

Be alert if you travel this trail on a sunny day or warm evening: Oodles

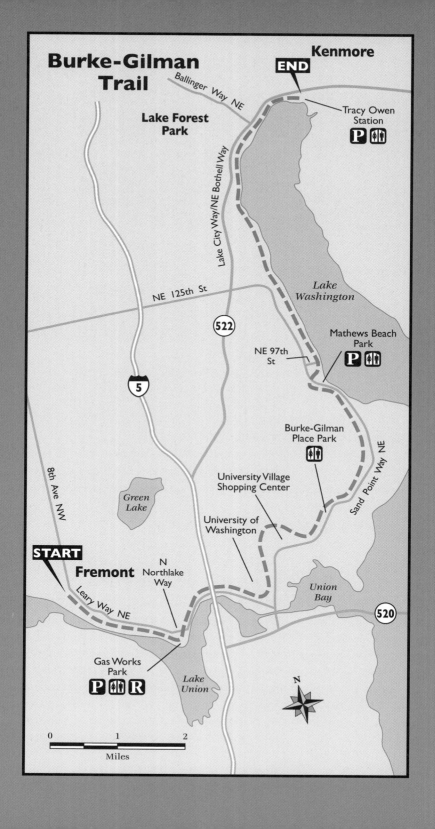

Burke-Gilman Trail

Kenmore

END

Ballinger Way NE

Lake Forest Park

Tracy Owen Station

P 🚻

Lake City Way/NE Bothell Way

NE 125th St

522

Lake Washington

NE 97th St

Mathews Beach Park

P 🚻

5

Burke-Gilman Place Park

🚻

8th Ave NW

Green Lake

University Village Shopping Center

Sand Point Way NE

University of Washington

START

Fremont

N Northlake Way

Leary Way NE

Union Bay

520

Gas Works Park

P 🚻 R

Lake Union

N

0   1   2
Miles

A cyclist in Tracy Owen Station.

of baby strollers, commuters, cyclists, skaters, and walkers will be right there with you. Be cautious and considerate.

The trail is described here from its southern terminus at Hales Brewery to the northern trailhead at Tracy Owen Station, but it can be accessed from many points along the way. A new section of trail has opened adjacent to Hiram Chittendon Locks.

Fremont Canal Park lies just 0.5 mile from the trail's beginning; here you'll find benches and a waterfront shelter with tile artwork. The trail then leaves Fremont city center to dip down to the edge of Lake Union.

You can make a side trip here to enjoy Fremont's street art and food, the "neon bridge lady," and the sign declaring Fremont the center of the known universe.

The trail passes Gas Works Park at mile 1.8; there's an uphill grade here. Stop for great views of the city, Mount Rainier, and Lake Union. Read the historical plaque posted on a bridge pillar as you approach the "Wall of Death" (a bright orange motorcycle velodrome) at mile 3. You'll cross several roads over the next 4 miles. As you pass University Hospital, the south campus, and Husky Stadium at 3.6 miles, a sign directs you to the

Cliffords is one of the restaurants along the trail boasting great lake views.

Lake Washington Loop. You are on the northern section of this loop. The sign points you to the southern section, which follows city streets around the south end of Lake Washington. Note the contrast here between the pointed tops of the university's stone architecture and the glass rectangles of the modern buildings. Arrive at 25th Avenue Northeast and the University Village Shopping Center at 5 miles. There are lots of treats and espresso to be discovered here.

The trail from here north is easy; it's especially good for beginner skaters and bikers. You'll find just a bit of grade, one wooden bridge crossing, and mostly small street crossings. A jogging path takes you as far as Lakeside Place Northeast.

At 40th Avenue Northeast you'll pass a grocery store and Burke-Gilman Place Park with picnic tables and restrooms, then enter a forested area. Benches are placed here and there for the next few miles. Maples, dogwoods, and trimmed hedges frame lake views north of Northeast 77th Street (mile 8). There's a fairly smooth trail surface with a slight grade and frequent small road crossings. A bridge crosses Sand Point Way to Mathews Beach Park at 9 miles. This lakeside park has swings, a play area, picnicking, and swimming. North of Northeast 97th Street, the character of the trail changes once again. Waterfront homes are sandwiched together much like the narrow streets of a European city; the small, sharp angles of gingerbread houses and brick Tudors offer an interesting contrast with modern square homes. Pass Lakeside Place Northeast at 10.6 miles. Northeast 153rd Street has parking for three cars. The trail reaches Lake City Way at Northeast Ballinger Way (mile 13.5). Take a drink of water from the serpent here.

Great eats and treats appear all along the remainder of the trail, though you don't need to leave the trail for entertainment. A small grassy park with water and restrooms sits 0.5 mile from Town Center on the trail. Just ahead and above the trail lies Cliffords. View floatplanes from this restaurant's cozy tavern and deck while you enjoy afternoon appetizers.

There are many coffee and fast-food spots on the main drag ahead. The Burke-Gilman Trail officially ends at Tracy Owen Station in Kenmore, although you can continue traveling to Marymoor Park from here on the Sammamish River Trail. Hop a bus to return to your starting point: The #372 will take you back to the University District.

2 SEATTLE WATERFRONT PATHWAY

This pathway and the connected Elliott Bay Trail (Trail 3) provide a scenic tour of the downtown Seattle waterfront. Park the car, grab your bike, skates, or walking shoes, and head for the water. The trail runs through a lively tourist area, past the ferry docks, along a trolley line, and adjacent to Safeco Field.

Activities:

Location: Downtown Seattle, King County

Length: 2 miles

Surface: Paved

Wheelchair access: The entire trail is wheelchair accessible.

Difficulty: Easy

Food: There are many restaurants and fast-food places along the waterfront.

Restrooms: Restrooms and drinking water are available at Myrtle Edwards Park.

Seasons: The trail can be used year-round.

Access and parking: To reach the Seattle Waterfront Pathway, head west from Interstate 5 to Alaskan Way; the trail runs along Alaskan Way from South Royal Brougham Way (its southern end) to Broad Street (the northern terminus). You can access the trail anywhere along its length. Metered parking is available on streets. Myrtle Edwards Park, at the trail's northern end, also offers limited parking.

Rentals: See Appendix A for a list of bike rentals in Puget Sound.

Contact: Bicycle Alliance of Washington, (206) 224–9252, www.bicycle alliance.org.

The Waterfront Streetcar service runs parallel to the pathway.

Bus routes: Waterfront Streetcar service—For current update, streetcar
.htm; ktransit.com/transit/uspnw/seattle/sea_orbus#8. Call Metro Transit
at (206) 553–3000, or visit transit.metrokc.gov.

Tour the heart of the bustling Seattle waterfront on this lively urban
pathway. The 8- to 10-foot-wide trail runs mostly along the east side of
Alaskan Way; it shifts to the west between Cedar and Broad Streets, near its
northern end. Pedestrians can use either the sidewalk on the west side of
Alaskan Way or this trail, as can bikers and skaters. The trail is a better choice
if you're on wheels, however. Plan to go slowly and to stop and start and
yield to pedestrians. Experienced cyclists may opt to ride the roadway.

This description runs from south to north, but you can access the trail
anywhere along its length. As you embark from South Royal Brougham
Way, grab a peek at Safeco Field. The sports arena features a retractable
roof that alternately protects fans from rain and welcomes the sun into the

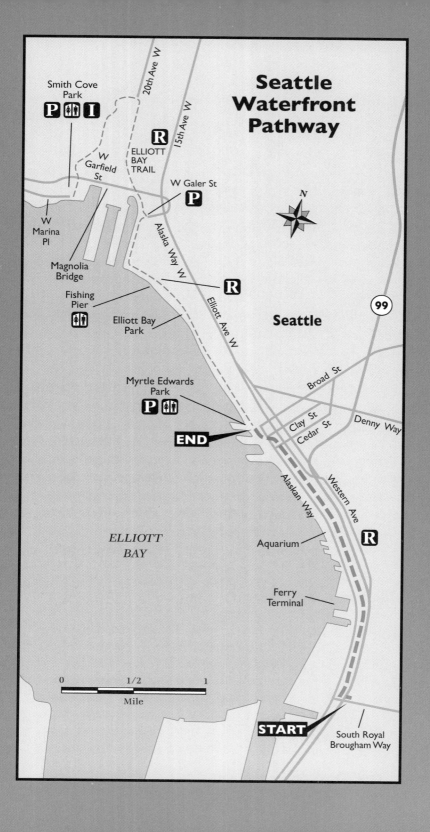

Seattle Waterfront Pathway

20th Ave W

15th Ave W

Smith Cove Park

P 🚻 **I**

W Garfield St

R

ELLIOTT BAY TRAIL

W Galer St

P

W Marina Pl

Alaska Way W

Magnolia Bridge

Fishing Pier

🚻

Elliott Bay Park

Elliott Ave W

R

Seattle

N

99

Myrtle Edwards Park

P 🚻

END ▶

Clay St

Cedar St

Broad St

Denny Way

ELLIOTT BAY

Alaskan Way

Western Ave

Aquarium

R

Ferry Terminal

0   1/2   1

Mile

START ▶

South Royal Brougham Way

game. (The Seattle Mariners' former venue, the Kingdome, was destroyed in 2000 when this controversial multimillion dollar stadium opened.) You'll then pass the ferry terminal and the aquarium as you head north and enjoy casual outdoor eating on the waterfront.

Look back when you're about 0.5 mile north of the ferry terminal to see the active tracks of the Burlington Northern Santa Fe Railway disappear into a tunnel beneath the city. The Waterfront Streetcar service runs on what once were the Seattle, Lakeshore & Eastern tracks, which were purchased by the Northern Pacific Railway Company. You can hop the trolley every 2 blocks for a rolling view of the activity. However, the service has been temporarily suspended due to the Olympic Sculpture Park construction.

If you're on foot, you might want to make a detour up the Pike Place Hillclimb at Pike Street to the market, shops, and more restaurants and activities. Stop to catch a peek at one of Pike Place Market's most popular attractions: fish vendors in white aprons hawking their wares by tossing them back and forth in a verbose game of catch.

Shift to the west side of the street from Cedar to Broad Streets. If you'd like to combine this trip with the Elliott Bay Trail, which takes you farther north, just continue straight into the Myrtle Edwards parking lot. Whenever you're ready, turn around and return the way you came.

Cyclists may also want to extend this trip southward from Royal Brougham on Alaskan Way. Pedal this street south to Spokane Street, then turn right on Spokane to cross the lower West Seattle Bridge. This will connect you with the Duwamish and Alki Trails and the beach, bakeries, restaurants, and cafes at Alki Point.

Expect possible disruptions toward the southern end of this trail as Alaskan Way is ripped up and rebuilt over the next several years. A trail extension south to Atlantic Street will be included in this renovation.

3 ELLIOTT BAY TRAIL

The Elliott Bay Trail provides a picturesque tour of Seattle's downtown waterfront. It connects with the Seattle Waterfront Pathway (Trail 2) for a longer stroll or ride along the waterfront.

Activities:

Location: Downtown Seattle, King County

Length: 3.35 miles

Surface: Paved

Wheelchair access: The entire trail is wheelchair accessible.

Difficulty: Mostly easy, although the pavement may be bumpy for novice skaters and bikers. There are a few little hills and one short, narrow, steep hill.

Food: Numerous restaurants abut the Myrtle Edwards parking lot and other points along the trail, including at the Fishing Pier.

Restrooms: There are restrooms and water at Myrtle Edwards Park and the Fishing Pier. You'll also find restrooms at Smith Cove Park.

Seasons: The trail can be used year-round. Smith Cove Park is open from 4:00 a.m. to 11:00 p.m. year-round. Both gates (under Magnolia Bridge and at 20th Street) are locked at dusk. Don't get trapped between them when they close!

Access and parking: To reach the Elliott Bay Trail, head west from Interstate 5 to Alaskan Way. You can park on the street at metered parking spots at Alaskan Way and Broad Street (this trail's southern terminus at Myrtle Edwards Park).

You can also park on West Galer Street for free. Continue north on Alaskan Way; after the Magnolia Bridge, the street name changes to 15th Avenue West. Turn west onto West Galer Street 1.3 miles north of the corner of Western and Denny, and park where Galer ends along the water.

Another option is to begin your tour at Smith Cove Park, at the trail's northern end; this will allow novice skaters and bikers to avoid a steep, narrow overpass and a railroad crossing. To reach the park, turn west onto West Galer Street from 15th Avenue West, cross the Magnolia Bridge, and continue to the Smith Cove Park exit.

Rentals: See Appendix A for a list of bike rentals in Puget Sound.

Contact: Bicycle Alliance of Washington, (206) 224–9252, www.bicycle alliance.org.

Bus routes: #15, #18. For more information, call King County Metro Transit at (206) 553–3000. Or try the Web site at transit.metrokc.gov.

|||||||||||||||||||||||||||||||||||||||||||||||||||||||||||||||||||||||||||||||||

The Elliott Bay Trail winds through two contiguous parks as it passes between the waterfront and the active Burlington Northern Santa Fe Railway line. The trail can be accessed from many points along the way; this description begins at Myrtle Edwards Park and continues north to Smith Cove. Starting from Myrtle Edwards, the trail is separated into different sections for wheels and for pedestrians. Both trails are narrow but picturesque.

Visit the rose garden at 0.55 mile or work your way through the par course while you watch the activity on the sound. Sunsets can be spectacular here. At mile 1 you may want to stop by the Fishing Pier for a candy bar or a soda; you'll also find restrooms and drinking water. You'll reach the Galer Street parking area at 1.35 miles. Cross in front of the entrance to terminal 91 and turn left on the sidewalk to pass under the Magnolia Bridge. Plans are under way to reroute this final section of the trail and make it a direct waterfront route.

As it leaves the waterfront beyond Galer Street, the trail becomes bumpy. It crosses old railroad tracks, quickly and briefly becomes very narrow, then climbs and descends a steep overpass. Cyclists and pedestrians, beware of skaters: They have less control than you and need more room. Beyond this overpass, however, the trail is flat and wide.

Several popular bike routes take off from 20th Avenue West at mile 1.68 (0.8 mile beyond Galer Street), including trips to the Chittenden Locks or to Fremont (see Trail 1 for more information on the funky town of Fremont). After 20th Avenue the trail curves around a huge parking lot, where cars

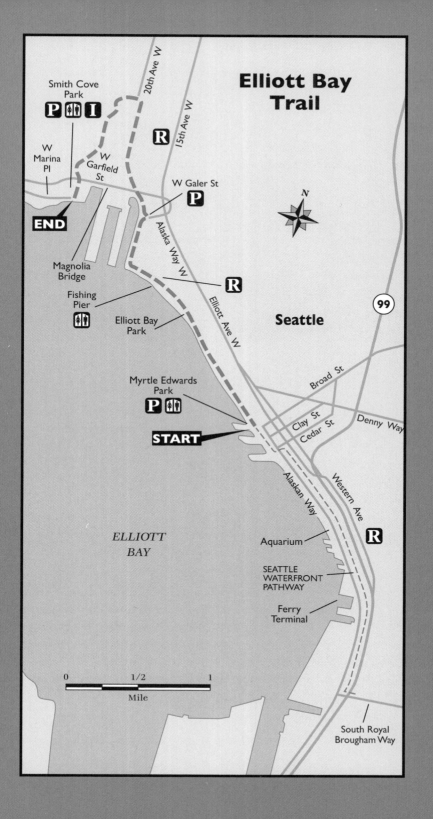

Elliott Bay Trail

Smith Cove Park

P 👫 I

20th Ave W

15th Ave W

R

W Marina Pl

W Garfield St

W Galer St

P

END

Magnolia Bridge

Alaska Way W

R

Fishing Pier

👫

Elliott Bay Park

Elliott Ave W

Seattle

N

99

Broad St

Myrtle Edwards Park

P 👫

Clay St

Cedar St

Denny Way

START

ELLIOTT BAY

Alaskan Way

Western Ave

R

Aquarium

SEATTLE WATERFRONT PATHWAY

Ferry Terminal

0   1/2   1
Mile

South Royal Brougham Way

View from Smith Cove Marina.

are delivered from overseas. Cross again under the Magnolia Bridge; a sign directs you to Smith Cove Park across the street and down the sidewalk at mile 3.35 (1.75 miles from Galer Street). Mount Rainier stands white and tall across the water, dwarfing the freighters attached to the pier.

From here you may want to continue 0.5 mile to the restaurants at Smith Cove Marina. The sidewalk and road end at a narrow strip of grass displaying a spectacular view of the Olympic Mountains across the sound. The marina allows public access until dusk.

The kiosk outside Smith Cove Park highlights some interesting rail and shipping history. The Northern Pacific coal bunker pier was completed here in 1891. Steamers and sailing vessels berthed on either side of this 2,500-foot trestle, loading coal from railroad cars until 1899, when the Great Northern Railway built Piers 88 and 89. This linked the transcontinental railroad to the Orient. In 1912 the Port of Seattle bought the tidal flats that were to become Piers 90 and 91. These 2,530-foot piers, completed in 1921, were the longest earth-filled piers in the world. The U.S. Navy owned them from 1942 to 1976.

When you're ready, turn around and return the way you came.

4 COAL CREEK PARK TRAIL

This trek along the Coal Creek Park Trail takes you through a bit of coal-mining history on your way to spectacular Cougar Mountain Park. It offers woodsy tranquility and a great workout close to town.

Activities:

Location: Cougar Mountain, Bellevue, King County

Length: 3 miles

Surface: Dirt and ballast

Wheelchair access: The trail is not wheelchair accessible.

Difficulty: This is a primitive trail that is moderate on the southern end due to bridge crossings, a few hills, and some downed logs. The northern end is easy.

Food: No food is available along the trail.

Restrooms: There is a portable toilet at the Red Town Trailhead.

Seasons: The trail can be used year-round; conditons vary and are affected by weather.

Access and parking: You can park your car and access the trail at either the Coal Creek Parkway Trailhead (the trail's northwestern terminus) or the Red Town Trailhead (its southeastern end). To reach the Coal Creek Trailhead, take exit 10 (Coal Creek Parkway) off Interstate 405 and drive east 1.3 miles to an unmarked pullout on the left. (This pullout is 0.8 mile past the light at Factoria Boulevard Southeast and 0.2 mile past the light at Forrest Drive, at a low point in the road.)

For the Red Town Trailhead, take exit 13 off Interstate 90 and turn south onto Lakemont Boulevard Southeast. Drive 3 miles. Where the road curves sharply right, turn left; the trail begins across the street.

Rentals: There are no rentals along the route.

Contact: Bellevue Parks and Community Services, (425) 452–6881, www .bellevue.gov.

Bus routes: #219. The #219 bus passes the Red Town Trailhead and travels within 1 mile of the Coal Creek Parkway Trailhead. Flag it down for a ride. For more information, call Metro Transit at (206) 553–3000, or visit the Web site at transit.metrokc.gov.

||||||||||||||||||||||||||||||||||||||||||||||||||||||||||||||||||||||||||||||||||||||

Newcastle coal was once the best in the Northwest, and the mining industry reached its heyday here from the late nineteenth century through the early twentieth. Unfortunately, Washington State let owner-ship of the mines fall into the hands of San Francisco moguls. While they reaped the mining profits, Seattle businessmen made what money they could by moving the coal—via the Seattle Walla Walla Railroad—from the mines to steamers destined for transport to San Francisco and beyond. This railroad, Seattle's own, ran to Renton and to the bunkers at the King Street Pier. Due to the powerful politics of railroading and the interests of the Tacoma-based Northern Pacific, however, it never actually reached Walla Walla.

The Coal Creek Park Trail offers a 3-mile trip through this rich his-tory. Much of the land in this area and in surrounding neighborhoods was mined for coal; it's now riddled with underground, artificial caves. In the mines' heyday, disposal of coal tailings built the ravine walls you'll see above the trail. Due to unstable ground and slides, little of the pathway remains on the railroad grade. But it will take you up and down small hills, beside a creek, and to a waterfall on your way to Cougar Mountain Park. You'll cross a variety of bridges that range from a questionable strip of wood, to an artful log with a single rail of round timber, to what looks like a suburban patio.

The trail can be accessed from either end. This description begins at the northwestern terminus and travels southeast to Cougar Mountain. Leaving the Coal Creek Parkway Trailhead, the trail descends into a man-made ravine as it follows the creek, rising above it and crossing it several times. You'll leap over mossy fallen logs and tree roots on this narrow end of the trail; it can be muddy. Leave the creek to climb to an open plateau at about 1 mile.

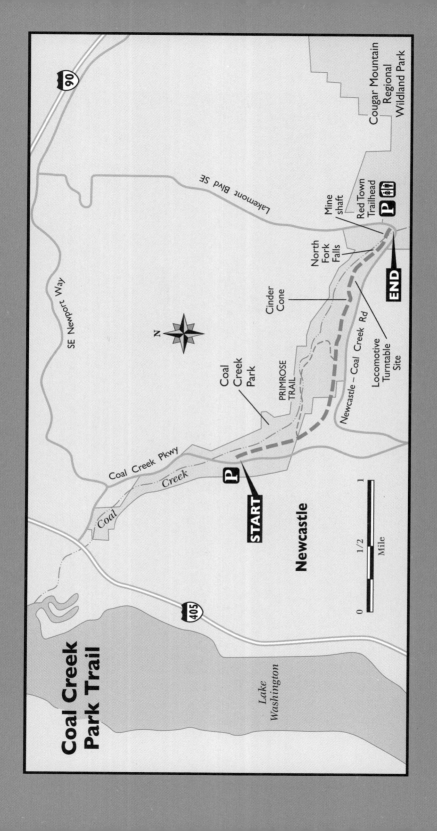

Coal Creek
Park Trail

90

405

Cougar Mountain
Regional
Wildland Park

Lakemont Blvd SE

Mine
shaft

Red Town
Trailhead

P 🚻

SE Newport Way

North
Fork
Falls

N

END

Cinder
Cone

Coal
Creek
Park

Locomotive
Turntable
Site

PRIMROSE
TRAIL

Newcastle – Coal Creek Rd

Coal Creek Pkwy

Coal   Creek

Coal

P

START

Newcastle

Lake
Washington

0   1/2   1
Mile

You'll find a wide variety of interesting bridges along the Coal Creek Park Trail.

The Primrose Trail intersects the trail several times, offering an alternate route. You'll find an intersection of both trails at mile 1.7, and the Cinder Cone 0.2 mile beyond. The Coal Creek Trail is well signed until it meets the railroad right-of-way. Turn right onto the right-of-way, then left after a few yards. Cross a fancy bridge and return to a narrow wooded trail. Trains turned around at the roundhouse here.

Before climbing up to Newcastle–Coal Creek Road and the Red Town Trailhead, you'll arrive at a peaceful rest stop. Watch a waterfall slide down a rock face into the creek. Just beyond, cross a bridge to the left to view an old mine. At the trail's end, cross Lakemont Boulevard Southeast (which becomes Newcastle–Coal Creek Road) to reach the Red Town Trailhead. Here, check the trail map to review a century of coal mining on Cougar Mountain. In 1883 the Red Town Trailhead was a mining town, population 750.

You're now in Cougar Mountain Park, which covers more than 3,000 acres and is the largest of the King County parks. The Issaquah Alps range here predates the Cascade Mountains, possibly dating back 8,000 years. There are 36 miles of hiking trails and more than 12 miles for equestrians. Wetlands and creeks originate within the park, which is forested by western red cedar, western hemlock, Douglas fir, Sitka spruce, and big-leaf maple. Keep your eyes open for black-tailed deer, black bears, bobcats, coyotes, bald eagles, ravens, sharp-shinned hawks, and pileated woodpeckers.

Other Cougar Mountain attractions include coal-mining shafts, spectacular waterfalls, a restored meadow (it was a baseball field in the 1920s), the former townsite, mountaintop views, large glacier boulders, numerous caves, and—surprisingly—a former missile site. After World War II, anti-aircraft guns were placed on Cougar Mountain. During the Cold War, these gunbases were upgraded to Nike missile and radar sites. The park offers interpretive programs to guide you through all of the history and natural resources of the park.

When you're ready, turn around and return the way you came.

5 KING COUNTY INTERURBAN TRAIL

This 15-mile trail offers a study in contrasts: from the bustling Supermall with its endless shops to small-town Algona, which looks straight out of the nineteenth century; from the imposing architecture of the Emerald Downs Race Track to the majesty of Mount Rainier; from industry to agriculture, it's all here.

Activities:

Location: King County, from Tukwila to Pacific, and including the towns of Kent, Auburn, and Algona

Length: 15.5 miles

Surface: Asphalt with soft shoulders

Wheelchair access: Yes, along most of the trail. There are two handicapped parking spots at South 277th Street in Kent, and there's easy access to the trail from the Kent Transit Center at James Street, Kent.

Difficulty: Easy

Food: In the town of Algona, you'll find restaurants, grocery stores, and espresso shops adjacent to the trail. The Supermall in Auburn has multiple restaurants. Downtown Kent (with lots of fast food) is several blocks east of the trail at Smith Street.

Restrooms: You'll find both restrooms and drinking water at Fort Dent Park, Kent Uplands Playfield, and General Services Administration (GSA) Park in Auburn (where the restrooms are located across an active railroad track).

Seasons: The trail can be used year-round.

Access and parking: You can access the trail from several points along the way. At its northern terminus in Tukwila, you can park at Bicentennial Park, located on the west side of the Green River on Strander Boulevard, 1 block west of West Valley Highway. Cross West Valley Highway on Strander to dead-end at the trail. (It extends north for 0.42 mile from here.) A second starting point is near Fort Dent, near the trail's intersection with the Green

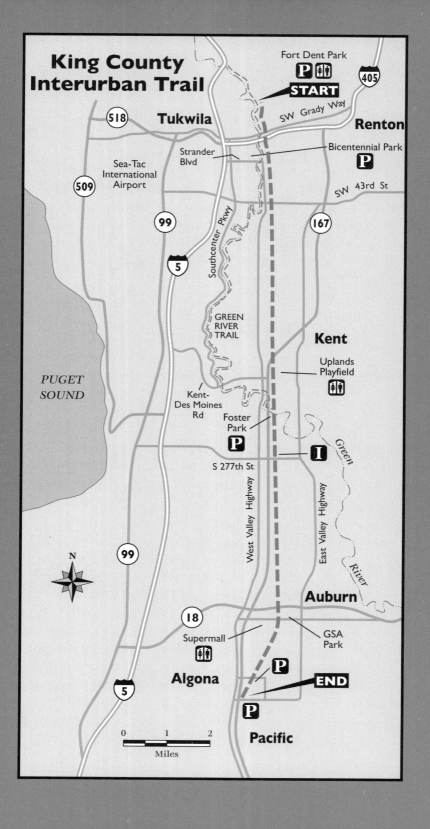

River Trail. The Green River Trail—which is depicted on the map but not described here—also passes through Bicentennial Park. You can head south on this trail and loop north on the Interurban or the reverse. The trails intersect again at Foster Park.

To start at the Foster Park Trailhead, exit Washington Highway 167 at Willis Street in Kent. Head east to Central Avenue. Turn right and head south to 259th Street. Turn right (west) and pass under a trestle to reach a parking lot on your left.

You can also start at either Algona or Pacific, at the southern end of the trail. To park in Algona, exit WA 167 at Algona-Pacific and head east on Ellingson Road. Then turn north onto Milwaukee Boulevard South to park on First Avenue in Algona. To reach the tiny lot at the trail's southern terminus in Pacific, head south on Milwaukee Boulevard, then west on Third Avenue.

Finally, street parking or small dirt lots are available at many intersections along the way.

Rentals: For bike rentals in Puget Sound, see Appendix A.

Contact: King County Parks Division, (206) 296–4232, www.metrokc.gov /parks/trails.

Bus routes: Bus #150 runs from Seattle and Tukwila. It can be easily reached from the trail in Tukwila and at the Kent Transit Center. For more information call Metro Transit at (206) 553–3000, or visit the Web site at transit .metrokc.gov.

The electric Interurban Railway transported people from Seattle to Tacoma from September 1902 until December 1928. It ran first as the Interurban Railway, then the Seattle Electric Company, and finally the Puget Sound Electric Railway. At sixty cents one way (a dollar round trip), this was a highly successful run until automobiles arrived in the 1920s. The transportation of goods from the productive soil of the Green River Valley to local markets accounted for 20 percent of the load.

Farming and manufacturing still dominate this route. Large warehouses, office parks, highways, malls, and hotels will follow you south from

The Big Brother and Little Brother trestles of the King County Interurban Trail can be seen from the Green River Trail at Foster Park.

Tukwila to Pacific on the King County Interurban Trail. Pastureland, rivers, and parks parallel the trail as well. People magnets like the Supermall, Emerald Downs Race Track, and Boeing back up against your pathway. The location of the trail near industry, highways, and buses allows commuters to travel via a combination of trails, buses, and cars. It also provides miles of parkland for residents of industrial neighborhoods.

Although the trail can be accessed from many points along the way, this description carries you from its northern end, in Tukwila, south to Pacific. Depart from Tukwila heading south. Begin where the trail intersects with the Green River Trail at a bridge crossing the river near Fort Dent Park (Interurban Avenue at Fort Dent Way). Cross the bridge to the south and continue under Interstate 405 past several hotels. You'll travel between an active railroad and office parks, under power lines, and through open fields.

At mile 5.5, pass under WA 167 and continue to the playing fields and the skate park at Smith Street in downtown Kent. To cross Willis Street at mile 6.5, jog right to cross at the light, then jog back left, crossing 74th Avenue South, to regain the trail.

Arrive at Foster Park at 7 miles. The park lies at the base of a teal-colored trestle. Pause for a view of the Green River below and notice an active railroad trestle beside you. Look closely: The trail bridge was built in the image of its big brother. (Indeed, it's called the Little Brother.) Two active tracks straddle the trail to the south. Some carry new cars, some open boxcars. Down the track, a yellow caboose rests still and alone. You're standing in an outdoor museum amid the steel rails of the Union Pacific, the Burlington Northern, and the old path of the Interurban.

The portions of the trail that pass under power lines are supported cooperatively by Puget Sound Energy and the cities along the trail. At South 277th Street, mile 8.5, approach a kiosk and cross a bridge over the wetlands. Horseback riding is allowed from this point southward on an unmaintained shoulder. Mount Rainier fills the sky here, as it does along most of your route.

At mile 10 you are dwarfed by a bright blue-and-green building crawling with contrasting shapes. The Emerald Downs Race Track looms like the Emerald City Palace, high above the gray and brown structures along the pathway. (Some folks take this trail to the races and avoid the traffic!)

A railroad crossing for trail users in Kent.

The friendly neighborhood of Algona is a welcome change of pace from the urban bustle that surrounds it.

After you cross under several highways, you're suddenly hit by orange neon signs. This is the popular Supermall (check out all the tour buses!). Shop, eat, rest—it's all here. If you can't resist the stores here, you'll be happy to know you can hop a bus back to your car. Otherwise, cross the four lanes of 15th Street Southwest at the light as you continue on the trail.

Once you push on past the mall, every sense of urban life disappears. All at once, at mile 14.5, you enter a picture from the past—a grassy little park with a gazebo, people meandering in the small street ahead, kids riding back and forth on their bikes, a restaurant in a timeworn wooden building, and, to your left, an espresso shop along with the local grocery. This is Algona. (Locals tell me, by the way, that there's a second espresso shop down the road.) This little town isn't far from the city of Auburn— just a few blocks. But it seems disconnected from the rest of the world. The residents are friendly and proud to share their history. They'll tell you about the railroad or about their own favorite spots along the trail. The nearby town of Pacific is 1 mile down the trail, but you'll recognize it only by the trails end. Between the two towns you'll cross several roads, most small with little traffic. Utility trucks may be on the trail now and then.

When you're ready, turn around and return the way you came.

Future Plans

The King County Interurban Trail will eventually extend into Pierce County via the cities of Edgewood and Puyallup. The Green River Trail and Interurban Trail make a nice loop. Ultimately the Green River Trail will extend to the city of Seattle, offering a great river-to-sound, suburb-to-city tour.

6 SNOHOMISH COUNTY INTERURBAN TRAIL

This excursion takes you down a historic corridor in and out of view of busy Interstate 5, whose sea of red taillights competes in autumn with the orange-gold of maple trees, a forest of deeply colored evergreens, and tangles of blackberry bushes.

Activities:

Location: The cities of Everett, Lynnwood, and Mountlake Terrace, all in Snohomish County; and Snohomish County Parks

Length: 15.4 miles

Surface: Asphalt

Wheelchair access: Most of the trail is wheelchair accessible.

Difficulty: Easy. The trail is mostly flat, with several hills and several areas that run on the roadside shoulders.

Food: You'll find things to eat in the Alderwood Mall, at Beverly Boulevard, at 164th Street Southeast, and 128th Street Southwest. There are roadside eateries along the way, too.

Restrooms: Restrooms and drinking water can be found in commercial establishments along the way and in the parks.

Seasons: The trail can be used year-round. Some sections may be closed for short periods of time while the Public Utility District (PUD) works on power lines.

Access and parking: There are numerous access points beside the trail. To reach the South Lynnwood Neighborhood Park near the trail's southern end, leave I–5 at exit 179 and drive west on Southwest 220th Street. Turn north onto 66th Avenue West, east onto Southwest 212th Street, north onto 63rd Avenue West, east onto 211th Street, and north onto 61st Avenue. Leave your car beside the park.

The southern terminus of the trail is about 1.25 miles south of the park in Mountlake Terrace. There is limited parking along this southern end of the trail. If you are commuting from the southern end, you can park on the

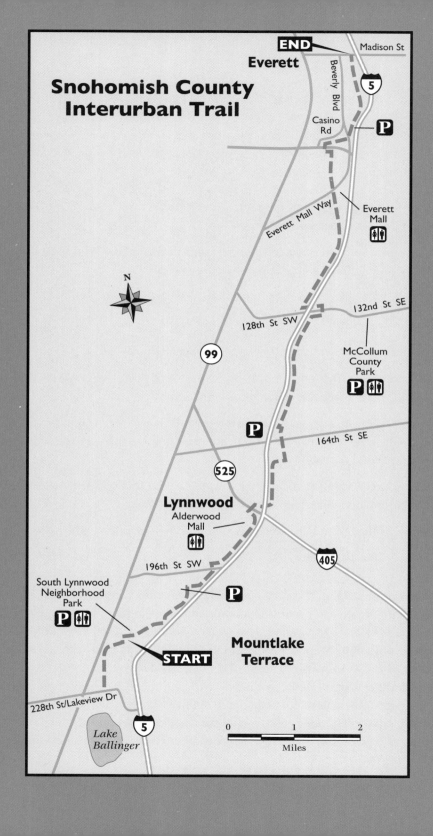

residential streets that cross the trail or you can park at Ballinger Park next to Lake Ballinger at 228th Street/Lakeview Drive. From Ballinger Park you can walk or ride along 74th Avenue north to the trailhead at 226th Street.

To begin toward the northern end of the trail, leave I–5 at exit 189 and follow Washington Highway 526 westbound toward Evergreen Way. Turn right onto Campus Parkway, then right onto Casino Road to park at Cascade High School in Everett. The trail passes across Casino Road. Or park at the northern terminus of the trail at Madison Street and Commercial Avenue in Everett.

You can also park along the residential streets in Mountlake Terrace; at the Alderwood Mall Boulevard Park & Ride (46th Avenue West and 202nd Street Southwest); at the McCollum County Park (600 128th Street Southwest); or at the 164th Street Park & Ride.

Rentals: For bike rentals in Puget Sound, see Appendix A.

Contact: Snohomish County Parks and Recreation, (425) 388–6600, www.snoco.org; Snohomish County Tourism Bureau, (425) 348–5802

Bus routes: For information, check out the Community Transit Web site at www.commtrans.org. You can also call them at (425) 353–RIDE.

||||||||||||||||||||||||||||||||||||||||||||||||||||||||||||||||||||||||||||||||||||

People came to town first by canoe, then riverboat, and finally train. With the rail lines in place across the Northwest, trains and mosquito fleets shuttled the settlers from town to town, but passengers had to compete with freight schedules, and most inland areas were without service. Then, on April 30, 1910, the Everett-Seattle Interurban introduced an elegant and effective way to move people between neighborhoods. This—the longest-lasting interurban line in Washington—connected Seattle with Everett for twenty-nine years, over a distance of 29 miles. The trolley carried residents to the Playland Amusement Park at Bitter Lake and to the Snohomish County Fairgrounds near Silver Lake; it hauled soldiers and it transported paving bricks for the construction of the Bothell-Everett Highway. In the end, however, it could not compete with cars and buses. "The line, which once traversed beautiful stands of virgin timber and skirted

> "The Everett-Seattle Interurban, the last in the state of its kind, will be but a memory, having served long and well, to be replaced at last by modern modes, which too, in all probability, will eventually pass away."
> —*Everett Daily Herald,* February 20, 1939

limpid lakes, will be abandoned and the customers along the right of way will be served by sleek gasoline-burning buses, whose coming years ago foretold the doom of the Interurban cars," said the *Everett Daily Herald* in 1939.

Now a public utilities corridor, the portion of this trail that reaches from South Lynnwood north to Everett lets you overtake I–5 gridlock on a historic route. The maple trees and blackberry bushes help distract you from the traffic, and as you approach the northern trailhead, the trail moves away from the highways. The quiet small-town ambience will greet and soothe you.

You can access the Snohomish County Interurban Trail from many points along the way; this description will guide you from South Lynnwood Neighborhood Park at its southern end northward. As you depart the park, the Interurban logo guides you through the park, onto the roadside, and finally between Alderwood Mall and I–5. At Alderwood Mall Boulevard (also 26th Avenue West) at South Maple Road, a trail sign points right. Go uphill on South Maple Road for 0.5 mile. Beware the occasional glass, gravel, and dirt on the shoulder. Cross the freeway bridge and take the next right, Butternut Road. Turn right onto the trail. Now on the east side of I–5, you pass a sea of red taillights. In autumn the orange-gold of maple trees highlights the forest of deeply colored evergreens and blackberries. The trail is well marked in most places.

You'll next head uphill, curving sharply east just south of 164th Street. Turn left (north) where the trail reaches a T-intersection at 13th Street, which becomes Meadowbrook (this left turn is unmarked). Pass through a light on 13th, then turn left at 160th Street Southwest. The trail sign is on your left, just after you start downhill. Use caution crossing the road. As you return to the I–5 corridor, blue spruce, tall firs, and banks of blackberry bushes shield you from the highway.

At exit 186 (Paine Field) the trail escapes I–5 and passes by an old drive-in, now the Puget Park Swap Meet and Drive-In. Turn left at Third Avenue Southwest where the trail becomes a sidewalk, then turn left on 128th Street (a stoplight) to find espresso, granita, and snacks at Sydney's Coffee Company.

Cross I–5 on 128th Street Southwest. Use caution on the ramp. You'll regain the trail on the west side of the interstate after crossing the off ramp. The light there makes this a safer crossing.

Now a high cement wall separates you from the freeway. The tall cedars and firs all but block the traffic noise.

The trail continues straight as a sidewalk at West Mall Drive and crosses Southeast Everett Mall Way. Turn left at 84th Street, then right at Seventh Avenue Southeast (a stoplight) and right at East Casino Road (another stoplight). Pass under the highway.

The trail takes a right across from Cascade High School. Enjoy the calm of a residential neighborhood and some picnic tables. Head downhill into the Pinehurst neighborhood and cross Beverly Boulevard. You'll discover a restaurant or two and the neighborhood convenience store in a nifty old building. Use the crosswalk here—not only for safety, but also to enjoy the unusual signal: It flashes a bicycle symbol just like the ones found in downtown Zurich. Pass through the Beverly Park substation to the trail's end at Interurban Park on Madison Street and Commercial Avenue in Everett.

When you are ready, turn around and return the way you came.

Future Plans

The city of Mountlake Terrace will ultimately extend the trail south to the King County line. Edmonds is contemplating alternative alignments for the corridor. Snohomish County will have a pedestrian/bicycle overcrossing connection north of 128th Street at about 124th Street and 3rd Avenue to bypass the I–5/128th Street crossing. Anticipated completion is 2008 to 2009. Everett plans to extend the trail to the downtown neighborhood. Portions of the corridor are reserved for a passenger rail line.

7 CEDAR RIVER TRAIL AND CEDAR TO GREEN RIVER TRAIL

Beginning as a narrow path below the streets of Renton, the Cedar River Trail ascends to street level to head east toward Maple Valley and Landsburg Park. The final miles of rural, wooded pathway visit the Cedar River at its most dramatic. A side trip to Lake Wilderness offers the chance for a waterfront picnic.

Activities:

Location: The cities of Renton and Maple Valley, along with Lake Wilderness, all in King County

Length: The Cedar River Trail runs 17.5 miles; the Cedar to Green River Trail is a 4-mile round trip.

Surface: Asphalt, ballast (some of it heavy), and dirt

Wheelchair access: There are paved portions of trail at Liberty Park, North Sixth Street, Wells Street, and Cedar River Park.

Difficulty: Mostly easy, although several miles between Cedar Grove Road and the Washington Highway 18 overpass are difficult due to large, deep ballast.

Food: Grocery stores and restaurants can be found in Renton, Lake Wilderness, and Maple Valley.

Restrooms: Most of the park facilities listed under Access and parking have vault toilets or restrooms, along with drinking water, phones, picnic tables, barbecues, and picnic shelters. Check the Web sites listed under Contact for more facilities.

Seasons: The trail can be used year-round.

Access and parking: You can park your car and access the trail at any of the following park facilities:

- North Sixth Street at the Cedar River: If you're coming from Interstate 405 South, take exit 5 (Park Avenue/Sunset Boulevard Northeast). Turn

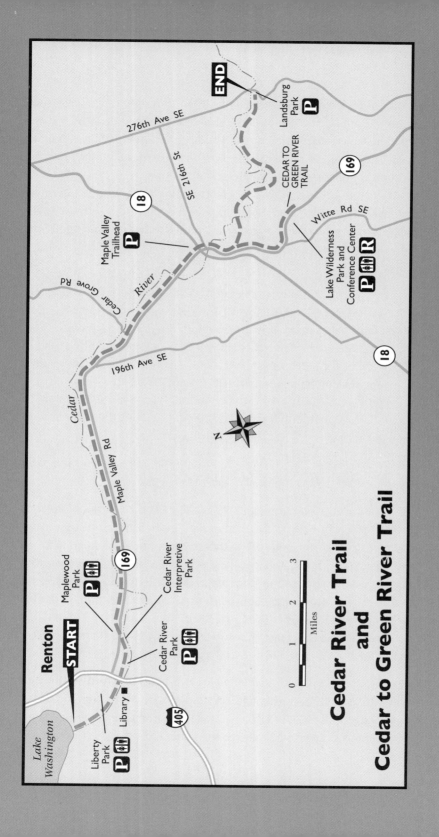

Cedar River Trail
and
Cedar to Green River Trail

right from the exit onto Park Avenue, then turn right onto North Sixth Street. Continue straight for several blocks until you dead-end at the trail. You'll pass a large trail sign at Logan Street. The road turns right to parallel the trail. You can park at the edge of Puget Sound. This is the western terminus of the Cedar River Trail.

If you're arriving from I–405 North, take exit 5 (Issaquah/Sunset Boulevard Northeast). Turn left onto Sunset Boulevard, which will eventually turn into Park Avenue. Turn right onto North Sixth Street and continue as directed above.

- Cedar River and Cedar River Interpretative Parks on Washington Highway 169: From I–405 South, take exit 4 (Maple Valley). This will bring you onto Sunset Boulevard Northeast. Turn left at the second traffic light onto Maple Valley Road (WA 169). Get into the right lane, travel a short distance, and turn right into Cedar River Park. Cedar River Intrepetative Park is 1 mile farther, on your right, down a lightly wooded, paved trail. Read about salmon habitat in this little roadside facility.

  From I–405 North, take exit 4A (Renton/Maple Valley). Turn right at the end of the exit onto Maple Valley Road (WA 169), then continue as directed above.

- Maple Valley Trailhead: The Maple Valley Trailhead is at an unmarked pullout on WA 169 just west of the WA 18 overpass.

- Landsburg Park: Leave Interstate 90 at exit 17 and drive south on Front Street, which turns into 276th Avenue Southeast. Pass through the town of Hobart and south of Southeast 216th Street, 13 miles in all, to the river. Watch for the hang gliders on Tiger Mountain and enjoy the Bavarian setting of Boehms Chocolates in Issaquah along the way. Park in the lot on 276th Avenue Southeast across from Landsburg Park. This is the eastern terminus of the Cedar River Trail.

  You can also drive east on 216th Street from WA 169 in Maple Valley to its end at 276th Avenue. Turn right to reach the river in 2.5 miles.

- Lake Wilderness Park in Maple Valley: From WA 169, turn south onto Witte Road Southeast, then left onto Southeast 248th Street after 0.8 mile. The park is on your left in 0.5 mile. The trail begins at the Wilderness Center Lodge; it's 1.8 miles to the Cedar River Trail.

Rentals: See Appendix A for bike rentals in Puget Sound. Boat rentals are available at Lake Wilderness.

Contact: King County Parks, (206) 296–4232, www.metrokc.gov/parks. Or contact City of Renton Parks, (425) 430–6600, www.ci.renton.wa.us.

Bus routes: Buses #143 and #149 take you from Seattle to Renton and Maple Valley. The bus depot is at Third and Burnett in Renton. For more information, visit the Metro Transit Web site at transit.metrokc.gov, or call them at (206) 553–3000.

|||||||||||||||||||||||||||||||||||||||||||||||||||||||||||||||||||||||||||||||||||||||

From 1884 to the 1940s, the rail lines you'll be traveling on this jaunt served the coal industry, which was largely responsible for the area's economic growth. The Columbia & Puget Sound Railway, once called the Seattle Coal & Transportation Company, moved coal from the mines of Maple Valley and Renton to Seattle starting in 1884. One hundred coal cars traveled this route in 1891; by 1913, 236 were making the trip. The Chicago, Milwaukee & Puget Sound Railway, part of the same parent company, ran the lines from Maple Valley to Cedar Falls and Rattlesnake Lake. The mines in Puget Sound produced most of Washington's 1.25 million tons of coal in 1890, and the best coal was from this area—in particular, the Newcastle mine on this line just north of Renton. (See Trail 4, Coal Creek Park Trail.) The coal was taken to the coal docks in Seattle for transport to San Francisco.

You can access the set of trails discussed here from many points; this description begins at the western end, in Renton, and proceeds eastward. In the city of Renton, the Cedar River Trail originates as a narrow path on the banks of the canal-like Cedar River; the city library floats above the water like a modern Ponte Vecchio. The trail then ascends to street level at Liberty Park to head east beside WA 169 on paved trail. This is a safe alternative to a narrow highway, great for commuters, and complete with bus service from Seattle to Maple Valley.

Dressed with treed parks, this section is especially popular with skaters; horseback riding is allowed once you're outside the Renton city limits. It's

The Cedar River Trail follows the scenic Cedar River.

hard to believe you're only a few hundred yards from WA 169. The trail follows the Cedar River along WA 169, dropping below the highway at times to provide a respite from traffic. It continues close to the highway for the next 5 miles, with the river coming up to meet you now and again, then wandering off, only to return under an old trestle or running along beside you once again. Continue past 196th Avenue Southeast and beyond.

Pass through a tunnel under Southeast 216th Street, then cross a trestle over the Cedar River. Retreat from the highway here and travel though a quiet, rural corridor near the river and its rural riverfront homes all the way to Landsburg Park. You'll reach the Lake Wilderness cutoff 0.8 mile from the WA 18 overpass (the high overpass above the trailhead pullout). If you like, you can take a soft right uphill on the 1.8-mile trail here to reach Lake Wilderness on the Cedar to Green River Trail, which is paved. (See Alternative Trail, below.)

This description, however, continues straight 4.8 miles to Landsburg Park. Along the final 2 miles of this pathway, the Cedar River leaves the trail then sneaks back, crossing back and forth, sometimes wandering with you for a while. Stop on the trestle to watch the river rush, especially when the waters are high. Watch the kayakers fighting the whitewater. The turbulence and speed of the Cedar River is impressive and frightening during high waters and flood stage. The surrounding terrain is hillier here, near the Cascade Mountains. In Landsburg Park itself you can walk beside the dam. When you're ready, turn around and return the way you came.

Alternative Trail

To enjoy the rural portion of this outing by foot, horse, or mountain bike, try a trip between Lake Wilderness Park and Landsburg Park. Both parks offer pretty waterfront places to picnic, and Lake Wilderness is the site of a large 1890s resort. The early 1900s brought a homestead for fishermen and hunters, which then gave way to the resorts of the 1920s. Some 9,000 guests per day could enjoy the skating rink, dance pavilions, beach slides, trapezes, and diving towers at Gaffney's Grove Resort in 1939. Peek in at the award-winning Lake Wilderness Center to see the modern replacement.

To reach the Cedar River Trail from the lodge, turn left once you reach the wide trail. A gate points you toward the Cedar River Trail, 1.8 miles ahead. The trail surface is easy to ride on a bike or a horse and pleasant to walk. This is an equestrian area. Be kind to the horses. Pass through the forest and the South King County Arboretum with its wandering interpretive trails, under Witte Road Southeast, and beside a housing development. At mile 1.5 you can take a right to enjoy some lovely water views. Trees frame the view of Lake Wilderness from the north bank. It's a great spot for a stroll or a mostly flat ride. Then return to the trail, pass under WA 169, and intersect the Cedar River Trail; Landsburg Park is 4.8 miles to your right.

Future Plans

The trail will be paved an additional 5 miles toward Maple Valley as funds become available. Farther in the future is a connection from Landsburg Park to the Snoqualmie Valley Trail (see Trail 10) and the John Wayne Pioneer Trail (see Trail 25) at Rattlesnake Lake in North Bend.

8 TIGER MOUNTAIN STATE FOREST

Tiger Mountain State Forest has several trailheads and miles of trails. Three multiuse rail trails and one hiking trail follow old railroad grades. The Preston Railroad Trail, the Northwest Timber Trail, and the Iverson Railroad Trail can be traveled individually or as a continuous loop. The Preston Railroad and Northwest Timber Trails take you on an exhilarating up- and downhill ride; the Iverson Trail, which makes a nice side trip, takes you through lowlands. Many volunteer groups maintain these trails and use them heavily. Mountain bikers, hikers, and equestrians enjoy the trails.

Activities:

Location: King County

Length: 8 miles

Surface: Crushed stone, rocks, gravel, and dirt. You'll find tree roots, puddles, and (on the Preston Railroad Trail section) running water on the pathway.

Wheelchair access: The trail is not wheelchair accessible.

Difficulty: Difficult to expert

Food: No food is available along this trail.

Restrooms: You'll find facilities at the Tiger Summit Trailhead.

Seasons: Tiger Mountain State Forest trails are open from April 16 through October 14.

Access and parking: To reach the Tiger Summit parking lot, get off Interstate 90 at exit 25 (Washington Highway 18). Head west 4.3 miles to the TIGER MOUNTAIN SUMMIT sign. The lot is just beyond on the right.

Rentals: See Appendix A for bike rentals in Puget Sound.

Contact: Washington State Department of Natural Resources, South Puget Sound Region Office, (360) 825–1631, www.dnr.wa.gov

Bus routes: None

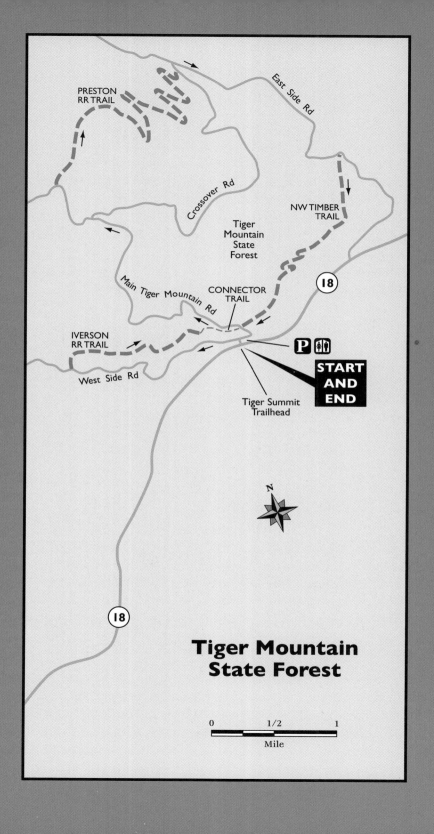

PRESTON
RR TRAIL

East Side Rd

Crossover Rd

NW TIMBER
TRAIL

Tiger
Mountain
State
Forest

18

Main Tiger Mountain Rd

CONNECTOR
TRAIL

IVERSON
RR TRAIL

P 👫

**START
AND
END**

West Side Rd

Tiger Summit
Trailhead

N

18

**Tiger Mountain
State Forest**

0   1/2   1
Mile

II

Logging in Tiger Mountain State Forest started in the 1920s and continues today. Timber was transported by switchback or incline railways
to the base of the mountain and by local railroads to mills in Preston,
Issaquah, Hobart, and High Point. Both the Preston and Northwest Timber Trails were originally switchback railways. Where the trail now turns
sharply at each switchback, a tail track once extended straight ahead to
allow trains to move past the switchback, then back up to continue downhill. The Iverson Trail was part of the Wooden Pacific incline railway, which
climbed 2 straight miles to the summit. The trails are named for the companies that logged them. The last of them, the Preston Mill, burned down
in 1990. The Department of Natural Resources, together with mountain
bikers, built the trails in the early 1990s. The West Tiger Railroad Grade, a
hiking trail, starts at the inner reaches of the West Tiger Natural Resources
Conservation Area and is reached from the High School Trail (see More
Washington Rail Trails for information).

While you're on the road, watch out for logging trucks and communi-
cations vehicles for the radio, television, and cell-phone towers. Gates are
locked year-round, blocking other traffic. The trails are closed during the
wet season, because costly damage can occur when they're muddy.

There are many trails and routes to take as you explore Tiger Mountain. This description takes you up the Preston Railroad Trail, whose summit
(at 1,230 feet) lies 3.4 miles above the parking lot via Main Tiger Mountain
Road. Once you complete the Preston segment, you'll descend the Northwest Timber Trail back to the parking lot or (if you'd like to stretch your legs
some more) to the Connector Trail, which leads to the Iverson Railroad Trail.

Preston Railroad Trail, 3.7 miles

IIIIIIIIIIIIIIIIIIIIIIIIIIIIIIIIIIIIIIIIIIIIIIIIIIIIIIIIIIIIIIIIIIIIIIIIIIIIIIIIIIIIIIIIIIIIIIIIIIIIIIIIIIIIIIIII

Tough, wet, and fun: That's the expert-level Preston Railroad Trail. You've
got to like to biff and bounce on a bike, wade through puddles, straddle
streams, and rocket off roots. A single-track downhill grade that turns into
a series of switchbacks, the trail is currently a drainage, though culverts are

The moist and wooded trails of Tiger Mountain.

being added to dry it out. The Backcountry Bicycle Trail Club has adopted the trail; we have its members to thank for maintenance.

From the Tiger Mountain Summit parking lot, pass through the right-hand gate. On your way up Main Tiger Mountain Road, you'll pass both the lower trailhead for the Northwest Timber Trail and the Connector Trail that leads to the Iverson Trail. Prepare for a steep climb. The clear-cuts are ugly but allow far-reaching views of Mount Rainier and the Green, Cedar, and White River Valleys. You'll find mile markers on the road and along the trail. At the T-intersection, turn left. The trailhead is a wooden gate on your right. The trail heads briefly and gradually uphill before it begins the long descent. It's narrow, a bit curvy, and fun for an experienced biker. At 0.7 mile, it finds the railroad right-of-way. The roots and obstacles thicken. You're in a forest of fir, cedar, hemlock, alder, and maple trees with bears, bobcats, grouse, ducks, and more than a hundred species of birds.

At approximately 1 mile, look for the first switchback—a hard left. The trail appears to continue straight here. If you miss the switchback, you'll end up at a major drainage; turn back. The trees at switchbacks are often marked with flagging and brush. The switchbacks are quite obvious from here on. Enjoy the challenge of this bumpy, wet descent.

Congratulate yourself when you reach the wooden gate at the bottom of the trail. Turn left onto Crossover Road, then right 0.2 mile later onto East Side Road, toward the Northwest Timber Trail. Roads and trails are well signed. Take rocky East Side Road about 2 miles. Relax. Enjoy the rushing water at creek crossings and the valley views. At just under 2 miles, the Northwest Timber Trail departs on your right for some rolling single-track. (East Side Road continues straight to end at WA 18 more than a mile west of the parking lot. Don't continue downhill on this road unless you enjoy a highway stroll!)

Northwest Timber Trail, 2.3 miles

The Northwest Timber Trail runs deep in the forest. Small bridges cross drainages and large bridges cross creeks as the pathway winds around the edge of the hillside. The lower end of the trail passes through archways canopied by brightly mossed deciduous trees; the spot captures the colors and essence of a Grimm Brothers fairy-tale painting. Lots of large puddles straddle the trail—prepare for wet feet—which is rugged in places but definitely an octave down from the Preston Railroad Trail in grade, surface, wetness, and obstacles. Check out the open views of the valleys below. Remember: Bikes yield to hikers yield to horses (though this is really bike territory). Use caution on your descents.

At the end of the Northwest Timber Trail, you have two choices. You can either turn left to reach the main parking lot and the end of your outing, or you can cross Main Tiger Mountain Road and find the Connector Trail just uphill. Take this to the Iverson Trail and more exercise.

By the way, you can also travel just the Northwest Timber Trail in an out-and-back trip. From the parking lot, head 0.25 mile up Main Tiger Mountain Road (right-hand gate), then turn right onto the Northwest Timber Trail. You'll ascend to East Side Road, 30 feet higher. Don't let this deceive you: You'll have plenty of little ups and downs on the way. From the road, turn around and return the way you came.

Iverson Railroad Trail, 2 miles

Get ready for a single-track with a long climb and a sometimes difficult descent. Bounce over roots, ride through streams, cross over bridges, and struggle to stay on switchbacks. Cyclists, prepare to walk.

You can explore the Iverson Railroad Trail on its own, or as a continuation of your Northwest Timber Trail jaunt. Start from the main parking lot and pass through the left gate (it is signed). After a bit of an uphill grade, pass through the locked gate onto West Side Road and continue for 1.5 miles to the signed Iverson Railroad Trail, on your right. Climb through the forest for just under 1.5 miles. The climb is steepest in the first 0.5 mile. Light filters through the dark forest at the top of the trail. Start your descent at a bridge crossing. Prepare to hop or dismount at the treacherous tree trunks and timber across the trail. You'll parallel the West Side Road as you descend the final portion of the trail. Turn right at the T-intersection to return to the trailhead, or head left to continue onto the Connector Trail.

9 PRESTON-SNOQUALMIE TRAIL

This peaceful, wooded trail in the Cascade foothills ends with a view of spectacular Snoqualmie Falls. For a romantic walk, an evening ride, your daily jog, or a pleasant skate, this trail is the ticket.

Activities:

Location: Preston, King County

Length: 6.2 miles

Surface: Asphalt with brief, steep gravel switchbacks

Wheelchair access: The trail is wheelchair accessible except for the descent and switchbacks listed below.

Difficulty: Easy, except for a steep paved descent to a road crossing and gravel switchbacks back up to the trail.

Food: In Preston you'll find a mini mart and restaurant at the Interstate 90 interchange. There are restaurants and grocery stores in Fall City.

Restrooms: There is a chemical toilet at the Lake Alice Trailhead.

Seasons: The trail can be used year-round.

Access and parking: You can access the trail from either the Preston or the Lake Alice Trailheads. To reach the Preston Trailhead, near the trail's western terminus, leave I–90 at exit 22 (Fall City). Turn north and drive to the T-intersection with Preston–Fall City Road. Turn right (east), drive 2 blocks, and then turn left onto Southeast 87th Street. The small parking lot is on your right.

To avoid the trail's switchbacks and get the grand view, start at the Lake Alice Trailhead (near its eastern end). To reach this trailhead, follow Preston–Fall City Road northeast for 3.5 miles past 87th Street (the location of the Preston Trailhead), then turn right onto Lake Alice Road. You'll find the trailhead on your right in 0.8 mile.

Rentals: There are no rentals along the route. See Appendix A for rentals in Puget Sound.

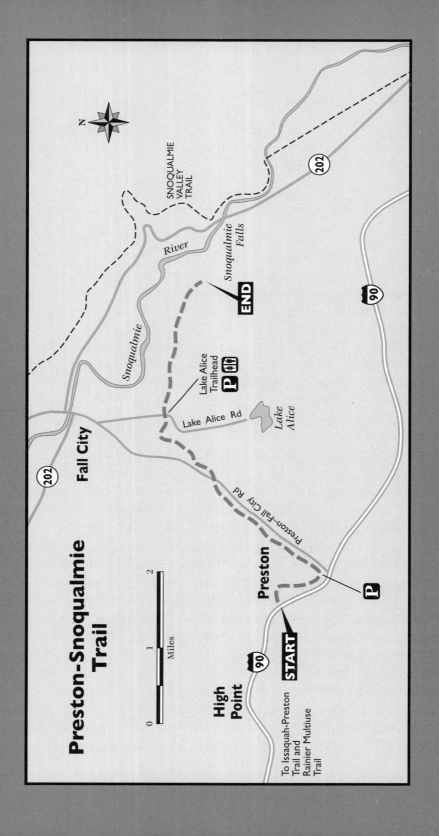

Preston-Snoqualmie Trail

N

SNOQUALMIE VALLEY TRAIL

202

Snoqualmie River

Snoqualmie Falls

END

Snoqualmie

Lake Alice Trailhead
P

Lake Alice Rd

Lake Alice

Fall City

202

Preston-Fall City Rd

Preston

P

High Point

90

START

To Issaquah-Preston Trail and Rainier Multiuse Trail

0   1   2
Miles

Contact: King County Parks Division, (206) 296–7800, www.metrokc.gov/parks/

Bus routes: Contact Metro Transit at (206) 553–3000, or visit the Web site at transit.metrokc.gov/parks/trails.

||||||||||||||||||||||||||||||||||||||||||||||||||||||||||||||||||||||||||||||||||

Only a twenty-minute drive from the suburbs on the east side of Lake Washington, the Preston-Snoqualmie Trail makes for a pleasant, woodsy outing. Parents stroll the pathway with their children as locals walk their dogs, enjoying the valley views. The trail ends with a view of Snoqualmie Falls, which drop 268 feet into the Snoqualmie River—100 feet more than the drop at Niagara Falls. The pavement is smooth and relatively flat except for a road crossing with a steep hill on both sides, one paved and the other featuring gravel switchbacks. This Seattle, Lakeshore & Eastern railway was built in 1890; the trail opened in 1978.

This description follows the trail from west to east. The trail actually extends 0.9 mile farther west from its western trailhead in Preston. If you'd like to explore this section, leave the trailhead parking lot and cross Southeast 87th Street; your route parallels the road and winds along the path of a corporate complex. You'll find a few small street crossings, a bit of grade, and some rough pavement here and there—just enough to intimidate a beginning skater.

To head east toward Snoqualmie Falls, start at the edge of the parking lot. The trail traverses a sidehill. The hillside down to the streets of the Preston Mill town and the valley below affords fine views and brightens your jaunt. You may see deer and stellar jays, cougars and bears. Locals mostly ignore the presence of cougars and bears. Though the animals retreat when humans are around, please do read the wildlife guidelines at the trailhead.

A large trestle once crossed the Raging River Valley 2.5 miles out. It has been replaced with a steep descent to the road. Watch for traffic veering around the curve as you cross Preston–Fall City Road. The trail parallels the road briefly, turns left, and climbs back up several steep gravel switchbacks to the hillside. Arrive at the Lake Alice Trailhead 3.5 miles from Preston.

The final 1.8 miles of trail south from Lake Alice Road offer valley views and a distant view of Snoqualmie Falls, framed by tall fir and cedar trees. Far from the tourist experience at the Salish Lodge, you'll observe the scene from a secluded bench in the forest.

Visit the nearby town of Fall City for a meal—perhaps beside the Snoqualmie River—or head up to the Salish Lodge for a bird's-eye view of the falls from the attic lounge. Above the trail and to the right is the new Snoqualmie Ridge community. Several soft-surface side trails climb the ridge and provide neighborhood access. Markers and restaurants are available by following these side trails and local roadways.

When you're ready, turn around and return the way you came.

Future Plans

The Snoqualmie Valley Trail and the Snoqualmie Centennial Trail are across the river from the Preston-Snoqualmie Trail. Currently, the Snoqualmie River is uncrossable. The right-of-way beyond the end of the Preston-Snoqualmie Trail is presently used by the Puget Sound Railroad Historical Society. Sightseeing trains run from the old Snoqualmie depot of the Great Northern Railway to the ledge above the falls. Perhaps in the future this right-of-way ledge can be shared in a way that would allow the Preston-Snoqualmie Trail to cross the river and connect to the other trails of the Snoqualmie Valley, along with the town of Snoqualmie. For now, the train ride from the depot—also a railroad museum—makes for an enjoyable, historical look above the falls.

Eventually the Issaquah-Preston Trail will connect to the Preston-Snoqualmie Trail, the Rainier Multiuse Trail in Issaquah, and the planned Lake Sammamish Trail (see More Washington Rail Trails). These will all be linked when a new highway interchange is built.

10 SNOQUALMIE VALLEY TRAIL

Wander the foothills of rural Snoqualmie Valley from Duvall through Carnation, to Snoqualmie Falls near Snoqualmie, on to North Bend, and finally to the John Wayne Pioneer Trail. You'll travel near the highway, through wetlands, along ridges, above the valley, through a golf course, minutes from Snoqualmie Falls, and into charming and historic downtown areas. Enjoy a teahouse, an elegant lodge, a 268-foot waterfall, bakeries, bridges, rivers, and lakes.

Activities:

Location: Duvall to North Bend, King County

Length: 31 miles

Surface: Crushed rock and original ballast

Wheelchair access: The trail is not wheelchair accessible.

Difficulty: Easy to moderate. The ballast and trestle gravel is a bit heavy in places. The 2.6 percent average grade above the valley floor requires a few climbs. The roadside trail detour from Tokul Road to Mount Si Golf Course also has some climbs.

Food: Restaurants, cafes, and grocery stores are all found within 1 mile of the trail, in Snoqualmie, Duvall, Carnation, Snoqualmie Falls, and North Bend. Mount Si Golf Course is along the trail as well.

Restrooms: Public restrooms are available at Duvall Park and at Rattlesnake Lake Recreation Area. There is also drinking water at Rattlesnake Lake.

Seasons: The trail can be used year-round.

Access and parking: To start at the northern end of the trail in Duvall, take Woodinville-Duvall Road east to Washington Highway 203, then turn north into the parking area nearby. To start in North Bend, turn north off North Bend Way onto Ballarat Avenue to reach the Park & Ride lot on Northeast Fourth Street, near the library.

To start at Nick Loutsis Park in Carnation, take WA 203 to Entwistle Street and turn east.

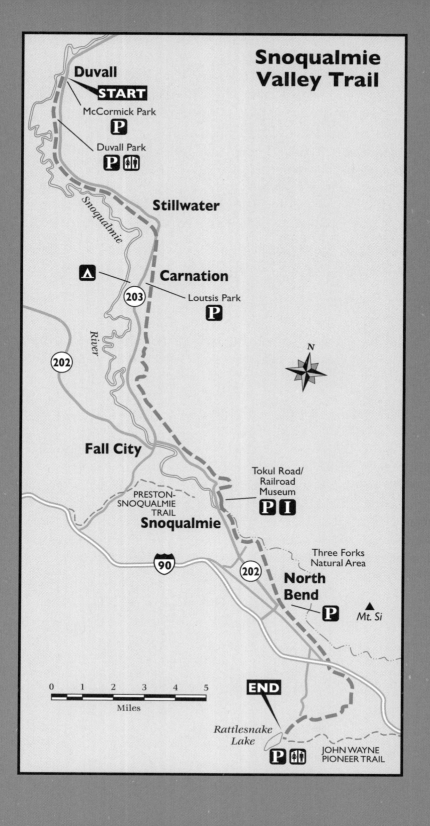

If you want to start the trail at Tokul Road, take Washington Highway 202 to Tokul Road near Snoqualmie Falls. Turn north on Tokul Road and continue 0.6 mile to the trail underpass. Turn right onto the single-track trail down to the railroad grade. You can also descend the steps to the trail, found on Tokul Road at the tunnel.

To begin at Rattlesnake Lake, take exit 32 (436th Avenue Northeast) off Interstate 90 eastbound. Turn south and follow the curves of the road for 2.9 miles to park at Rattlesnake Lake. Find the trail directly across the street.

Rentals: There are no rentals along the route. See Appendix A for bike rentals in Puget Sound.

Contact: King County Parks Division, (206) 296–4232, www.metrokc.gov /parks/trails

Bus routes: On weekdays only, take bus #929 from Duvall to North Bend, or #209 from Preston to Fall City to North Bend. Check the Metro Transit Web site at transit.metrokc.gov, or call them at (206) 553–3000.

You can choose from among many spots to hop on the Snoqualmie Valley Trail; this description follows it from Duvall (at its northern end) to Rattlesnake Lake in the south. You may wish to travel from Carnation to Duvall for a flat ride; head to Snoqualmie Falls for some hills and ridge views; or depart from North Bend for a lowland ride away from the highway. Start at Rattlesnake Lake for a longer trip with a bit of downhill grade.

Duvall to Carnation, 9 miles

Enjoy the town of Duvall; watch it hanging on to its rural feel despite recent growth. Look for the antiques shops and ice cream parlor. From McCormick Park, head north a few blocks for a peek at an old Chicago, Milwaukee, St. Paul & Pacific Railroad depot.

The trail travels southeast on the west side of WA 203, close to the road yet separated by wetlands and open fields. You'll pass driveway crossings of the working farms and lots of blackberry bushes. Watch for waterfowl and listen for songbirds. Bird hunters sometimes stalk their prey near the trail, but this is not generally a problem. Use caution at a couple of road crossings.

The trail crosses WA 203 just north of Carnation. Reach the Nick Loutsis Trailhead at mile 9 at Entwistle Street. Turn west (right) for a neighborhood tour of Carnation, an espresso at Starbucks, a snack at QFC grocery, or tea and fresh muffins at Rosebuds Tea Room and Antique Shop. Take a side trip to the riverfront at Tolt-McDonald Park, just south of the shopping center.

Carnation to Tokul Road, 10 miles

From Carnation the trail rises above the Snoqualmie Valley, crossing over trestles and enjoying views of the river and valley through a canopy of evergreens. Cross the Tolt River 0.5 mile from the town of Carnation. You'll pass Remlinger Farms 0.5 mile farther on. Cross the 356th Drive Southeast Trailhead at 7 miles. A high bridge crosses Tokul Creek at 9 miles, affording valley views and a peek at the creek below. The trail climbs near Snoqualmie Falls

This 1912 depot station in Duvall used to serve the Chicago, Milwaukee, St. Paul & Pacific Railroad.

and ends 3.3 miles from 356th under the Tokul Road underpass at mile 10. Exit the trail via the single-track, heading left up to Tokul Road.

To visit Snoqualmie Falls and take the Snoqualmie Centennial Trail to the Northwest Railroad Museum for a side trip, water, restrooms, a snack, or a meal, turn south on Tokul Road. To view the falls, turn right at the T-intersection with WA 202 at 1.2 miles. Ride the shoulder briefly to the parking lot on your right. Take the bridge to the falls. Do not cross the highway. To reach the museum, turn left after you cross the bridge to the falls for a brief jaunt and a bridge crossing on the road. Leave the road at the light at Snoqualmie Parkway to ride the Snoqualmie Centennial Trail 0.8 mile to its end at the museum.

Tokul Road to Meadowbrook, 5 miles

To continue on the Snoqualmie Valley Trail through North Bend and on to Rattlesnake Lake, follow Tokul Road south for a ride on a country road. Turn east on Stearns Road and continue on Mill Pond Road, then Reinig Road. The former Weyerhauser mill site is nearby. It was the second all-electric mill in the United States and the first to reduce the incidence of forest fires by electrifying the steam donkey logging trains. The abandoned mill looms in the midst of rural rolling hills and valleys. It lies north of the Snoqualmie River and on the historic Seattle, Lakeshore & Eastern main line, which hauled timber for shipping. The line reached into Seattle from North Bend and connected to what is now the Snohomish Centennial Trail North, in Snohomish County.

The city of Snoqualmie Falls—the Weyerhauser Company town— dominated the landscape here until 1958. The mill workers' homes were then sold and transported, on a temporary bridge, to the valley below. Beyond the mill the Snoqualmie River and the town of Snoqualmie across the river come into view. Use the Meadowbrook Bridge off Mill Pond Road to visit the town. Continue on Reinig Road to find the old railroad bridge across the river. Ascend steps to continue east on the trail. The trail passes the Meadowbrook Slough near the confluence of the three forks of the

Snoqualmie River. Mount Si Golf Course will appear, surrounding the trail. Pass through the golf course. Look up at Mount Si towering above the upper Snoqualmie River valley.

If it's time for lunch, try the deck at the golf course restaurant. It's a friendly place that serves good food. They'll even reserve a table for you and your cycling buddies.

Continue southeast from the golf course, beside fields, along the Snoqualmie River, and below the steep wall of Mount Si. Cross several small roads before you reach the parking lot at Fourth and Ballarat. For a bit of railroad history, visit the library across the street; you might also wish to head downtown to visit George's Bakery or the main street of downtown North Bend, just a few minutes away. The factory outlet mall is up the street a couple of miles.

North Bend to Rattlesnake Lake and the John Wayne Pioneer Trail, 7.3 miles

The Snoqualmie Valley Trail continues north of the parking lot. Mount Si remains in sight as you pass soccer fields, cross several streets, and watch the skate rats at the skateboard park. Cross North Bend Way at 2 miles and then cross under I–90. Arrive at Rattlesnake Lake 4.75 miles from here. To reach the John Wayne Trail, hop off the trail onto the road and through the gate. Look for the gated trail on your left at 0.6 mile. You can ride east on the John Wayne Trail or enjoy the Rattlesnake Lake Recreation Area.

Trail Connections and Future Plans

You don't have to cross the country to discover differences, find surprises, and witness dramatic changes in scenery, terrain, culinary treats, and perspective. Existing trails in Washington State combine to create a diverse and

A stretch of trail from Duvall to Carnation.

scenic experience. For instance, you can travel from Duvall to the Columbia River on the Snoqualmie Valley Trail (SVT) and the John Wayne Pioneer Trail.

You could also spend a day touring Seattle neighborhoods and rural towns, breweries and wineries, espresso shops and bakeries, lakes and rivers, mountains and desert on one continuous trail. Eventually the SVT will be linked to the Snohomish Centennial Trail through Monroe in Snohomish County. The connection between the SVT, the John Wayne Trail at Rattlesnake Lake, and the proposed Cedar River Trail will take you to Renton and Lake Washington. If the SVT becomes linked to the Preston-Snoqualmie Trail, you'll be able to continue into Issaquah, up the East Lake Sammamish Trail to Redmond, and all the way to Seattle for a multiday tour of the Snoqualmie Valley and Seattle. You'll be able to start this tour from the east at the border of Idaho or from the north in Skagit County, once the work is done. Our counties, cities, and the state are working vigorously to develop future trails and connections that will provide an even greater trail network suitable for multiday tours.

The Snoqualmie Valley Trail parallels the Snoqualmie River.

11 IRON GOAT TRAIL

This interpretive hiking trail in the Stevens Pass historic district climbs a constant 2.2 percent grade. Kiosks guide you through a trail decorated with wildflowers and forests of ferns, alders, and evergreens. The route offers you views of the Alpine Lakes Wilderness and mountain peaks, rivers and streams, remnants of the railroad, and the 7.8-mile Cascade Tunnel. Mileage markers reflect the original railroad signs, indicating mileage to St. Paul, Minnesota. The trail is named for the logo on the Great Northern trains.

Activities:

Location: King County, near Stevens Pass

Length: 10 miles

Surface: Gravel with binder and crushed limestone on barrier-free sections

Wheelchair access: The 2.2-mile lower grade is barrier-free and wheelchair accessible from Martin Creek Trailhead to Scenic Iron Goat Trail Interpretive Site. Also, 3 miles of barrier-free trail (moderate difficulty) is available from the Wellington Trailhead to the Windy Point Tunnel.

Difficulty: Easy to moderate

Food: No food is available along this trail.

Restrooms: There are restrooms at the Martin Creek and Wellington Trailheads, and the Scenic Iron Goat Trail Interpretive Site; there is a pit toilet at Windy Point.

Seasons: Winter travel is discouraged due to avalanche risks and snow-covered access.

Access and parking: To reach the Martin Creek Trailhead, take U.S. Highway 2 to milepost 55, 6 miles east of the town of Skykomish, or to milepost 58.3 at Scenic, 5.6 miles west of the summit. Turn north onto Old Cascade Highway, Forest Road 67. Proceed to Forest Road 6710 (2.3 miles from milepost 55 or 1.4 miles from milepost 58.3). Take FR 6710 1.4 miles to the trailhead.

To access the trail at the new Scenic Iron Goat Trail Interpretive Site Trailhead, drive US 2 to milepost 58.3, at Scenic. Turn north onto Old Cascade Highway, then immediately turn right into the new trailhead. Look for the caboose.

To reach the Wellington Trailhead, drive to the Stevens Pass parking lot on the north side of US 2 (opposite the ski area). Heading west, take the first right (0.3 mile) onto Old Stevens Pass Highway at milepost 64.4. After 2.8 miles, turn right onto a short gravel spur road marked WELLINGTON TRAILHEAD.

A Northwest Forest Pass is needed at the Martin Creek and Wellington Trailheads when parking at these sites. You can purchase a one-day ($5) or annual ($30) permit via the Internet, the Skykomish Ranger Station, or hiking stores.

Rentals: No rentals are available along this trail.

Contact: U.S. Forest Service, Skykomish Ranger Station, (360) 677–2414. To order the trail guidebooks, contact Volunteers for Outdoor Washington at (206) 517–3019 or visit www.irongoat.org.

You can also visit the Mount Baker-Snoqualmie Forest Service Web site at www.fs.fed.us/r6/mbs/.

Bus routes: None

The route of the Iron Goat Trail is best known for two things: for the impressive engineering of the mountainside switchbacks and the Cascade Tunnel, and for the tragedy of 1910, when an avalanche knocked fifteen cars off the rails and killed ninety-six people. The tragedy was but the final blow for the train's passengers, who had been stalled for seven days watching hillsides of rocks, snow, and trees sliding over the tracks.

The drama of the railroad started back in 1891 when engineers like Charles Haskell and John Stevens forced their way to Stevens Pass through

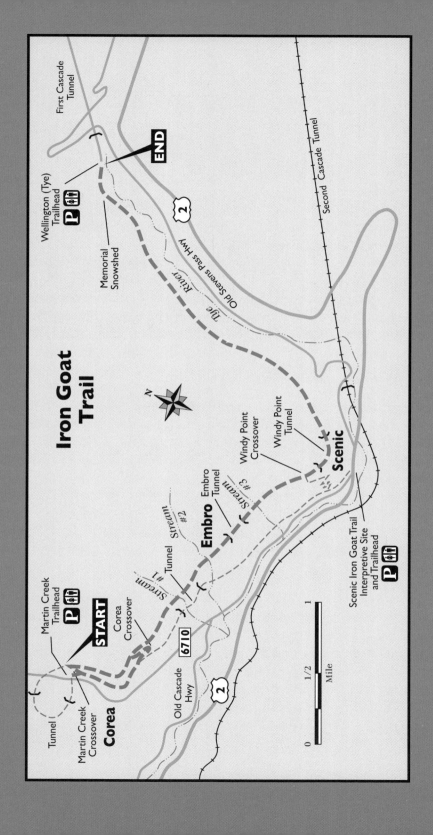

Iron Goat Trail

N

START

END

First Cascade Tunnel

Second Cascade Tunnel

Wellington (Tye) Trailhead

Memorial Snowshed

Tye River

Old Stevens Pass Hwy

Windy Point Crossover

Windy Point Tunnel

Scenic

Embro Embro Tunnel

Stream #3

Stream #2

Tunnel #1

Stream #1

Scenic Iron Goat Trail Interpretive Site and Trailhead

Martin Creek Trailhead

Corea

Corea Crossover

6710

Old Cascade Hwy

Tunnel I

Martin Creek Crossover

1

1/2

Mile

0

This concrete snowshed was built in 1910–11 at the site of the 1910 avalanche disaster.
(Courtesy Tom Davis, U.S.F.S.)

challenging terrain and difficult weather. Then came the construction of intricate switchbacks cut into the mountainside. In 1900 the completion of the original 2.6-mile Cascade Tunnel eliminated the tedious use of the switchbacks. Though snowsheds were added to protect trains from avalanches, trains were still halted for days at a time in winter storms. These historic events are documented in the *Iron Goat Trail Guidebook*.

Many of the tunnels are collapsed or covered with slide debris. They can be viewed from the trail, but do not attempt to enter any tunnels or to walk on rotten timbers. Please stay on the trail to protect the wildflowers.

Although you can access the trail from either end, this description begins at the Martin Creek Trailhead. Trains once climbed through a 170-degree horseshoe-shaped tunnel (now collapsed) at Martin Creek, creating an upper and a lower track. The trailhead lies at the elevation of the lower section of the tracks. This is called the lower trail.

For a short, flat hike, take the lower trail 1.5 miles. Listen for the rustling leaves of hardwood trees as you travel across Stream #1, to the Twin Tunnels and the 96-foot-high concrete arch of a snowshed. A trail extension was completed in 2006, adding 1.5 miles to the prior 1.5-mile

One of many tunnels and snowshed back walls along the trail. (Courtesy Ruth Ittner)

segment. The trail now goes to the town site of Scenic, the new trailhead, and the Scenic Iron Goat Trail Interpretive Site.

For a longer outing from the Martin Creek Trailhead (elevation 2,380 feet), you can take either of two crossover trails (which avoid the collapsed tunnel) up to the upper grade. From the trailhead, the trail crosses wetlands on a boardwalk. The Martin Creek Crossover appears after the boardwalk and takes you up a short, steep trail to the upper trail. You can take this crossover and turn right when you reach the upper grade, or (for a longer trail with less slope) continue on the lower grade to the Corea Crossover at 0.5 mile. This crossover is a third of a mile long; turn right at the top.

At just under 2 miles from Martin Creek, you'll find one of the remaining back walls of eleven massive concrete snowsheds, just before Embro, once the site of a telegraph station and workers' shacks. A spur trail leads you to the spillway and reservoir built to manage fires caused by sparks from passing trains.

Just beyond, follow the spur trail around the Embro Tunnel. After the tunnel's east portal, head to the Windy Point Crossover, where a trail option is to take the switchbacks down to the Iron Goat Trail Interpretive

Center at Scenic. You could end your journey at the interpretive center, having enjoyed Windy Point and the loop trails from Martin Creek. Otherwise, continue on the Iron Goat Trail past the Windy Point Crossover, around Windy Point Tunnel, and east to Wellington.

At the Windy Point Tunnel, the trail follows the original grade around the tunnel on the edge of the mountainside. Check out the active tunnel below from the viewpoint and follow the trail on the 2-foot-wide ledge of the snowshed archway to view the east portal. Continue east past several snowsheds.

At mile 6 you'll come upon a snowshed that now serves as a memorial to those who died here in the avalanche of 1910. The Wellington depot was built just beyond this point, in 1883. It was moved east when this snowshed was built. A year after the avalanche disaster, both the depot and the town of Wellington were renamed Tye: The railroad knew that passengers simply would not want to pass through "Wellington."

Pass a runaway track and cross Haskell Creek to reach the Wellington Trailhead, 3,100 feet in elevation. Continue 0.25 mile to view the west portal of the Cascade Tunnel.

When you're ready, turn around and return the way you came. For a longer outing, consider a drive or an overnight to the town of Leavenworth. Or you might want to visit the rail trail at Wallace Falls.

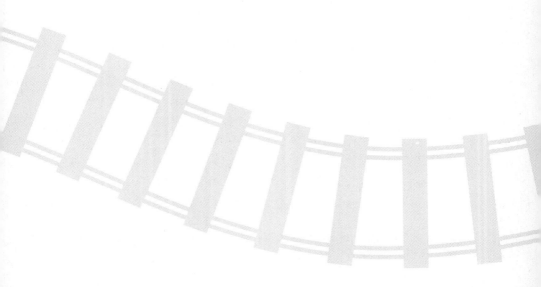

12 CASCADE TRAIL

The Cascade Trail reaches into the Cascade foothills in rural northwestern Washington. It parallels Washington Highway 20 on the flats until it climbs to a wooded hillside near Concrete. The trail crosses twenty-three trestles, which range from 10 to 2,200 feet long.

Activities:

Location: Sedro Woolley to Concrete, Skagit County

Length: 23 miles

Surface: Crushed rock and ballast; some portions are made of compacted sawdust

Wheelchair access: This trail is not wheelchair accessible.

Difficulty: Easy, although the ballast is difficult to ride on a bike in most areas, and equestrian use deteriorates it further.

Food: You'll find things to eat in the towns of Sedro Woolley and Concrete.

Restrooms: Public restrooms are available at all trailheads.

Seasons: The trail can be used year-round.

Access and parking: To reach the western trailhead at Sedro Woolley, take Interstate 5 to exit 232 (Cook Road) and turn right. Take a left onto WA 20 and drive several miles to Fruitdale Road. Parking is between Fruitdale Road and Polte Road.

To reach the trail's eastern trailhead, drive WA 20 to Concrete. Turn north into town on E Avenue, then turn right onto Railroad Street and drive to the senior center.

To access the trail at Birdsview, turn left off WA 20 onto Baker Lake Road. Horse trailer parking is available at all trailheads.

Rentals: No rentals are available along this route.

Contact:

- Skagit County Parks and Recreation, (360) 336–9414, www.skagitcounty .net/offices/parks/index.htm

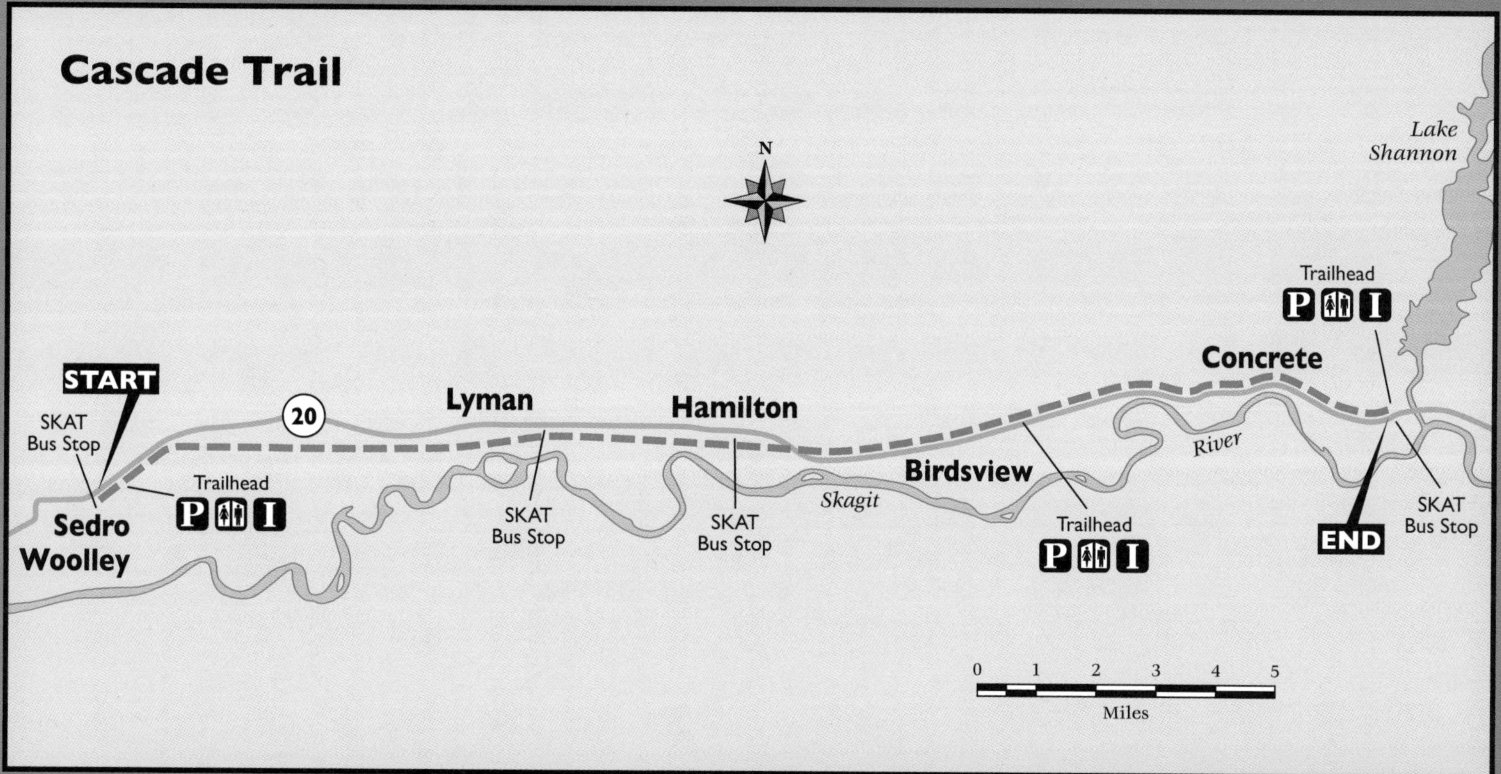

Cascade Trail

START

SKAT Bus Stop

Sedro Woolley

Trailhead P 🚻 ℹ️

20

Lyman

Hamilton

SKAT Bus Stop

SKAT Bus Stop

Birdsview

Trailhead P 🚻 ℹ️

Skagit River

Concrete

Trailhead P 🚻 ℹ️

Lake Shannon

SKAT Bus Stop

END

N

0 1 2 3 4 5
Miles

- Sedro Woolley Chamber of Commerce, (360) 855–1841, www.sedro-woolley.com

- Concrete Chamber of Commerce, (360) 853–7042, www.concrete-wa.com

Bus routes: Skagit Transit #717, (360) 757–4433, www.skagittransit.org

The Great Northern Railway (GN) once connected downriver towns with the wooded areas along the upper Skagit where the Cascade Trail now runs. Independent businessmen sought their riches among the forests of cedar trees that filled the valley. In Sedro Woolley, P. A. Woolley made a fortune supplying ties for the GN; merchants prospered, too, from the passengers traveling through town. The line transported cement, lumber, and shakes. The town of Concrete shipped cement as far as the Pacific during World War II. The GN arrived in town in 1900. The cement plants, opened in 1904 and 1907, supplied the Grand Coulee Dam, Baker River Dam, and Ballard Locks. Eleven miles of the line—from Sedro Woolley to Hamilton—ran freight until 1990. The trail was completed in 1999. The railroad right-of-way extends to Anacortes, where a trail is being developed.

You can access the trail from several points along the way; this description takes you from west to east. The pathway starts on the outskirts of Sedro Woolley among the trees. Mileage is well marked. At mile 7 the Skagit River comes up to the trail for a brief, scenic passage. Three miles out of Lyman, you'll cross Lyman-Hamilton Road; there's a SKAT bus stop here if you're ready to turn back. You'll next cross numerous creeks before reaching WA 20. The trail runs beside the highway here. Just past mile 14, pass Lusk Road. (Head south on Lusk Road to reach the 120-acre Rasar State Park on the Skagit River.) Just down the trail, pull off to the Baker Lake grocery and gas station for an ice cream. Detour onto the bridge walkway on WA 20 to cross Grandy Creek at Baker Lake Road. Return immediately to the trail on Birddog Private Lane.

You can ride beside the trail on Challenger Road between Russell Road and mile 19 if you find the trail surface difficult for a bike. At mile

One of the cascading streams near the eastern edge of the trail. (Courtesy Lou Petersen, Skagit County Parks and Recreation)

18 you're on a lush hillside and can begin to see the mountains to the east. Once you spot the unusual building that bridges the road (it's a high school), you're nearing downtown Concrete. Pass the concrete silos where concrete dust was stored, and cross E Avenue to the trail's end at the Concrete Senior Center.

Turn up E Avenue to tour Concrete and get a snack, dinner, or an espresso. You'll find public restrooms adjacent to the old schoolhouse. Built in 1936, it served a population double the 800 residents of today. Cross the historic Thompson Bridge to rest at the riverside picnic tables at the Baker River Fish Facility Visitors Center. This bridge connected the towns of Baker and Cement City in 1918; at the time, it was the longest single-span cement bridge in the world.

Enjoy this little town and ride the bus back to your starting point.

13 SNOHOMISH COUNTY CENTENNIAL TRAIL

This trail comes in two parts. A paved trail leaves the city of Snohomish and travels north through farmland, wetlands, and fields. At Lake Stevens the pathway runs through rural and wooded country. Skaters savor the wide, smooth pavement, while equestrians enjoy the soft, 6-foot-wide parallel path. Multiple access points, fun towns, and several parks and lakes contribute to a relaxing day or a weekend getaway.

Activities:

Location: Snohomish, Lake Stevens, Marysville, and South Arlington, all in Snohomish County

Length: 17.5 miles

Surface: Asphalt for 17.5 miles, with parallel dirt path for equestrians that runs for 10.5 miles

Wheelchair access: At trailheads; special "disabled parking only" located at Lake Cassidy Wetlands Trailhead

Difficulty: Easy

Food: Snohomish and Lake Stevens have restaurants, espresso shops, and markets within a mile of the trail. Vending machines and covered seating are available at Division Street in Machias.

Restrooms: Developed restrooms are at the Pilchuck Trailhead, Machias Trailhead, and Bonneville Ballpark. Chemical toilets are at the 20th Street Trailhead, Lake Cassidy Trailhead, and at 152nd Street East Trailhead.

Seasons: The trail can be used year-round.

Access and parking: Moving from the southern end of the trail to the northern terminus, there are six main trailheads with vehicle access points. The corner of Maple Street and Pine Avenue in Snohomish marks the southern terminus of the trail. Exit Interstate 5 at U.S. Highway 2 eastbound to Snohomish and Wenatchee, then exit US 2 at Snohomish. Turn left onto Second Street, then left (north) onto Maple Street, and drive about 1 mile to Pine Avenue. From Washington Highway 9, exit at Snohomish and drive

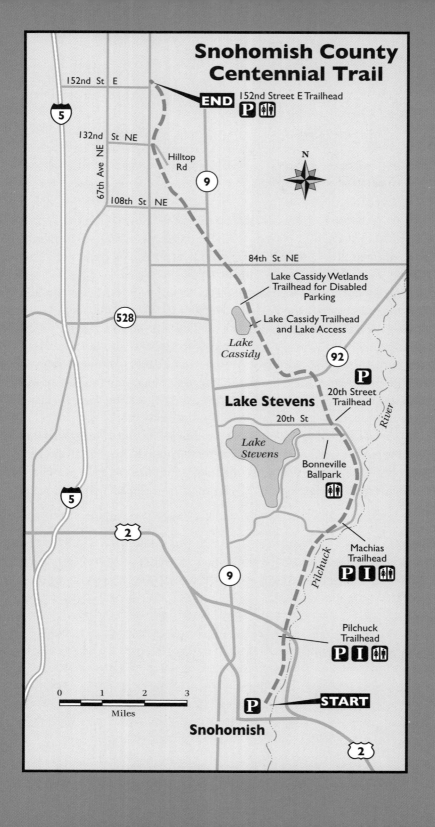

Snohomish County Centennial Trail

152nd St E

END 152nd Street E Trailhead

5

132nd St NE

67th Ave NE

Hilltop Rd

9

108th St NE

N

84th St NE

Lake Cassidy Wetlands Trailhead for Disabled Parking

528

Lake Cassidy Trailhead and Lake Access

Lake Cassidy

92

P

20th Street Trailhead

Lake Stevens

20th St

Lake Stevens

River

Bonneville Ballpark

5

2

Pilchuck

Machias Trailhead

P I

9

Pilchuck Trailhead

P I

0   1   2   3
Miles

P   **START**

Snohomish

2

north to Second Street. Turn left, then left again at Maple, and proceed to Pine. You can park on the street here.

To reach other trailheads, drive north on Maple, which becomes Machias Road. The Pilchuck parking area is 1.5 miles up the road, on the right. To reach the Machias Trailhead, continue north on Machias Road to Division Street and turn west; you can park about an eighth of a mile ahead. The trailhead is on the right.

To get to the 20th Street Trailhead near Lake Stevens from WA 9 north of Frontier Village, turn right on Washington Highway 92. Then turn right onto Machias Road and go south for about 3.5 miles. Turn right onto 20th Street. The trailhead is on the right, with parking for one hundred vehicles.

Access the Lake Cassidy Wetlands Trailhead, which is used for disabled parking only, by going on WA 9 north of Frontier Village. To park here you must have a disabled parking pass issued by your home state. Turn right onto 60th Street Northeast, then right onto 99th Avenue Northeast and left onto 54th Street Northeast. Turn left onto 105th Avenue Northeast and follow the signs to the trailhead. Trail users already on the Snohomish County Centennial Trail can access Lake Cassidy by leaving the trail via the Lake Cassidy Trailhead and Lake Access point on the trail.

A new trailhead at 152nd Street East marks the end of the paved trail and the present northern terminus. From WA 9 north of Frontier Village, turn left onto 108th Street Northeast, then right onto 67th Avenue Northeast. Continue north to just beyond 152nd Street. The trailhead is on the right.

Contact: Snohomish County Parks and Recreation Department, (425) 388–6600, www.snoco.org

Bus routes: Take bus #201 or bus #202 from Smokey Point to Marysville. For information, call (425) 353–RIDE; TDD (425) 778–2188. Or visit the Web site at www.commtrans.org.

If the sunny summer crowds of Seattle are not your style, head north. The Snohomish Valley lies 40 miles northeast of Seattle. The valley's hundred-year history of dairying and farming is evident along the

The northern portion of the trail is still undeveloped. Design plans are under way to continue to the Skagit County line.

Snohomish County Centennial Trail, which begins in Snohomish and presently ends between Marysville and Arlington. Take the time to enjoy the antiques shops and eateries of Snohomish, along with the tiny town center and the huge Lake Stevens. Or try the trail on the weekend of the Snohomish car show. Downtown roads are closed and the band is playing; it's one very big block party.

This trail is peaceful, paved, and well planned. Smooth, wide pavement attracts skaters, and a 6-foot-wide soft trail is mowed and brushed for equestrians. The presence of horses and the calm, rural setting take you back to the heyday of the dairy and farming industries, when this area was served by the Seattle, Lakeshore & Eastern Railroad. Past years of heavy logging have left no scars. Well-placed benches and picnic tables and occasional interpretive and historical signs invite you to stop, look, and imagine. Wheelchair travelers and walkers will enjoy these spots for breaks.

You can access the trail from many points along the way; this description begins in Snohomish, its southern end, and proceeds northward. From the trailhead at Pine Avenue and Maple Street, take in Snohomish's flower boxes and benches, then begin your journey along the Pilchuck

Snohomish County Attractions and Events

- Blackmans' House Museum, (360) 568–5235.

- Arlington NWEAA Fly-in & Airshow at the Arlington Airport, (360) 435–5857. Experimental aircraft and hot-air balloons contribute to this event's status as the largest in the county.

  For information on rodeos, farmers' markets, music festivals, and more, contact the Snohomish County Tourism Bureau at (888) 338–0976 or www.snohomish.org.

River. Benches and picnic tables are thoughtfully placed for views and serenity—you'll find them at the edge of a field, beside the river, below a bridge, and at a display describing the critters that wander the wetlands and rivers.

The railroad's history, locations of the old train stations, and trail mileage are all listed at the Pilchuck parking lot 1.5 miles up the trail. The Snohomish–Arlington run of the Seattle, Lakeshore & Eastern Railroad's Sumas line came to town in 1889 and continued through the 1950s. In 1989 the rail trail was planned and named for this hundred-year history. It opened in 1991, with the final mile completed in 1994. Additions are continuing.

The train came from Woodinville to Snohomish, Arlington, and Bryant—the site of a big mill and a 100-foot-high trestle—through the town of Pilchuck and on to the Canadian border. The Seattle–North Bend run completed the route to Seattle for shipping lumber and carrying mail and livestock. Shingle mills were big business in the railroad's peak years; they required little investment, and the Snohomish Valley had plenty of cedar. Snohomish had four shingle mills; Marysville had seven. You can still see the mill beside the trail in Lake Stevens.

The Machias Trailhead at Division Street, 4 miles up the path, provides a sense of heritage. Restrooms are housed in the pretty blue replica of a depot built in the late 1890s. The photos of the town of Machias take

Equestrians travel the soft path near Pilchuck Trailhead in Snohomish.

you back to the early 1900s. Hitch your horse, check out some history, let the kids loose in the grassy area, or snack at the covered picnic tables. At 4.5 miles, just past the Machias cutoff, a kiosk introduces the woodchuck, Pacific salamander, belted kingfisher, great blue heron, and other members of this wetland community.

Head north for a sign that relates some amusing and historical cow tales of the turn of the twentieth century, when "No udder business was better than dairy." You can learn the prolific peculiarities of Miss Sadie and Rose, which led to their local fame. Try to guess how many offspring they had or how much milk they produced in a year before you reach the sign. Farther on, you can learn what swims, flies, and slithers here. Settle in at a pretty spot on the river and find out what a mountain beaver or a northern flicker looks like.

The maintained trail continues past the 20th Street Trailhead in Lake Stevens. Or turn left here or at the previous crossing at 16th Street. To grab an espresso or a meal, continue 0.25 mile to the old section of town. You'll find a bike shop, a library, a market, restaurants, some shops, and a community park on the lake itself.

If you'd like to continue your trek northward, return to the trail and travel to the new trailhead at 152nd Street East, south of the city of Arlington.

The trail goes straight through with no road detours. Ride or walk the path, thick with maples and alders, birds fluttering about. Near Lake Cassidy Wetlands, take the access path to the lake. You'll find bass and trout here.

At 84th Street Northeast, a main thoroughfare, use caution with the vehicle traffic when crossing the road. You'll cross under WA 9 at about 6 miles, and then under Lauck Road. Streets are named twice in this area: old names and new names. Lauck Road, for instance, is also 108th Street Northeast, while 84th Street Northeast is also Getchell Road. The 911 emergency service needed numbers, and the residents wanted their history. Get some views of valley farms as the trail traverses a ridge. Finish at the 152nd Street East Trailhead.

Plans to pave the trail farther are in the design phase. The final plan will extend the Centennial Trail another 16 miles, through Arlington and north to the Skagit County line. Cyclists will finally have an alternative to WA 9, which has no shoulder north of Arlington. The 44 miles of the Centennial Trail will be complete when it connects with the Snoqualmie Valley Trail (Trail 10) south of Monroe.

Trail users navigate the falling foliage along the paved trailway.

14 WHATCOM COUNTY AND BELLINGHAM INTERURBAN TRAIL

The Interurban Electric Trolley motored passengers between Mount Vernon and Bellingham Bay from 1889 to 1903. The trolley route takes you high above Chuckanut Drive and Bellingham Bay, on a path amid evergreens, deciduous trees, and the occasional home. Though Chuckanut Drive is a hilly, curvy street, the trail is quite flat except for one section.

Activities:

Location: Larrabee State Park to the historic Fairhaven district in Bellingham, Whatcom County

Length: 7 miles

Surface: Crushed stone; one difficult section south of Old Samish Way has dirt.

Wheelchair access: Fairhaven Park and the trail north of Old Samish Way is wheelchair accessible.

Difficulty: Easy in the southern portion and north of Arroyo Park; difficult through California Street from Arroyo Park.

Food: You'll find things to eat in Fairhaven.

Restrooms: All trailheads except Arroyo Park offer both restrooms and drinking water.

Seasons: The trail can be used year-round.

Access and parking: Follow the signs for Larrabee State Park from exit 250 (Fairhaven Parkway) off Interstate 5. Drive west on Fairhaven Parkway for 1.5 miles to 12th Street.

To start in Fairhaven, turn left into the Rotary Trailhead before you reach 12th, or turn into Fairhaven Park on Chuckanut Drive. To reach Larrabee State Park and trailheads on Chuckanut Drive and Old Samish Way, turn left onto 12th Street; after 2 blocks, bear left onto Chuckanut Drive. (Fairhaven Park is on your left.) To reach Arroyo Park, turn left onto Old Samish Way (there's a gallery on your right). The North Chuckanut Mountain Trailhead and California Street are just beyond this turnoff. Cyclists may wish to park here and climb up the steep quarter-mile grade on California Street to avoid the single-track in Arroyo Park.

To start at the southern trailhead at Larrabee State Park, stay on Chuckanut Drive, turning left into the Clayton Beach Trailhead 0.5 mile past the main entrance to the park (5 miles from Fairhaven Parkway). You can also park on neighborhood streets and access the trail from there.

Rentals: Try Fairhaven Bike & Mountain Sports at 1108 11th Street, (360) 733–4433, www.fairhavenbike.com; or Jack's Bicycle Center at 1907 Iowa Street, (360) 733–1955.

Contact:

- City of Bellingham Parks and Recreation, (360) 778–7000, www.cob.org/parks.htm

- Whatcom County Parks and Recreation, (360) 733–2900

- Bellingham/Whatcom County Tourism, (800) 487-2032, www.bellingham.org

- Historic Fairhaven District Information Line, (360) 738–1574 (for merchant and historical information)

Bus routes: Contact the Whatcom Transit Authority (WTA), (360) 676–RIDE.

In 1915 the Larrabee and Gates families donated the twenty acres that became Larrabee State Park, the first state park in Washington. The park's Chuckanut Mountain includes a network of signed hiking and mountain biking pathways that take off from the Interurban Trail. To explore these trails, purchase the "Happy Trails" map at Village Books on 11th Street.

You can park your car and access the trail from many points along its way; this description begins at its southern end, the Clayton Beach Trailhead. Look for the trail sign at the northwest corner of the parking lot. Once you're on this short access trail, take a right to continue on the Interurban Trail. (From the parking lot, about 3 miles of flat trail stretch

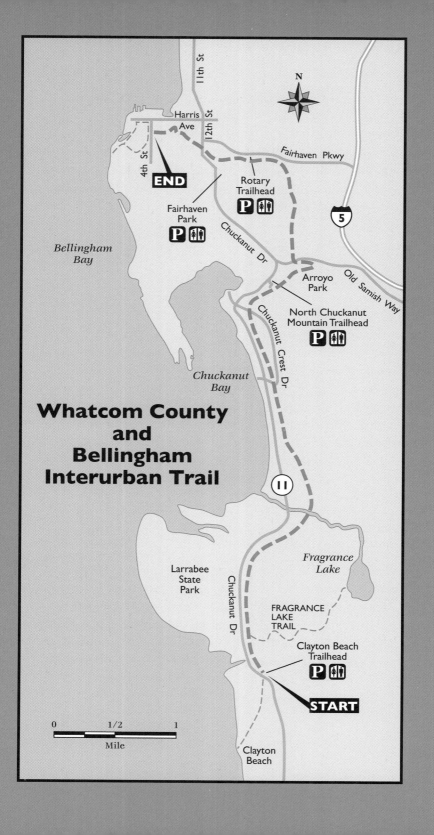

11th St

Harris Ave

12th St

N

Fairhaven Pkwy

4th St

END

Rotary
Trailhead

P 🚻

5

*Bellingham
Bay*

Fairhaven
Park

P 🚻

Chuckanut Dr

Arroyo
Park

Old Samish Way

North Chuckanut
Mountain Trailhead

P 🚻

Chuckanut Crest Dr

*Chuckanut
Bay*

Whatcom County
and
Bellingham
Interurban Trail

11

*Fragrance
Lake*

Larrabee
State
Park

Chuckanut Dr

FRAGRANCE
LAKE
TRAIL

Clayton Beach
Trailhead

P 🚻

START

0   1/2   1

Mile

*Clayton
Beach*

northward; you have the option of turning back at a difficult section or continuing on to Fairhaven.)

You can also head left at this intersection for a side trip to the beach on a rugged, undeveloped section of trail. Cross the street and follow the trail over logs and through brush to reach the water's edge. The Burlington Northern Railroad may grant rights to Larrabee State Park to develop and maintain this access to Bellingham Bay.

Heading north on the main trail, you'll run into hikers coming from the Fragrance Lake Trailhead at 0.5 mile.

The forest of second-growth and deciduous trees begins to open up to a view of the bay and the islands in 2 miles. Cross several streets and meet Chuckanut Drive where it rises up to the level of the trail at Chuckanut Crest Drive. If you want to avoid steep hills, exit the trail to a second car parked on the road here or turn back.

After this brief encounter with civilization, you'll reach a couple of hills and then a drop to a sudden stop sign at California Street at 4.5 miles. Cyclists have two choices. One option is to turn left onto California, then right onto Chuckanut Drive to Old Samish Way for a roadside detour of about a mile. Turn right and regain the trail across the street from the Arroyo Park lot.

If you're looking for a forest hike or a single-track route accented by a couple of sharp switchbacks and steep hills on a narrow, muddy trail, however, the second option is just your ticket. Continue across California to the trail. Take the right fork and head into a deep mossy forest crossed by creeks and bridges, decorated by a small waterfall, and orchestrated by Chuckanut Creek.

When all this fun is done, stop to enjoy the sounds and smells of Chuckanut Creek and the forest as you cross the long wooden bridge. Turn left at the trail across the bridge for an uphill haul to Old Samish Way, a parking area, and the trail. Cross Old Samish Way to continue. The pilings from the large railroad trestle that once crossed here now support a bench for trail users. (This is where you arrive if you take a left on California to avoid the park.) Head into a pleasant, more open area on the fringes of town. Cross several small streets and parallel Fairhaven Parkway.

You'll cross 20th Street 1 mile from the Arroyo Park Trailhead. Head straight, following the yellow-striped brown posts on the sidewalk beside

Julia Street. The trail heads right as the street curves left. Pass the Rotary Trailhead on your right and leave the neighborhood to enter the wooded Padden Creek area. You'll reach Donovan Avenue and 10th Street at Padden Creek less than 1 mile from the Rotary Trailhead. You can turn onto 10th Street to head into Fairhaven, and to reach the South Bay Trail (Trail 15).

To wind around the bay for a mile before returning to Fairhaven and to the South Bay Trail, continue on the trail beside Padden Creek. Cross Sixth Street and wind down around the wastewater plant to a trail paralleling the waterfront. This is an off-leash dog exercise area, with bags for waste disposal available at the trailhead to your right. Turn left for a 0.2-mile detour to the active rail and some secluded waterfront. Turn right to the wastewater parking lot and onto Fourth Street. Turn left onto Harris Avenue. (This is more or less a dead end—there's only one way to go.) Take a moment to smell the coffee—Starbucks is straight ahead at the ferry terminal.

Or you can turn right onto Harris and then left at 10th, which dead-ends at the South Bay Trail in 1 block—about 0.6 mile from Starbucks. For a reading and feasting treat, head up to 11th Street and turn right to rest at Village Books and the Colophon Café. African peanut soup, espresso, and Moosetracks ice cream sound good?

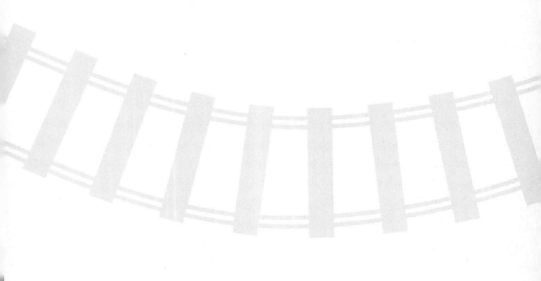

15 SOUTH BAY TRAIL

Read about local history, see a sunset, walk the waterfront, pass through a park, and enjoy the shops and eateries of downtown Bellingham. Starting at the historic Fairhaven district, most of the South Bay Trail hugs the shore of Bellingham Bay.

Activities:

Location: Bellingham, Whatcom County

Length: 2 miles

Surface: Asphalt, crushed stone, concrete

Wheelchair access: Boulevard Park is wheelchair accessible.

Difficulty: Easy, except for steep section on the historic Taylor dock, and a railroad crossing or two

Food: You can stock up in downtown Bellingham and the historic Fairhaven district.

Restrooms: There are restrooms and drinking water at Boulevard Park, the Fairhaven Village area, and Taylor dock.

Seasons: The trail can be used year-round.

Access and parking: Take exit 250 (Fairhaven Parkway) off Interstate 5, then drive west on Fairhaven for 1.5 miles to 12th Street. Turn right, then left in 4 blocks onto Mill Avenue. It dead-ends at the trailhead on 10th Street. You can park on the street.

South State Street has several pullouts; steps lead down to the trail for an evening stroll. To reach South State Street, continue on 12th. It becomes Finnegan Way, then 11th, and then State.

Boulevard Park (midtrail) can be reached from Bayview Drive off of South State Street. This is a nice spot for a quick trip south along the prettiest portion of the trail. The northern terminus is downtown at East Maple Street west of Railroad Avenue; you can park on the street to access the trail.

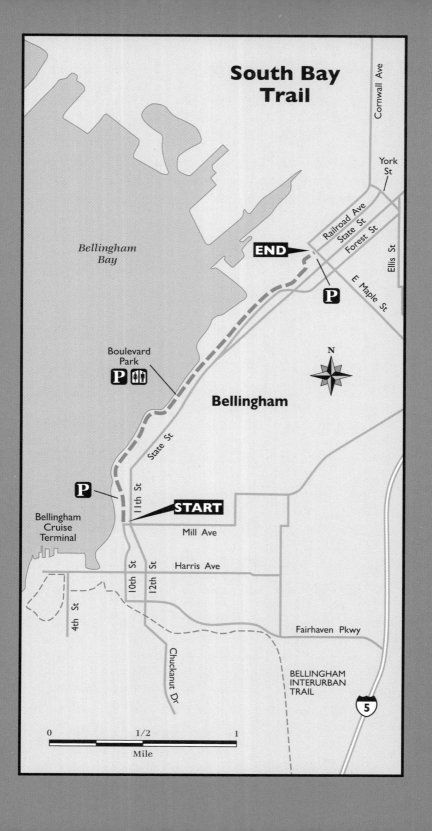

South Bay Trail

Cornwall Ave

York St

Railroad Ave
State St
Forest St

Ellis St

END

P

E Maple St

Bellingham
Bay

Boulevard
Park

P 🚻

Bellingham

N

State St

11th St

P

START

Mill Ave

Bellingham
Cruise
Terminal

10th St

12th St

Harris Ave

4th St

Fairhaven Pkwy

Chuckanut Dr

BELLINGHAM
INTERURBAN
TRAIL

5

0   1/2   1
Mile

Rentals: Try Fairhaven Bike & Mountain Sports at 1108 11th Street, (360) 733–4433, www.fairhavenbike.com; or Jack's Bicycle Center at 1907 Iowa Street, (360) 733–1955.

Contact: City of Bellingham Parks and Recreation, (360) 778–7000, www.cob .org/parks.htm; or Bellingham/Whatcom County Tourism, (800) 487–2032, www.bellingham.org

Bus routes: Contact the Whatcom Transit Authority, (360) 676–RIDE.

|||||||||||||||||||||||||||||||||||||||||||||||||||||||||||||||||||||||||||||||||

This line of the Bellingham Bay & Eastern Railway once pulled coal, saw-logs, and lumber from the Lake Whatcom watershed to ship to developing West Coast cities. The first mill in the area—Henry Roeder's Mill—was built in 1850, and there were no fewer than sixty-eight shingle mills in Whatcom County by 1900. The largest mill in the world, the Puget Sound Sawmill and Timber Company, operated in Fairhaven.

You can park your car and access the right-of-way—now the South Bay Trail—from many spots along its way. This description takes you from its southern terminus, 10th Street and Mill Avenue, northward. As you head north, the trail takes you onto 10th briefly until you reach Taylor Avenue Dock, a refurbished wooden trestle and reconstructed boardwalk. Cross over the tracks and enjoy the 0.25-mile over-water walkway. Bicycle riders should move slowly or consider dismounting.

For an alternate bike route, continue north on 10th. Travel 1 block on State Street/11th and turn left at Bayview Drive into Boulevard Park—a great spot for sunsets.

The interpretive signs along the trail are interesting and fun, especially when combined with a historical tour of Fairhaven. Cross the tracks (carefully) at the north end of Boulevard Park to continue north, or hike up the steps to the overpass. The paved trail takes you past pulp mills and other industries until you reach East Maple Street, where the trail ends.

If you'd like to extend your trek, you have many options. Turn right onto Railroad Avenue and then left to pass the Orchard Street brewery,

South Bay Trail near Fairhaven.

restaurants, and cafes. You can also cross Maple and continue straight into the alley for an alternate bike route.

A mile and a half on city streets will take you to the Railroad Trail (Trail 16). Turn right off Railroad onto York Street and left onto State. State becomes James Street. Turn right on East North Street (1 block north of the light at Alabama Street) and left at the T-intersection onto King Street to find the trailhead on your right.

If you're traveling southbound on the South Bay Trail, you can connect with the Interurban Trail (Trail 14). From 10th and Mill, continue south on 10th, then turn right onto Harris Avenue and left onto Fourth Street. Turn right into the wastewater plant parking lot. The trail begins at the doggy bag stand.

Whale-watching tours and ferries to the San Juan Islands, Victoria, and Alaska leave from the Bellingham Cruise Terminal at Fourth and Harris. A nearby boat launch is convenient for kayaking, sailing, and pleasure boating. Rentals are available.

The city and county consider these trails to be works in progress. Some signage is missing. Links have been proposed to connect the trails and create a better route through the city.

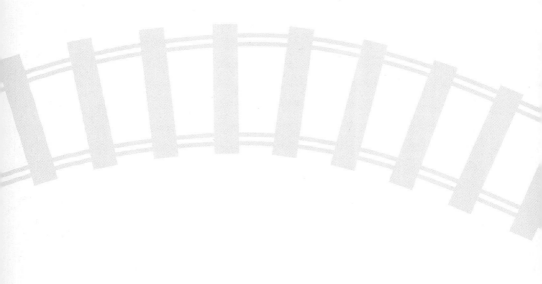

16 RAILROAD TRAIL

The Railroad Trail leaves Bellingham to make a gradual climb through quiet neighborhoods and Whatcom Falls Park. (If you prefer to head downhill, start from the park.) The trail is lightly wooded for most of its length. The 251-acre park has a network of trails that can get you off track. You might enjoy a planned detour to the creekside; picnic facilities are available at both Whatco Falls and Bloedel Donovan Parks, while the former has a kids' fishing pond and hatchery.

Activities:

Location: Bellingham, Whatcom County

Length: 3.5 miles

Surface: Crushed stone

Wheelchair access: The trail's wheelchair access is found at Whatcom Falls Park and Bloedel Donovan Park.

Difficulty: Easy to moderate. Traveling from west to east, the trail offers a gradual uphill grade with one moderate slope.

Food: Barkley Village Shopping Center on Woburn Street offers things to eat.

Restrooms: There are restrooms and drinking water at Bloede Donovan and Whatcom Falls Parks.

Seasons: The trail can be used year-round.

Access and parking: To reach the western trailhead near Memorial Park, get off Interstate 5 at Sunset Drive (exit 255). From I-5 southbound, go straight, down James Street. From I-5 northbound, turn left onto Sunset to cross the highway, then turn left onto James. After several blocks, turn left onto East North Street, then left again onto King Street. The trailhead is on your right.

Find the eastern trailhead by turning east onto Sunset Drive/Mount Baker Highway, south (right) onto Orleans Street, and east (left) onto Alabama Street. Turn right onto Electric Avenue at Lake Whatcom. The trailhead is immediately on your right.

Rentals: Try Fairhaven Bike & Mountain Sports at 1108 11th Street, (360) 733–4433, www.fairhavenbike.com; or Jack's Bicycle Center at 1907 Iowa Street, (360) 733–1955.

Contact:

- City of Bellingham Parks and Recreation, (360) 778–7000, www.cob.org/parks.htm

- Whatcom County Parks and Recreation, (360) 733–2900

- Bellingham/Whatcom County Tourism, (800) 487–2032, www.bellingham.org

Bus routes: Contact the Whatcom Transit Authority, (360) 676–RIDE.

||||||||||||||||||||||||||||||||||||||||||||||||||||||||||||||||||||||||||||||||||||

You can travel the Railroad Trail in either direction; this description takes you from west to east. Starting from King Street, the trail crosses I–5 and enters a quiet neighborhood with several streets to cross. There is a

Remnants of a trestle on the path near Lake Whatcom.

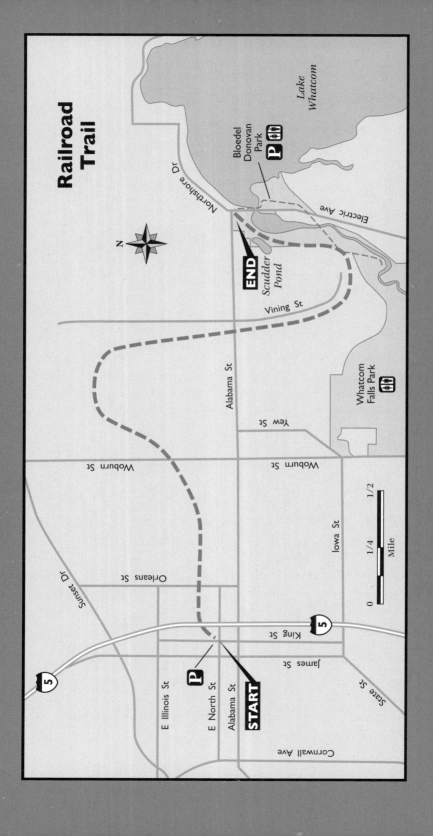

Cyclists near the duck pond on the Railroad Trail.

nice buffer between the small homes and the trail. Cross Woburn Street at 0.9 mile. Get ready for a Pacific Northwest moment: A well-used side trail lures you to the Starbucks at Barkley Village. From here on, pedal hard and burn calories. You'll want to stop here on your way back to chow down. You can create your own smorgasbord of salads, Chinese food, pizza, and other prepared foods at Haagens grocery store and cafe, or choose from a variety of restaurants.

Food fantasies behind you for the moment, push on to pass some pilings from an old trestle. In years past the Bellingham Bay & Eastern Railway occupied the Railroad Trail for 4 miles from New Whatcom to Lake Whatcom. In 1882 the Blue Canyon Mines used the railway to send coal to bunkers on Bellingham Bay. Later the tracks brought lumber from Lake Whatcom to the docks of New Whatcom and Fairhaven for transport to developing western cities, such as San Francisco. Remnants of trestles can be found along the trail to Lake Whatcom, around Lake Whatcom, and even across Lake Whatcom. The BB&E merged with the Northern Pacific Railway in 1903.

Just past these pilings, head up a hill to an opening beside a pond at 1.4 miles. A bench provided here makes this a peaceful spot from which to watch the ducks, the walkers, and the cyclists. As the trail curves north beyond the pond, take in views of town and the bay below. A new overpass takes you safely over Alabama Street. The trail parallels Vining Street before it heads up a short, steeper hill into Whatcom Falls Park. Turn left at the fork (2.9 miles) to go north to Scudder Pond, or follow the signs to cross the bridge and Electric Avenue to Bloedel Donovan Park.

To catch a glimpse of an old railroad trestle crossing, head straight for a few hundred yards before taking the left fork. You'll see a trail to the right heading downhill before you reach the edge where the trestle lies. You can take a side trip and explore the park and the creek on this trail. (You'll appreciate having a mountain bike.) Turn right at the T-intersection with a wide trail, and then turn left at the first trail *without* steps (the second left). The narrow trail takes you down and across the bridge over Whatcom Creek. Wander around to find a view of the little waterfall below the bridge. Turn left after the bridge. The trail curves around the creek, past a trestle and a kayak practice area. It ends at a small road. Turn right to cross Electric Avenue. Continue on a short trail to the left into Bloedel Donovan Park, then through the park to Alabama Street. Find the eastern trailhead at the corner.

Turn around and return the way you came. The trip back is downhill. Bear right when you reach the first fork at mile 0.5. And don't forget Barkley Village at mile 2.37. After crossing Woburn, you've got 0.9 mile to the western trailhead at King Street near I-5. There's enough of a grade to cruise happily downhill. Beware of pedestrians.

17 WALLACE FALLS RAILWAY TRAIL

On this trek you'll head uphill on a railroad grade for 2.5 miles. Then a 1.5-mile ascent continues on a narrow walking trail up steep switchbacks, through deep woods, and over wooden bridges to spectacular views of Wallace Falls. Get ready for a great workout while you enjoy a rural road trip and a scenic trail with the convenience of camping and the proximity of good food.

Activities:

Location: Wallace Falls State Park, town of Gold Bar, Snohomish County

Length: 2.5 miles. An additional 1.5-mile hiking trail takes you to the waterfalls. A 4.75-mile side trail takes you to Wallace Lake.

Surface: Dirt, somewhat rocky

Wheelchair access: This trail is not wheelchair accessible.

Difficulty: The rail trail is moderate; the hiking trail to the falls is steep.

Food: You'll find restaurants, grocery stores, bakeries, and espresso shops in Gold Bar and other towns along U.S. Highway 2. Also check out the Sultan Bakery in Sultan.

Restrooms: There are bathrooms and water at the trailhead.

Seasons: The trail can be used year-round, from dawn to dusk.

Access and parking: Access the trail from Wallace Falls State Park. To reach this park, take US 2 to Gold Bar, 30 miles east of Everett. Follow signs to the Wallace Falls State Park entrance. Turn left into the park; travel 0.3 mile to the trailhead. The trailhead is adjacent to the restrooms in the parking lot.

Rentals: No rentals are available along this trail.

Contact: Wallace Falls State Park, (360) 793–0420, www.parks.wa.gov

Bus routes: Bus #271, #270 from Everett. For information, check the Community Transit Web site at www.commtrans.org, or call (425) 353–RIDE. Or in Washington, call (800) 562–1375.

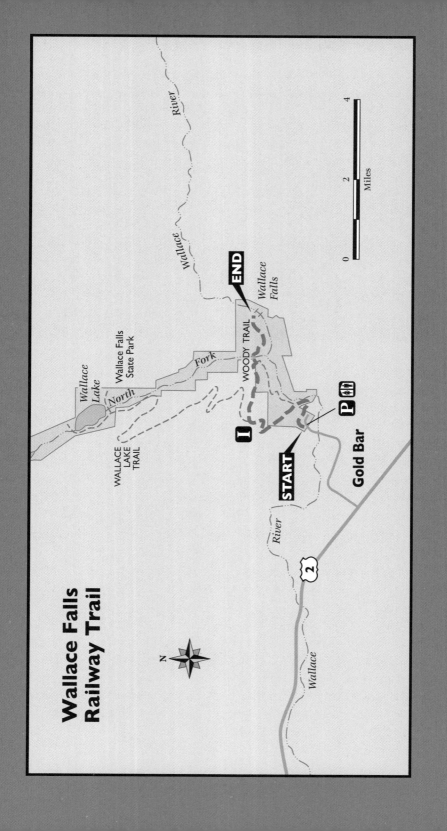

The narrow walking trail meanders through deep woods to spectacular views of the falls.

The Wallace River rushes, plummets, and jams up against large river boulders along its course. Nine waterfalls, ranging in height from 50 to 265 feet, plunge into the river from tributaries along its walls, while the waterway itself drops 800 feet in half a mile. Wallace Falls State Park, the site of this riverside trek, is located near several small towns in the Cascade foothills, in Gold Bar off US 2.

The trail runs along one of several logging railroad routes built in these hills. The railroad grade is steeper than most rail trails because it was built for wood-fired trains known as steam donkeys, which reached high into the hills after timber. Indeed, it was the invention of the steam donkey and the arrival of the Great Northern Railway in 1882 that put Gold Bar on the map as a "great northern town." The timing was good, because the increasing number of gravel bars in the Skykomish River was making steamboat travel more and more difficult. Success of the logging industry here then became a sure thing when Frederick Weyerhauser bought 900,000 acres of land from J. J. Hill, Great Northern's owner. The logs were taken to a nearby mill and shipped out from the depot at Gold Bar.

Steam Donkey

The steam donkey was a wood-fired engine with a wire rope winch mounted on a log sled. When anchored to a stump, it could pull logs out of the woods to a loading site. Unfortunately this "ultimate techological triumph" sent logs flying through the air almost as often as it dragged them across the ground, resulting in numerous injuries and deaths. This precipitated the first phone in the Wallace Falls area—line between the doctor in Sultan and the logging camps of the Gold Bar Lumber Company and the Wallace Lumber and Manufacturing Company.

Washington State eventually purchased the park site from the Weyerhauser timber company; the park opened in 1977. It was built through the efforts of the Youth Development and Conservation Corps programs, thanks to the legislative initiative of Senator Frank Woody, for whom the Woody Trail is named.

Find the trailhead near the parking lot. After 0.25 mile the trail forks. To your right is the Woody Trail, which departs here to hug the river for 1.5 miles. Stay left to continue on the railroad right-of-way. The surface is good for mountain biking.

Stop to examine the mosaic of the bright green, fuzzy moss that carpets each branch of the forest and each stump top in pleasing designs. You'll hear the distant sound of the river as you climb through the woods on broad switchbacks. If you're lucky, you might see some wildlife. It's not only birds and deer that roam here: This area is also home to coyotes, bobcats, bears, and cougars. There are interpretive signs along the way.

At 1.5 miles you'll arrive at the intersection with the Wallace Lake Trail, which departs on your left. There's a kiosk and a picnic table here. Look back through the forest at the old railroad pilings.

Two trails beyond this intersection cut down to the Woody Trail. The right-of-way continues to the North Fork of the Wallace River, where it once crossed on a trestle. Use caution: Steep banks and a steeply dropping

Nearby Attractions

Visit the Gold Bar Depot Museum (closed in winter) to discover the connection between the town name and Chinese
railroad workers. After your workout, treat yourself to pas-
tries or dinner at the Sultan Bakery in Sultan. You can also
get lunch to go before your trip. In Index, 9 miles east, view
the breathtaking Mount Index. Climbers frequent the cliffs.

river prohibit a safe crossing. Enjoy the view and backtrack to the cutoff
down to the river. If you're riding, secure your bike and continue on foot.

Turn left when you reach the river. A bridge crosses the North Fork
here, and the trail climbs to the falls. Steps are built into some of the
steeper portions. Benches are placed along the way—some, thoughtfully,
between switchbacks. Signage is good.

The riverside picnic shelter is your first viewpoint, 0.3 mile from the
bridge. Less than a quarter mile ahead is a dramatic view of Wallace Falls.
The trail steepens progressively into shorter switchbacks over the next 0.5
mile until you reach the upper falls viewpoint at 1,700 vertical feet. One
of the logging camps in this area was at 1,800 feet. After your trek uphill,
imagine the intense life lived by a logger and his steam donkey in this spot
one hundred years ago.

Enjoy the mountains peeking through the trees on your descent.
You'll deserve the crème brûlée or the chocolate cheesecake created by
the pastry chef at the Sultan Bakery, even if you didn't haul a single tree
down with you.

18 OLYMPIC DISCOVERY TRAIL: DEER PARK SCENIC GATEWAY CENTER TO SEQUIM

Leave U.S. Highway 101 to tour a pathway with wildflowers, a covered bridge, and a beautifully restored trestle. This segment of the Olympic Discovery Trail offers a combination of flat and rolling terrain with some steep hills.

Activities:

Location: Clallam County, east of Port Angeles

Length: 13 miles

Surface: Asphalt with a brief section of hard-pack gravel

Wheelchair access: Available at the Morse Creek Trestle, Deer Park Scenic Gateway Center, Robin Hill Park, and Railroad Bridge Park

Difficulty: Moderate

Food: C'est Si Bon on Cedar Park Drive and Sawmill Cafe in Carlsborg

Restrooms: Restrooms are along the trail at Morse Creek Trailhead, Bagley Creek, Robin Hill Park, Carlsborg Road, and Railroad Bridge Park.

Seasons: The trail can be used year-round.

Access and parking: The Morse Creek Trailhead lies 4 miles east of Port Angeles. Access it at the intersection of US 101 and Strait View Drive.

To access the new Deer Park Scenic Gateway Center east of Morse Creek Trailhead when westbound on US 101, exit directly into the center. If eastbound on US 101, turn north off US 101 onto Buchanan Drive, just west of Deer Park Cinemas. Turn left onto Cedar Park Drive and take the second left, signed SCENIC OVERLOOK AHEAD, into the lot.

To reach the Siebert Creek Trailhead, take Old Olympic Highway 1.5 miles to Wild Currant Way. The trailhead is at the cul-de-sac at the end of Wild Currant Way. The eastern trail terminus at Sequim is accessed by taking westbound US 101 to the first Sequim exit (Washington Street). Turn north onto Blake Avenue, go 0.5 mile north, and turn into Carrie Blake Park.

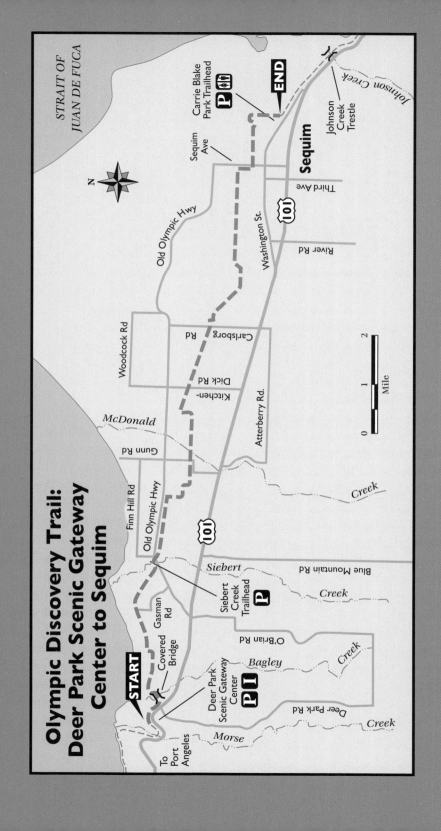

Olympic Discovery Trail:
Deer Park Scenic Gateway
Center to Sequim

STRAIT OF
JUAN DE FUCA

N

Carrie Blake
Park Trailhead

P

END

Johnson
Creek

Sequim Ave

Johnson Creek
Trestle

Sequim

Old Olympic Hwy

Third Ave

Washington St.

101

River Rd

Woodcock Rd

Carlsborg Rd

Kitchen-
Dick Rd

Atterberry Rd.

McDonald

Gunn Rd

Creek

Finn Hill Rd

Old Olympic Hwy

101

Blue Mountain Rd

Siebert

Creek

Siebert Creek
Trailhead

P

Gasman
Rd

O'Brian Rd

Covered
Bridge

Bagley

Creek

START

Deer Park
Scenic Gateway
Center

P

Deer Park Rd

Creek

To Port
Angeles

Morse

0   1   2
Mile

Rentals: Try Sound Bikes and Kayaks at 120 East Front Street (360) 457–1240, in Port Angeles.

Contact: Clallam County Public Works, (360) 417–2290; or Port Angeles Visitor Center (877) 456–8372, www.cityofpa.com. Or visit the Olympic Discovery Trail Web site, www.olympicdiscoverytrail.com.

Ferries: For information, contact Victoria Express Passenger Ferry, (360) 452–8088, www.victoriaexpress.com; or Blackball Transport (360) 457–4491, www.ferrytovictoria.com.

Bus routes: Contact Clallam Transit, www.clallamtransit.com, US Highway 101, Old Olympic Highway, (800) 858–3747.

The Olympic Discovery Trail is planned to eventually connect Forks, and LaPush on the Pacific Ocean with Port Angeles, Sequim, and Port Townsend. Sections of the trail run on old railroad rights-of-way. The completed trail segments extend from Ediz Hook, west of Port Angeles, to Blyn. See Trail 19 for another segment of this ambitious rail trail.

The Seattle, Port Angeles & Western Railway Company purchased the Seattle, Port Angeles & Lake Crescent Railway Company (1911–15) in 1916, then sold it to the Chicago, Milwaukee & St. Paul in 1918. Two round trips a day reached Discovery Junction from Majestic, with connections to Port Townsend. The line to Twin Rivers, west of Port Angeles, was built for logging; in the industry's glory days, three large logging concerns competed to bring a million board feet of logs to the trains each day for shipment to the Orient. When trucking logs became competitive, the rail line was abandoned. The current rail trail moves on and off the right-of-way to avoid private property. Be sure to check out the old No. 4 locomotive on Larridsen Boulevard.

Although you can access this segment of the Olympic Discovery Trail from either end, this description begins on the western side at Deer Park Scenic Gateway Center. Begin by exploring a brief section of trail to the west of the parking lot. The trail skirts the lot, just below it. Head west down a hill to cross Strait View Drive and then the Morse Creek Trestle,

The covered bridge over Bagley Creek.

built in 1915. The fully decked and railed trestle curves under a maple canopy and over Morse Creek. The trail extends west from Morse Creek for 5 miles to downtown Port Angeles, and another 4 miles west through Port Angeles to Ediz Hook (see Trail 19).

Return to the Deer Park Scenic Gateway Center parking lot, and this time head east, following the yellow stripes. Turn left with the road and right onto Cedar Park Drive to the T-intersection at Buchanan. The crosswalk takes you across to the trail entrance indicated by three yellow trail bollards. Travel beside US 101 briefly until the trail turns left at a second gate, just ahead.

Enjoy the paved trail down a steep hill to the covered bridge, formerly a Bainbridge ferry ramp. You can smell the moisture of the forested ravine. After crossing the covered bridge, you climb up a short, steep hill out of the Bagley Creek ravine. The next 4 miles are relatively flat. Once you've moved away from the highway, you'll hear birds chirping and see yellow, violet, and white wildflowers. A few cedar trees provide a green background in this open country.

The trail zigzags across a dirt road at 0.9 mile from the gate at US 101 and again at 1.3 miles. See bright red berries and horses beside the trail. You'll come to the intersection of the trail and Old Olympic Highway between mileposts 9 and 10. The Siebert Creek Trailhead is just ahead on the shallow Siebert Creek Ravine, near the end of Wild Current Way.

At milepost 9.5 the Siebert Creek Trail Bridge connects the forested western trail with the pastures and farms of the Dungeness Valley Trail segment. Proceed east on the paved trail and pass through the Schmidt Dairy Farm on Spring Road. Your next major attractions are the McDonnell Creek Bridge and the Robin Hill Farm County Park.

The trail heads north from Robin Hill Farm beside Vautier Road for 0.5 mile before turning sharply east past more pasturelands and the Sequim Valley Airport. Railroad Bridge Park and the Audubon Center are at milepost 17 beside the Dungeness River.

When you get near the end of the trail in Sequim, you will encounter a detour that takes you off the trail and east onto Hendrickson Road, then south onto Sequim Avenue for about 0.25 mile. Use the marked bike lanes. Then join Fir Street and go about 0.75 mile east into Carrie Blake Park, the east-end trailhead.

For a 2-mile extension to your journey, head east from the park toward Whitefeather Way. You will journey across the spectacular Johnson Creek Trestle, looming 100 feet above the creek near Whitefeather Way.

Future Plans

It is anticipated in future years that 3 more miles of trail east of Blyn to the county line will be completed.

19 OLYMPIC DISCOVERY TRAIL: PORT ANGELES WATERFRONT

What better place to tour Washington State's coast than on the turbulent Strait of Juan de Fuca? Especially when you can also see Victoria in front of you and the Olympic Mountain Range behind you. This stretch of the Olympic Discovery Trail also lets you stroll along the downtown waterfront, through lumber holding areas, and past an active mill.

Activities:

Location: City of Port Angeles on the Olympic Peninsula, Clallam County

Length: 9 miles

Surface: Asphalt

Wheelchair access: The entire trail is wheelchair accessible, although the trail runs on the roadside at Ediz Hook.

Difficulty: Easy

Food: According to locals, the best fish-and-chips in the world can be found at The Landing at the ferry dock along the trail. There's good Italian food at Bella Italia, and fine Thai food at the Thai Pepper, both a few blocks from the trail. Or try the fresh seafood at the Crabhouse Restaurant at the City Pier. There are wineries and many other restaurants in and near town.

Restrooms: You'll find restrooms at the marina on Marine Drive, at the tip of Ediz Hook, at the City Pier, and at Morse Creek Trailhead.

Seasons: The trail can be used year-round.

Access and parking: To start at the City Pier, follow U.S. Highway 101 into Port Angeles. It will become Front Street. At the intersection with Lincoln Street, turn north onto Lincoln, then drive 1 block to the waterfront and pier. You can also park at the tip of Ediz Hook (the spit), or in downtown Port Angeles; there's street lighting along Marine Drive. To add another 4 miles to your journey on the Port Angeles waterfront, park at the eastern portion of this trail segment at Morse Creek Trailhead. Access it at the intersection of US 101 and Strait View Drive.

Or you can continue a short distance to the new Deer Park Scenic Gateway Center east of Morse Creek Trailhead. When westbound on US 101, exit directly into the center. If eastbound on US 101, turn north off US 101 onto Buchanan Drive, just west of Deer Park Cinemas. Turn left onto Cedar Park Drive and take the second left, signed SCENIC OVERLOOK AHEAD, into the lot.

Rentals: Try Sound Bikes and Kayaks at 120 East Front Street (360) 457–1240, in Port Angeles.

Contact: Port Angeles Chamber of Commerce and Visitor Center, (360) 452–2363, www.cityofpa.com. Or visit the Olympic Discovery Trail Web site, www.olympicdiscoverytrail.com.

Ferries: For information, contact Victoria Express Passenger Ferry, (360) 452–8088, www.victoriaexpress.com; or Blackball Transport, (360) 457–4491, www.ferrytovictoria.com.

Bus routes: Clallam Transit, (800) 858–3747, www.clallamtransit.com

Port Angeles is the largest city on the northern Olympic Peninsula, headquarters for Olympic National Park, and site of the ferry dock for Vancouver Island. The Waterfront Trail here is one of three open sections of the Olympic Discovery Trail, which is planned to eventually reach from Forks to Port Townsend. Picnic tables are scattered along the trail, both in town and on the hook. You'll find the pathway lit at night from the marina east.

An ideal spot to start your trip is at the City Pier on Railroad Avenue near Lincoln Street. It is the starting point for the trail mileposts, which increase in number as you head east toward milepost 22 at Whitefeather Way on the south side of Sequim. (See Trail 18 for more information on the Deer Park Scenic Gateway Center to Sequim section.)

As you head east from the City Pier toward Morse Creek Trailhead, you leave the city life behind you. Along the way you will find benches, interpretive signs, and serenity. At 1 mile east of the City Pier, the trail dog legs around the former mill site. The paved trail continues eastward along the Strait of

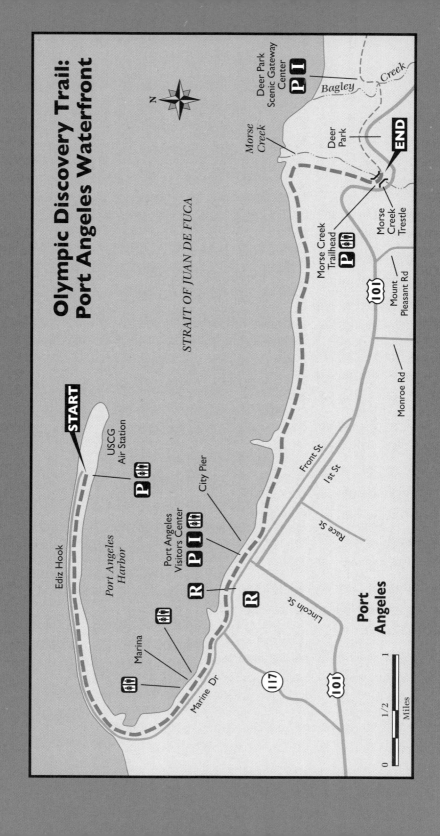

View of Port Angeles waterfront from Ediz Hook.

Juan de Fuca for 2 additional miles past the mill site before it turns south near Morse Creek. When you turn south away from the strait, you are less than a mile from the Morse Creek Trestle and the Morse Creek Trailhead.

If you opt to start your trip by heading west from the City Pier on Railroad Avenue, you will find the trail is a well-marked sidewalk. It follows Railroad Avenue, turns ninety degrees south, then turns west onto the sidewalk beside Marine Drive. Pass the marina, ducks, and a host of fishing boats. The trail sneaks into a little park and on toward the mill, an impressive operation. The pathway is a shoulder on the road from here to the tip of the spit, about 3 miles. Use caution. Check out the ships docked in the harbor and traveling through the strait, with Canada in the distance and the snowcapped Olympic Mountains above. The trail ends at the Coast Guard station.

For the grand coastal tour, continue west on US 101 to visit rail trails Spruce Railroad (Trail 20), Willapa Hills (Trail 23), and Astoria Riverwalk, Oregon (Trail 30). Or head north from Keystone to Bellingham for some rail trail tours through town and in scenic outlying areas.

20 SPRUCE RAILROAD TRAIL

This fun single-track trail runs along the shores of Lake Crescent in Olympic National Park. It's bounded by steep slate walls above and the water below. Check out a tiny "hole in the rock" tunnel and, after your workout, relax beside mountains reflecting in the turquoise lake.

Activities:

Location: Olympic National Park, 16 miles west of Port Angeles on the Olympic Peninsula, Clallam County

Length: 4 miles

Surface: Smooth dirt and gravel with some rocky areas. Most of the trail is 3 to 4 feet wide, although it has eroded to 2 feet and is banked toward the lake in places.

Wheelchair access: This trail is not wheelchair accessible.

Difficulty: Easy to moderate for walkers; moderate to difficult for bikers

Food: You'll find many restaurants in Port Angeles (see Trail 19). And in summer only, try the Fairholm General Store on U.S. Highway 101 at Camp David Jr. Road, the Log Cabin Resort near the eastern trailhead, and Lake Crescent Lodge on US 101.

Restrooms: There are vault toilets at the eastern end of trail off East Beach Road and at North Shore Picnic Area. You'll find flush toilets and water at Fairholm Campground, open May through September.

Seasons: The trail can be used year-round. At only 800 feet in elevation, snow usually isn't a problem. You may find that US 101 west of the trail has some icy hills when the snow level is low. Most services in the area are open May through September.

Access and parking: Take a ferry from Seattle, Edmonds, or Keystone to the Olympic Peninsula and drive to Port Angeles. Take US 101 west from town for 16 miles, then turn right (northwest) onto East Beach Road. Follow the signs to the Log Cabin Resort (accommodations are available here), turning

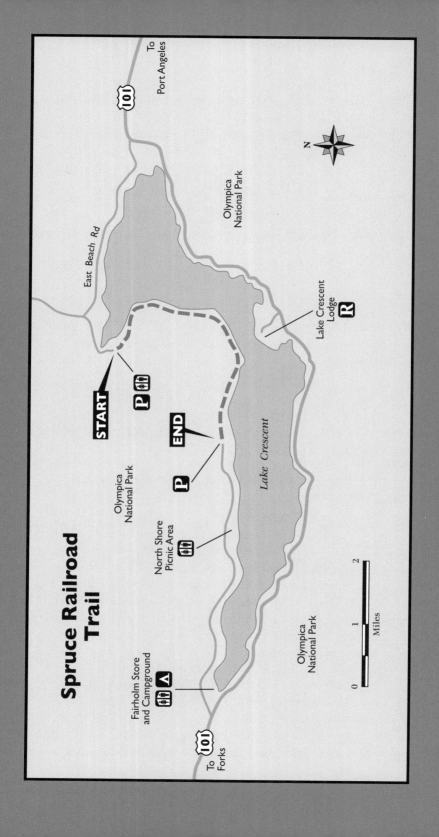

left after 3.3 miles at the trail sign. You'll reach the trailhead 0.8 mile beyond. This road is paved except for the final quarter mile.

You can also access the trail from the west. Turn left off US 101 at Camp David Jr. Road. This paved road goes 0.6 mile to the Fairholm Campground (eighty-eight sites for tents and RVs). Continue past the campground for just over 4 miles on a dirt road to reach the western trailhead; depending on the season and maintenance, this road may be rough.

Rentals: Try Sound Bikes and Kayaks at 120 East Front Street (360) 457–1240 in Port Angeles.

Contact:

- Olympic National Park Visitors Center is open from 9 a.m. to 4 p.m. Call (360) 565–3130; for TDD, call (800) 833–6388; for twenty-four-hour recorded information, call (360) 565–3131; check the Web site at www .nps.gov/olym.

- The Storm King Ranger Station can be reached at (360) 928–3380 or www.nps.gov/olym.

- For fishing regulations, contact the Department of Fish and Wildlife at (360) 902–2200.

- Olympic National Forest and Olympic National Park Visitors Center, Forks, (360) 374–7566.

Ferries: For information, call (800) 843–3779, or visit www.wsdot.wa.gov/ ferries/current/.

Bus routes: Visit www.clallamcountytransit.com.

The Spruce Railway was a war effort during World War I, when the army needed the light, strong wood of the Sitka spruce to build airplane frames. This tree grows only along the Pacific coastal region from northern California to Alaska, with vast stands located in the roadless Olympic Peninsula. The army's Spruce Production Division thus built the Olympic Spruce Railroad #1 around Lake Crescent in 1918. Armistice Day arrived on November 11, 1918; nineteen days later, the line was completed. The army sold the railway before a single log had been hauled. It was used for commercial logging until 1954, when it was abandoned. The current 4-mile rail trail was completed in 1981.

For more information about this trail or the national park itself, stop at the Olympic National Park Visitors Center on Race Street, a short distance east from US 101, in Port Angeles. It's fully accessible and contains a lowland

> "The 36 miles of main line construction through the tunnels and forests of solid rock, over spidery tressels, around dizzy rocky curves ...is being completed practically within five months! It is the most remarkable speed feat in the history of American railroading."
> —Loyal Legion of Loggers and Lumbermen, January 1919

forest display along with information on the natural and cultural history of the park. The park is designated a Man and Biosphere Reserve and a World Heritage Park. Pets are allowed only in parking areas and campgrounds.

About half of the Spruce Railroad Trail is curvy, narrow, rough, and sometimes rocky. You'll cross rockslide residue and drainage divets, some carrying streams; horses would have a tough time here. The other half of the trail, mostly in the west, is fairly flat and unobstructed. The park suggests wearing long pants to ward off deer ticks; bright-colored clothing will help you spot the critters. If one visits you, dress it in petroleum jelly. They suffocate in five minutes and can be scraped off.

Although you can access the trail from either end, this description begins at its eastern trailhead. From here the trail heads up into the woods and remains beside the lake, either at water level or on a bank 100 to 200 feet high. A lovely bridge detours around the collapsed 460-foot McFee Tunnel. All that remains is a pile of debris above the west side of the bridge. At 3 miles, look east to see the small Daley-Rankin bore. Observe from outside the tunnels only: The fallen timber and falling rocks here not only are dangerous but also pose a fire hazard to the hillside above.

Though Pacific madrone trees, with their peeling red bark, shade these lower slopes of Pyramid Peak, the southern exposure creates a dry

A bridge over a small inlet along the Spruce Railroad Trail.

microclimate. In addition to cougars, bears, deer, and raccoons, you might see a golden eagle or a peregrine dropping in from its nesting spot on Pyramid Peak. Look and listen for the pileated woodpecker, the world's largest. Mountain goats, introduced in 1921, remain in the area.

Emerge on Camp David Jr. Road. To extend your adventure, take the road to Fairholm or hike the rugged Pyramid Peak Trail, which climbs 2,400 feet to the peak. Leave from the North Shore Picnic Area about a mile down the road. Check with the ranger for conditions.

While you're in the area, you might also visit the Deer Park Scenic Gateway Center to Sequim (Trail 18) and Port Angeles Waterfront (Trail 19) sections of the Olympic Discovery Trail. Or you can continue west for the big ocean tour on the Willapa Hills Trail–Raymond to South Bend Riverfront Trail (Trail 23) and the Astoria Riverwalk (Trail 30). The largest Sitka spruce tree can be found near the Banks-Vernonia State Trail (Trail 31).

21 FOOTHILLS TRAIL

The foothills of Mount Rainier and the southern Cascades, green valleys, rivers, creeks, eagles and salmon, small happy towns, and families at play—this is the Foothills Trail. The community created this trail and the community enjoys it. Mount Rainier towers above at such close range that you can almost feel its 14,000 feet of rock, glaciers, and snowfields.

Activities:

Location: Puyallup to Buckley in Pierce County

Length: There are currently 15 continuous miles of paved trails between the northeast Puyallup (Meeker) Trailhead and South Prairie Trailhead. A paved 3-mile section of the Puyallup Riverwalk extends west to the city of Puyallup. Plus, there is a yet-to-be connected 2-mile segment of the Foothills Trail within the city of Buckley.

Surface: Asphalt with a narrow equestrian path

Wheelchair access: The trail is accessible wherever it's paved.

Difficulty: Easy, except one hill climb

Food: You'll find restaurants, espresso shops, and grocery stores in the towns of Buckley, South Prairie, and Orting.

Restrooms: Restrooms and drinking water are available at the trailheads.

Seasons: The trail can be used year-round.

Access and parking: There are several spots from which to access this trail. To begin at the northwest terminus and enjoy 15 miles of paved trail, use the Puyallup (Meeker) Trailhead, found on 80th Street 0.2 mile east of 134th Avenue East and Pioneer Way East, located 1 mile west of Washington Highway 162 in Puyallup.

This intersection can be reached from Washington Highway 512 by taking the Pioneer Avenue exit and turning east, continuing for 1.8 miles on Pioneer Avenue. Or continue south on WA 162 to the McMillin Trailhead just west of a concrete bridge over the Puyallup River. Another option is to continue on WA 162 to Orting Park and begin there, or at the South Prairie Trailhead off WA 162, east of Orting. Beyond that, dirt lots provide trail access near the Carbon River.

You can access the trail's 2-mile Buckley stretch from the town of Buckley. Washington Highway 410 will bring you to town; there are two trailheads on this road, one at the armory and one at Ryan Road.

Rentals: Bicycle rentals can be found at Trailside Cyclery in Orting on Van Scoyac Avenue, on the south side of Orting Park.

Contact: Foothills Rail-to-Trails Coalition, (253) 841–2570, Bugtrail@aol .com, or visit www.piercecountytrails.org.

Bus routes: Contact Pierce Transit at (253) 581–8000 or www.pierce transit.org.

|||||||||||||||||||||||||||||||||||||||||||||||||||||||||||||||||||||||||||||||||||||||||

While much of the Foothills Trail's eventual 30-mile length remains undeveloped, you can presently access a 15-mile asphalt segment that begins at Puyallup's eastern city limit and continues through the towns of McMillin and Orting and on to a newer trailhead at South Prairie. Along the way you cross rivers and wetlands. Additional trail sections continuing to Buckley and Carbonado are expected to be completed in 2009. Currently there is also a stretch of about 2 miles of paved trail through Buckley.

This description begins at the Puyallup Trailhead, although there are many other ways to enjoy the trail. From Puyallup, you'll be traveling to McMillin through open land featuring tree farms and fields of rhubarb, strawberries, and pumpkins. You can visit trailside farm stores along the way. An added bonus is the breathtaking view of Mount Rainier.

South of the McMillin Trailhead, the trail parallels WA 162 through a corridor of housing developments and schools for a distance of 2.5 miles into the Orting park and business district. Enjoy the landscaped greenway with hundreds of flowering fruit trees that were planted by the Foothills Rails-to-Trails Coalition. The trees separate the trail from the nearby highway.

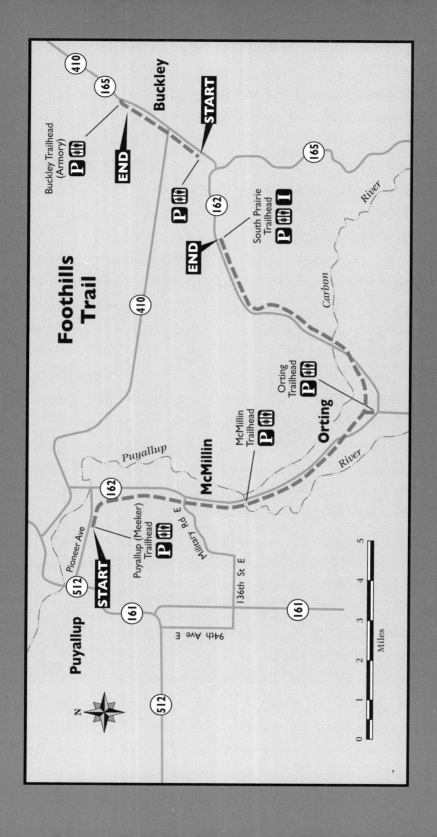

Mount Rainier provides a stunning backdrop for the Foothills Trail. *(Courtesy Ernest Bay)*

The grade on the trail is minimal, but you may notice it if you're a beginner skater or bicyclist. At 2.3 miles from the McMillin Trailhead the trail turns right and crosses Whitesell Street Northwest. Reach Orting Park and the trailhead at Calistoga Street West 0.4 mile beyond. You'll find a grocery store and restaurants here. To complete the picture of a rural Northwest town, the slogan IN D'BEAN WE TRUST frames the espresso shop. Stop to experience the history and local pride in the park.

Stop to enjoy the history of the area as depicted on a number of the building murals in town. Also visit the Foothills Rails-to-Trails Coalition kiosk. Names of trail supporters are inscribed in a brick bench, and there is a wooden sign featuring the city's former logo of many years: daffodils flanked by Orting's two rivers. The logo has been replaced with a design centered on the Foothills Trail.

The Orting parkland was purchased by the Northern Pacific Railway in 1887 for $1.00 from the city of Orting. Trains carried passengers to Spokane on one line and across the country on another. Coal and coke were transported from Carbonado, Fairfax, and Wilkeson; timber was shipped from the forestlands by the St. Paul & Tacoma Lumber Company. Burlington Northern took up the tracks starting in 1985, and the city and Pierce County Parks department bought the right-of-way in 1994. Trail construction began in 1996.

Continue through the park to the WA 162 crossing, where the highway turns north toward Buckley. Note the 1904 Odd Fellows Hall. Here the trail leaves WA 162, passes the city's skate park, borders a cattle pasture, and skirts a small forest. The trail meets the rushing Carbon River at Bernie's Place, a memorial rest stop. The trail crosses a paved timber bridge at Voights Creek and passes a buffalo farm.

The trail returns to the highway and heads uphill to a trestle crossing. A second trestle crosses the Carbon River. Dirt lots sit on either side of the trestle. (You can leave a car here to make this trail a shuttle trip.) The trail crosses a wetlands area on a long, paved timber bridge and continues along South Prairie Creek, which is one of the state's premier salmon-bearing streams. Shortly before Arline Road, you'll find a paved interpretive wetlands rest stop on your left. The twenty-acre man-made mitigation wetland was designed for salmon recovery. Continue on a paved trail past the

South Prairie Trailhead to a "bridge in waiting" over South Prairie Creek near the fire station that serves as a community center at South Prairie Park.

When you are ready, turn around and return to the trailhead you started from.

The 2-mile segment of paved trail in Buckley runs parallel to WA 410. It passes through a park, ending at the armory north of town.

Future Plans

Eventually the trail will extend from South Prairie to Buckley and from Cascade Junction to Wilkeson and Carbonado. At present it connects with the Puyallup Riverwalk via a dead-end paved farm road, 134th Avenue East. From there, across the Sumner Bridge, it accesses a short Sumner Trail section along the White River. Sumner Trail is planned to connect with the King County Interurban Trail (Trail 5). The trail in Buckley will continue east to Enumclaw and King County. The tremendous efforts of the Foothills Rails-to-Trails Coalition created this trail. Get in touch with the coalition (see Contact, above) to become part of this continuing effort.

22 CHEHALIS WESTERN TRAIL

This peaceful trail hides you from a commercial district near Interstate 5, just a few miles from the state capitol in Olympia. It passes beside homes, then farms and ponds, finally reaching the Woodard Bay Conservation Area near Puget Sound. Horses are accommodated with a separate path for most of the way, sometimes through the woods. The sights and sounds of ponds, pastures, forest, birds, ducks, and cows make this a delightful trail, well designed for all users.

Activities:

Location: Olympia, in Thurston County

Length: 5.5 miles

Surface: Asphalt with a dirt horse trail (separated for much of the distance)

Wheelchair access: The entire trail is wheelchair accessible.

Difficulty: Easy

Food: You'll find restaurants on Martin Way at the trail's southern terminus. If you complete the trail round trip, check out the Main Chinese Buffet several miles east on Martin Way. To purchase a gourmet picnic for the trail or indulge at a great salad bar, Top Foods is also east on Martin Way.

Restrooms: There are restrooms at the Woodard Bay lot and at midtrail, but no running water.

Seasons: The trail can be used year-round.

Access and parking: You can park your car and access the trail from several cross streets in the area, which have small parking areas. To reach these lots, exit I–5 at Sleater-Kinney Road and head straight (north) to South Bay Road. Turn left and then right onto Shincke Road to a trailhead. Turn left off Shincke at any of the small streets beyond (north) for other trailheads.

There's also a parking lot at the Woodard Bay Conservation Area. To reach this, turn left off Shincke Road at 36th Avenue Northeast, then turn right onto Boston Harbor Road NE, and right again onto Woodard Bay Road.

To reach the trail's southern terminus (no parking) at Martin Way, turn left onto Martin Way off Sleater-Kinney Road soon after exiting I–5 and look to the right for a bus stop within a few blocks. The trail leaves from the sidewalk here. A final option is to try to get permission to park at a commercial establishment along Martin Way.

Rentals: Olympic Outfitters is at 407 4th Avenue East in Olympia.

Contact: Washington State Department of Natural Resources, (360) 577–2025

Bus routes: None

A lthough you can access the pleasant Chehalis Western Trail from many points along its way, this description takes you from its southern terminus at Martin Way. The trail begins just off I–5 on a busy street. It's mostly flat with a bit of grade here and there.

A dirt equestrian path runs alongside the paved trail used by skaters and other trail users.

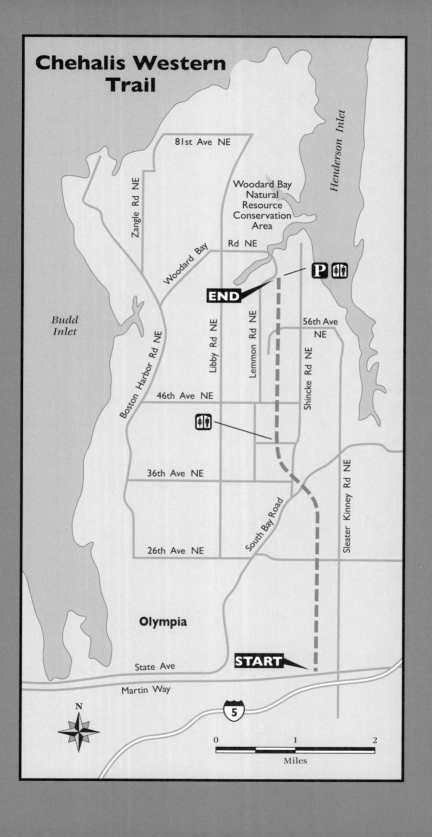

Once you depart Martin Way, you'll pass by homes and a little pond. Cross 26th Avenue Northeast at 1.5 miles; the horse trail starts here. You'll travel past horse pastures and wetlands and through evergreens and blackberry vines. Cross South Bay Road at mile 2.5, then Shincke Road soon after. Interpretive and map signs are placed at each intersection. See pictures of locomotives and read the history of timber transport along this route. Logs were hauled to Henderson Inlet by rail and then to the Everett mills by water.

Fields extend far in one direction, and a duck pond straddles the trail. Grab a bench to enjoy the serenity. Find a restroom at 3.25 miles, just north of 41st Avenue Northeast. After two more street crossings—46th and 56th—you'll arrive at the Woodard Bay Conservation Area. Walk 0.5 mile on the Overlook Trail to Henderson Inlet. Rest at this wooded waterfront spot, which was once a bustling logging transfer area. If you parked here, drive out to Boston Harbor for another waterfront view.

For more trail touring, you can continue on the southern part of the Chehalis Trail, which begins approximately 1 mile beyond I–5 at Chambers Lake. The southern section is administered by Thurston County Parks (360–786–5595) and extends 7 miles south to 103rd Avenue. Or you can try the Foothills Trail in Orting (Trail 21), or head to Olympia to tour the lake beside the capitol. For a unique and soulful experience, head farther south to Tenino and howl with the wolves at Wolf Haven.

23 WILLAPA HILLS TRAIL (RAYMOND TO SOUTH BEND RIVERFRONT TRAIL)

South Bend and Raymond, Washington, aren't on the way to anywhere (unless you're heading to Long Beach or Astoria for some oceanfront R&R). You have to *want* to come here. You have to like rural "unyuppified" communities with regional pride, history, and art. You have to appreciate blue herons and outdoor sculpture. A taste for fresh oysters might come in handy, too.

Activities:

Location: Between Raymond and South Bend, in Pacific County

Length: 3.5 miles

Surface: Asphalt

Wheelchair access: The trail is wheelchair accessible.

Difficulty: Easy

Food: You'll find things to eat in both South Bend and Raymond.

Restrooms: You'll find restrooms and drinking water at the Raymond Trailhead. Public restrooms are also located at the South Bend City Park at the southern end of town.

Seasons: The trail can be used year-round, but it's often windy and wet in winter.

Access and parking: The Raymond Trailhead lies in the park at the Willapa Seaport Museum. Turn north from U.S. Highway 101 on Heath Street (which turns into Alder Street) across from the Raymond Visitors Center. The museum and trailhead are on your left near the end of the road. Take a quick walk down the trail from the road's dead end to see the railroad bridge.

To start in South Bend, turn (north) toward the river on Summit Street just north of town.

Rentals: There are no rentals available along this trail.

Contact: Raymond Chamber of Commerce, (360) 942–5419; or Raymond City Hall, (360) 942–3451

Bus routes: None

Explore a pair of rewarding small towns on this trail, the Willapa Hills Trail (Raymond to South Bend Riverfront Trail). Your starting point, off-the-beaten-track South Bend, doesn't just claim to be the oyster capital of the world. The county courthouse is also on the National Register of Historic Places, and a bayside sculpture recognizes Joe Krupa, a resident who brought home the prestigious World War II Medal of Honor. The Joe Krupa Wayside Park also offers picnic tables and a portable toilet.

Raymond, on the other hand, boasts a Wildlife-Heritage Sculpture Corridor, funded by the U.S. Coastal Corridor Program to visually enhance WA 101. The community worked together to determine the essence of Raymond. Artists then developed images to portray that essence: Willapa Bay with its nearby hills and the native flora and fauna, the community's history, the logging, fishing, and farming. A steel fabricator produced the 200 designs except for the hand-sculpted three-dimensional works.

You can access the trail from either end, but this description takes you from South Bend northeast into Raymond. From the Krupa Wayside Park, the trail leaves the right-of-way and heads toward the town of Raymond. You'll parallel the highway at close range for a bit, then drop to the water. Just beyond, turn left onto the road and right at the stop sign. The trail begins again after a short pass through the Port of Willapa Harbor parking lot. You get a break from the highway before you cross the river on US 101. The trail then turns left onto Heath Street, taking you to the Raymond Trailhead and the interpretive area near the museum.

Explore Raymond's Third Street to see the old theater and more sculptures. The Willapa Seaport Museum and Northwest Carriage Museum at the trailhead offers more glimpses of local history.

When you're ready, turn around and return to South Bend for your reward: oysters at East Point Seafood, located in a cannery on the riverside, south of the trailhead at Summit. Barges bring them in fresh daily. The artistic highlight of this town is the 1911 Pacific County Courthouse, 2 blocks off US 101 on a hill overlooking the bay and the hills. Walk among the faux marble pillars; look down at the mosaic tile floor and gaze up at the lit art glass dome, 29 feet in diameter. Outside you can picnic by the duck pond and watch the trout swim about. The Pacific County Historical Society Museum also offers glimpses of local history.

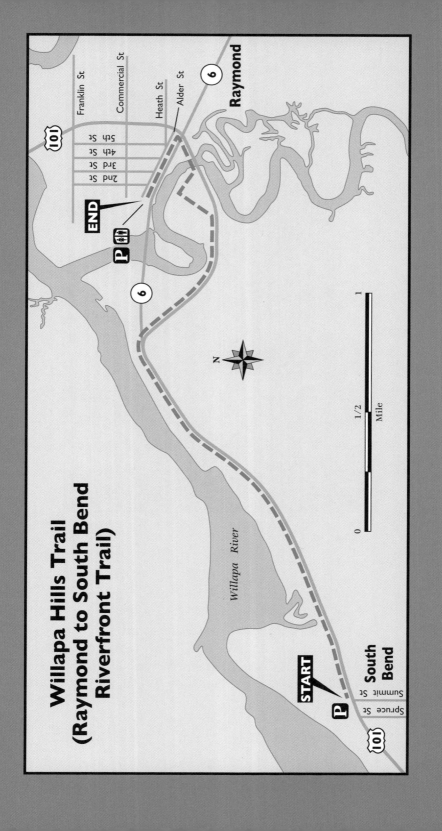

Willapa Hills Trail
(Raymond to South Bend Riverfront Trail)

Franklin St

Commercial St

Heath St

Alder St

Raymond

101

5th St

4th St

3rd St

2nd St

6

END

P

6

P

N

Willapa River

START

P

South Bend

Spruce St

Summit St

101

0   1/2   1

Mile

One of the many sculptures along Raymond's Wildlife-Heritage Sculpture Corridor.

If you're up for a mountain bike ride, Raymond is thirty-five minutes from Montesano and Lake Sylvia State Park (Trail 24).

The Raymond to South Bend Riverfront Trail crosses US 101 and follows Washington Highway 6 to Chehalis, ultimately connecting to the John Wayne Pioneer Trail. The redesign of the Third Street business loop of Raymond includes bike lanes all the way to Washington Highway 105 along the ocean.

24 LAKE SYLVIA STATE PARK

Lake Sylvia State Park has something for everyone: logging history and operations, a dam, a thirty-acre lake, camping, picnicking, and any number of great trails to explore. Two of these trails—the Sylvia Creek Forestry Trail and the Two Mile Trail—are featured here. Both are secluded in a forest of western hemlock and Dougls fir, some of which is part of a working tree farm. Though the trails are managed by two different agencies and for different purposes, they are contiguous with each other and offer a similar forest experience and a great workout.

Activities:

Location: Grays Harbor County

Length: 4.8 miles total. The Sylvia Creek Forestry Trail is 2.8 miles long; the Two Mile Trail is 2 miles.

Surface: Dirt and gravel; the trail can be very muddy.

Wheelchair access: The trails are not wheelchair accessible, but access is available at the park and lakeside.

Difficulty: The Two Mile Trail is easy along its 0.75-mile flat stretch, difficult along the 1.25-mile hiking trail. The Sylvia Creek Forestry Trail is difficult.

Food: There are vending machines in the park; you'll also find restaurants and groceries in Montesano.

Restrooms: The park features restrooms and drinking water.

Seasons: The trails are open year-round, though they can be wet in fall and winter.

Access and parking: To reach Lake Sylvia State Park, take exit 104 off Interstate 5 onto U.S. Highway 101 west toward Aberdeen. Where US 101 exits, stay on Washington Highway 8. Continue to Washington Highway 107, signed MONTESANO, LAKE SYLVIA STATE PARK. Turn right into town. Follow signs to the park: Drive through the stoplight, turn left at the stop sign (East Spruce Avenue), then turn right onto North Third Street. You'll arrive at the Lake Sylvia parking area 1.5 miles from WA 8.

Rentals: No rentals are available along the trail.

Contact:

- City of Montesano, (360) 249–3021, www.montesano.us
- Lake Sylvia State Park, (360) 249–3621
- Washington State Parks Reservations Service at (888) 226–7688, www .parks.wa.gov

Bus routes: None

||||||||||||||||||||||||||||||||||||||||||||||||||||||||||||||||||||||||||||||||||

Lake Sylvia State Park has a lot to explore. The park's thirty-acre lake contains native bass and stocked trout. Coho salmon and trout live in Sylvia Creek; beavers build dams along its banks, while otters play in the water. Bears and birds love the sweet grasses, berries, and bushes in the open replanted areas of the forestry trail. A play area, picnic sites, and a

A tree-tunnel on the Sylvia Creek Forestry Trail.

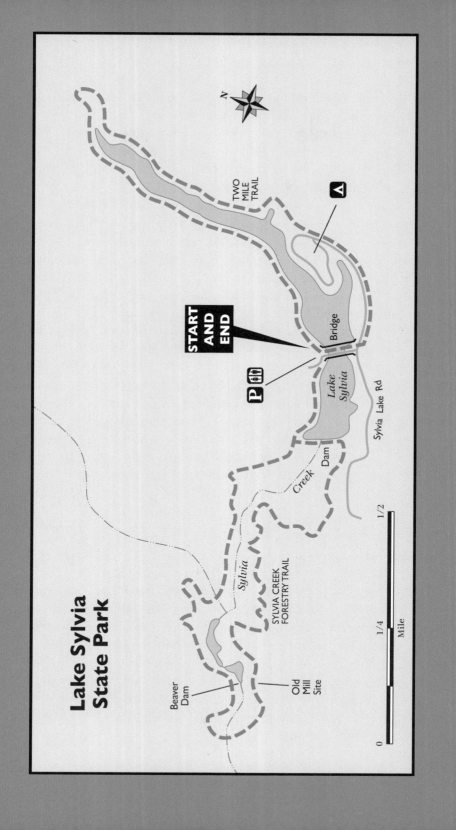

Lake Sylvia State Park

N

TWO
MILE
TRAIL

START
AND
END

P

Bridge

Lake
Sylvia

Sylvia Lake Rd

Creek

Dam

Sylvia

SYLVIA CREEK
FORESTRY TRAIL

Beaver
Dam

Old
Mill
Site

0   1/4   1/2

Mile

boat launch combine with interpretive trails to offer a full day of recreation; a campground lets you extend your visit.

History is highlighted throughout the park as well. The original dam was built in 1868 to power the first sawmill in Grays Harbor County. The backwater pond was used for log flotation. You can see the suprastructure when the lake is lowered. The present dam was built in the 1920s to provide Montesano with power. The land became a state park in 1936.

Look for a carved 4-foot sphere of wood used for leisure log rolling in the lake, the underwater log dam, remnants of the sawmill, and old trestles. These 3 miles of railroad were built to haul timber from the pond to the Chehalis County Logging and Timber Company in 1905. Oxen then hauled it to town. The hearty oxen were the sole method of timber transport before the railroad.

A vast network of trails will take you through the park. This description focuses on two of them: The Sylvia Creek Forestry Trail, built in 1991, is a rugged interpretive trail beside Sylvia Creek with short, steep hills and small bridges; the Two Mile Trail heads out 0.75 mile on the railroad right-of-way, then loops 1.25 miles around Lake Sylvia on a hiking trail. The undeveloped right-of-way continues straight into the forest as part of the network of mountain bike trails. The park has a map of the entire trail network; many offer especially desirable mountain biking. Some trails are also logging roads, so you may encounter logging trucks.

Sylvia Creek Forestry Trail (SCFT)

The SCFT is a rugged, challenging 2.8-mile-long trail. For the mountain biker, it's strewn with obstacles and hazards; for the hiker, it provides an interesting and hilly pathway through the forest. The land up against the park boundaries, including this trail, is owned by the city of Montesano and leased out for logging. Logging created this railroad bed over one hundred years ago, and it's still going strong today. The city developed an interpretive trail to exhibit this working forest. The clear-cuts, the second-growth forest, the old Chehalis mill site, and the wildlife and plant habitat are all part of this display.

Bridge across Lake Sylvia.

From the parking lot, head to the dam on the lakeside path. The SCFT starts on the uphill side of a short rock wall behind the restrooms. Bikers may prefer to cross the dam to the south side of Sylvia Creek and ride to the railroad bridge and back, avoiding the more difficult north side. If you do bike the north side, stop or slow at every blind curve to avoid collisions with hikers, and be cautious of steep banks below the curving trail, wooden steps placed in steep sections, narrow bridges, and mudholes. Ride in control.

From the north side, the trail heads downhill to a creek crossing at 0.65 mile and up a steep hill. The second creek crossing is on a short, narrow bridge. Steep steps follow; a short downhill leads to a burned-out tree that creates an archway on the trail at mile 1. Shortly after that, a gaping hole all but eliminates the trail. The riverbank is steep here. Be sure, if you're on a bike, that your brakes and rims aren't too muddy to keep you on the trail. At mile 1.15 the clear-cut opens the wooded trail up to sunshine. Steps take you downhill to the creek crossing at 1.4 miles.

The trail levels out to rolling terrain for a while. The flat area to your right is the site of the sawmill that operated in the late 1800s. The trestle pilings can be seen on your left. At 1.83 miles steps follow a curve that

Stream crossing on the Sylvia Creek Forestry Trail.

takes you downhill to a narrow bridge and onto a second bridge almost concealed by a curve in the trail. Walk up a long hill on steps. Wind around in the deep evergreen forest high on the banks of Sylvia Creek until you reach a dramatic view of the drop below the dam. Watch the edge here. Cross the dam to return to the park.

Two Mile Trail

The Two Mile Trail begins adjacent to the small parking area near the bridge that crosses the lake. It runs flat along the lake, a bench placed here and there. At the gate at 0.75 mile, climb up to a bridge (over the middle fork of Sylvia Creek) and turn right to continue the Two Mile Trail around the lake. The actual right-of-way, called B-line Road, goes straight ahead past another gate. It continues flat for 2 miles, then heads uphill. A steeper logging road heads off to the right. Be sure to take a bike map if you'd like to venture off to the many trails outside the park boundaries. The Two Mile

Trail loop climbs up steps and descends to narrow bridges, only to climb again to a bank high above the lake. The trail is narrow and pretty. Use the interpretive guide to follow the numbered posts to identify wildflowers, trees, and logging features. The trail drops you off at the campground, and from there the road returns you to your starting point.

On your way out of Montesano, be sure visit the historic county building on Broadway, 1 block downhill from Spruce. Other nearby rail trails include the Willapa Hills Trail (Trail 23), thirty-five minutes from Montesano, and the Chehalis Western Trail (Trail 22), north of Olympia off I–5.

Grays Harbor County has quite a number of abandoned railbeds. Meetings are in progress to work toward linking them together as trails.

25 JOHN WAYNE PIONEER TRAIL (WEST)

The John Wayne Pioneer Trail crosses most of Washington State. The developed portion lies within the Iron Horse State Park. It parallels Interstate 90 from Cedar Falls, near North Bend, to Kittitas, then drops south through army land to end on the edge of the magnificent Columbia River.

The trail passes through various climatic zones. West of the Cascades are the wet and green Cascade foothills. East of the mountains you'll find glacial valleys with pine and fir trees and ranchland. As you continue east, the landscape changes to sagebrush desert, arid scrublands, and the irrigated farmlands of the Columbia Basin. East of Thorp the trail is unshaded and dry, hot in summer and cold in winter. Bears, bobcats, cougars, rattlesnakes, eagles, ospreys, rodents, rabbits, and butterflies inhabit different parts of the trail.

Activities:

Location: Cedar Falls to the Columbia River

Length: 113 miles

Surface: Compacted ballast, gravel, and sand; the trail is 16 to 20 feet wide. The section from Cedar Falls to Easton has the most compacted surface.

Wheelchair access: This trail is not wheelchair accessible.

Difficulty: Easy to moderate, with some sandy and rocky surfaces. There's a constant 1.75 percent grade uphill from Cedar Falls to Hyak.

Food: You can find things to eat in Ellensburg, Easton, and Kittitas, and at the intersection with Thorp Prairie Highway.

Restrooms: You'll find restrooms at all trailheads except Easton, Ellensburg West, and Kittitas; they're also available along the trail between Cedar Falls and Hyak. Water is available at most trailheads.

Camping: You'll find campgrounds at Lake Kachess, Lake Easton State Park, the Wanapum Recreation Area, the Army East Trailhead, and Kittitas County Fairgrounds.

Seasons: The trail can be used year-round, although the Snoqualmie Tunnel is closed November 1 through April 30. Cross-country skiing or snowshoeing is fun here between December and March; the trail is groomed on weekends from Hyak to Crystal Springs or Lake Easton State Park.

Access and parking: You'll need a special Sno-Park permit to park at Hyak, Easton, or Lake Easton State Park in winter. Contact local outdoor stores or the U.S. Forest Service office adjacent to the Summit Ski Area at exit 52.

- Cedar Falls (exit 32): Take Cedar Falls Road off I–90 and drive 3 miles south to the Rattlesnake Lake parking lot. Park and continue up the road 0.5 mile to the trailhead on your left.

- Twin Falls (exit 38): If you're driving east on I–90, turn right at the end of the exit and park in the lot marked TWIN FALLS NATURAL AREA. If you're heading westbound, take a left off the exit ramp, drive 2 miles, and park in the second lot on your left.

- Hyak (exit 54): At the end of the ramp, make a soft left onto the frontage road. Turn right at the sign that reads IRON HORSE STATE PARK to enter the Lake Keechelus parking lot. A Sno-Park permit is required in winter.

- Lake Easton State Park (exit 70): To head west on the trail, get to the frontage road south of I–90 and drive east to the park entrance. Pass the ranger booth and take the first right. Park in the day-use area straight ahead. To reach the trail, turn left out of the lot, pass through a closed gate, turn left at the dead end onto a dirt road, and finally turn right onto the trail. A Sno-Park permit is required in winter.

- Easton (exit 71): To head east on the trail, follow the signs from the exit to Easton. Cross the railroad tracks and turn left at the trail sign. A Sno-Park permit is required in winter.

- South Cle Elum (exit 84): Follow the signs to South Cle Elum, turning left on the main drag and left again at the tourist office on your left and the flagged park on your right. Follow signs to Iron Horse State Park.

- Thorp (exit 101): Head 0.25 mile north on Thorp Prairie Highway. Turn left onto Thorp Depot Road and drive another 0.25 mile to the trail crossing and the trailhead beyond.

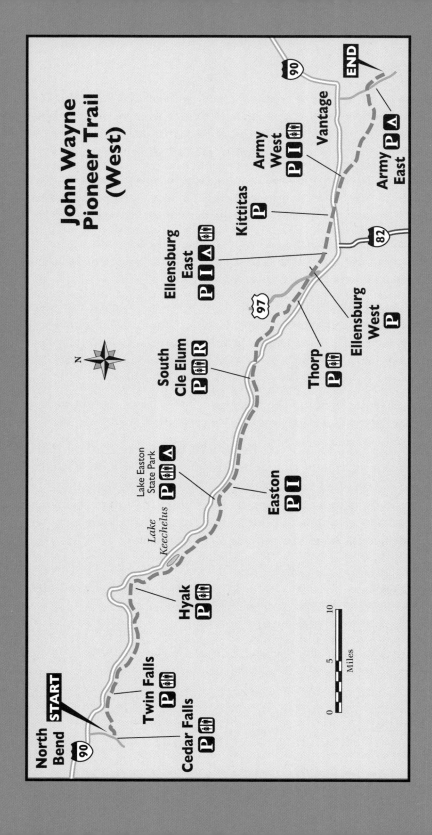

John Wayne Pioneer Trail (West)

N

North Bend **START**

90

Cedar Falls
P 🚻

Twin Falls
P 🚻

Hyak
P 🚻 🚻

Lake Keechelus

Lake Easton State Park
P 🚻 ⛺

Easton
P I

South Cle Elum
P 🚻 R

97

Thorp
P 🚻

Ellensburg East
P I ⛺ 🚻

Ellensburg West
P

Kittitas
P

82

Army West
P I 🚻

Army East
P ⛺

Vantage

90

END

0   5   10
Miles

- Ellensburg West (exit 106): To head west on the trail, follow signs to Central Washington University north of I–90. The trailhead is on Water Street near 14th Avenue.

- Ellensburg East (exit 109): Turn north onto Main Street. Head north for 2 miles, then turn right on Eighth Avenue. Drive 0.8 mile more, then look for the KITTITAS COUNTY FAIRGROUNDS sign on your right. Turn right at the Dairy Queen and go 1 block. The trailhead is on the left. Park at the fairgrounds.

- Kittitas (exit 115): Head north from the freeway. Turn left onto Railroad Avenue and park near the depot or in town.

- Army West (exit 115): Continue north on Main Street past the Kittitas Trailhead to First Street and turn right. First Street becomes Parke Creek Road and parallels the trail for 2.5 miles. Turn right onto Prater Road to cross I–90, then left onto Boyleston and right at the T-intersection with Stevens Road. The trailhead is on your left.

- Army East (exit 136): From the freeway, travel south on Huntzinger Road past the Wanapum Recreation Area. Go 2 miles farther. The trailhead parking is on the left.

Rentals: You can rent mountain bikes at Bike and Board in Cle Elum, (509) 674–4567.

Contact:

- For information on camping, call Washington State Parks Reservations Service, (888) 226–7688; for information about the trail and camping, visit www.parks.wa.gov.

- Lake Easton State Park can be reached at (509) 656–2586.

- The Wanapum State Park's phone number is (509) 856–2700.

- For information on camping at the Kittitas County Fairgrounds and for reservations, call the Kittitas County Events Center at (509) 962–7639.

- The number for tourism information in Ellensburg is (509) 925–3137.

- To learn about the history of the Milwaukee Road Railroad, visit www.mrha.com.

Bus routes: None

||||||||||||||||||||||||||||||||||||||||||||||||||||||||||||||||||||||||||||||||||||||||

Iron Horse State Park includes 113 miles of rail trail and more than 1,600 acres of adjacent land. The trail is isolated much of the way. There are no services on the trail east of Kittitas. There is presently no bicycle or pedestrian or equestrian crossing to the town of Beverly, where the eastern section of trail begins, across the river.

Snow cover for cross-country skiing and snowshoeing usually lasts from December through March and is most reliable from Hyak to Crystal Springs or Easton. Ski tracks are groomed in winter. Some areas east of the mountains have intermittent snow cover.

In 1917 the Milwaukee Road (of the Chicago, Milwaukee, St. Paul & Pacific Railroad) became the first electrified transcontinental railroad and the nation's longest electrified train. This not only helped clear smoke from the tunnels, but also eliminated the time-consuming job of setting the brakes on mountain switchbacks. The electric railway was so well designed that it operated from 1917 into the 1970s with few problems. Trains braking while heading downhill regenerated power back into the overhead catenary wires to power the uphill trains. The line opened for freight in 1909, and the *Olympian-Hiawatha* passenger train made its debut in 1911. The last Milwaukee train passed over the Cascades in 1980. The state opened the first segment of the rail trail in 1984 and added the trestle at Hall Creek in 1999. Only two trestles remain to be decked, east of Thorp.

Hyak to Cedar Falls, 22.5 miles

|||||||||||||||||||||||||||||||||||||||||||||||||||||||||||||||||||||||||||||||||||||||||

From Snoqualmie Pass to the lowland town of North Bend, this portion of the John Wayne Trail guides you through 2.25 miles of tunnel, above

A cross-country skier near the Lake Keechelus Sno-Park at Hyak.

the Snoqualmie River Valley on high trestles, and below mountain peaks. Pass beside creeks and waterfalls, under huge fir trees, and beside a large blue lake bounded by the vertical walls of Mount Si. It's quite a treat to be perched above the valley and dwarfed below the mountain peaks, watching the moving picture of the Cascade Mountains and valleys below you.

Although you can travel either way on the trail, this segment from Hyak to Cedar Falls is described going east to west. The constant 1.75 percent grade of 2,500 vertical feet makes this section an easier downhill ride going west for cyclists. Plus, many people visit the trail just to see the tunnel at the east end of this segment.

You can park cars at both trailheads. To reach the western trailhead, see Access and parking, above. Cedar Falls can also serve as the trailhead for a multiday trip across the state via bicycle, horse, ski, or foot. The Snoqualmie Valley Trail extension reaches Rattlesnake Lake for those connecting from other trails.

Descending this section of the old Milwaukee Railroad is as sad as it is scenic. Local history describes ski instructors boarding the Seattle train on Friday night for a weekend of work and play. They hopped off the train and trudged through the snow to their bunkhouse. These were the days of

Supports for the electric wires of the old Milwaukee Road still stand at Hansen Creek Trestle.

the tow rope and the Milwaukee ski jump. A few old boards remain on the hillside. Modern skiers couldn't be convinced to ride the rails; they wanted the convenience and flexibility of their cars.

Still, the abandonment of this railroad has given way to new adventures, new ways to raise our spirits and our heart rates. This 22.5-mile segment is the most heavily used. The rail station at Hyak now houses individual bathrooms, large enough for a small party—a great amenity for cold skiers. The Hyak ski area (called Summit East) lies directly uphill. The Summit Cross Country Ski Trail runs just above the rail trail and encircles Mount Catherine for a hillier, groomed ski tour.

From the Lake Keechelus parking lot, join the trail westbound. You'll shortly enter the east portal of the 2.25-mile Snoqualmie Tunnel. It is the longest tunnel in the United States open to non-motorized trail use. Bring a flashlight and a jacket. The ceiling drips water in several spots, and it's cold and dark. It's also spooky and a lot of fun. You'll be able to see the beams of light from oncoming walkers, horses, and cyclists. A miniature archway of light shines from the west end of the tunnel. The archway grows slowly until you exit under its 30-foot ceiling. You'll emerge on the edge of a river gully with Outlook Mountain in your face. Look back to see the engraved sign that reads SNOQUALMIE TUNNEL. Cyclists and walkers around you are removing their long sleeves and replacing their sunglasses. It's time to head down the trail and enjoy the view and the downhill grade. The trail is mostly open with great mountain views.

Pass beside a wooden snowshed at mile 5.5 before reaching the curving trestle at Hansen Creek at mile 8.5. Beware of missing cables on the bridge sides. You can see the overhead supports for the electric lines. A creek falls steeply down the center of a mountain cirque. It drops below the trestle and draws your eyes to the valley. Enjoy the scenery.

The Snoqualmie Tunnel at Hyak.

You'll cross creeks and valley views, seeing waterfalls against the steep hillsides. McClellan Butte comes into sight straight ahead, and you enter a lowland forest. The last few miles are rockier and steeper. Mount Si makes a pretty picture when it comes into view.

At mile 16, cross the modern trestle at Hall Creek. A collapsed link was replaced in spring 1999, so the trail is now passable without your having to leave the railroad grade. Just beyond, you'll pass a busy stream of rock jocks climbing Deception Crags.

A road cuts down to Olallie State Park from here. The next hiking trail that drops off to the right takes you to the 75-foot free-span wooden bridge over waterfalls in Twin Falls State Park.

At the gated end of the trail, turn right on the road to reach Rattlesnake Lake or to descend to North Bend on the Snoqualmie Valley Trail. Catch the trail across the street from the parking lot. (See Trail 10.) Don't forget to enjoy a pastry at George's Bakery on North Bend Way.

Hyak to Easton, 18 miles

Heading east from the Snoqualmie Tunnel or Hyak, enjoy 18 miles of gentle downhill and flat grade as you drop from 2,500 feet to 2,176 feet. The trail follows the edge of Lake Keechelus until you reach the Keechelus Dam. You will find yourself on a corridor bounded by bright green foliage, rock faces, and the deep blue Lake Keechelus, which is interrupted by the occasional tiny island. The gentle sound of water teasing the banks of the lake makes this a great place to stop. Little white wildflowers and tiny patches of lavender blossoms color the trail in summer, while frosted peaks and the icy lake change the landscape in winter.

Cross Meadows Creek and the road to Lost Lake at mile 6. Once past the lake, the conical, ivory heads of Bear Grass cluster here and there. The trail parallels the dirt Stampede Pass Road until crossing it at 7.5 miles. At mile 10, pass through the short, dark, and rocky Whittier Tunnel. Then head left at the fork. Between miles 14 and 15, you will pass over creeks and high above the Yakima River on the secluded, wooded trail. Detour left onto a dirt path at the sign to Easton and the Iron Horse Trail. The dirt road angles right onto a paved road beside Lake Easton. (From the gate here, it will be another 2.3 miles along the road until you reach the Easton Trailhead.) At the first intersection, you will find restrooms, water, a beach, and picnic tables to the right. Turn left to continue and left again to reach the park exit. Turn right (east) to exit Lake Easton State Park onto the frontage road. Arrive in the tiny town of Easton on Railroad Street. Pass CB's general store with snacks and sandwiches. Turn right at the post office and left at the IRON HORSE STATE PARK sign. A dirt road takes you to the park and the trailhead, where you'll find picnic tables, a hitching post, restrooms, and water. A kiosk provides trail information.

Easton to Cle Elum, 11.5 miles

As you depart from the downtown Easton Trailhead, you'll enjoy a slight downhill grade and a good surface. The trail runs close to I-90 in places, though it's buffered by pine and fir trees. The mountains shrink into

Trestle over the Yakima River west of Cle Elum.

rounded hills; an occasional ranch appears on the landscape. Cross Golf Course Road and an I–90 interchange at 6 miles and twin trestles just beyond. Listen for the clicking of grasshoppers on the trail. At mile 9.5 the Yakima River rushes under the trail and leaves just as quickly. Violet and yellow wildflowers accompany the wild, white daisies.

Marshes and creek crossings give the trail some interest as you approach the old Cle Elum railroad station and the substation, which now has a restaurant. This is one of two remaining depots; the second still stands in Kittitas. As you pass the depot, the substation, and a trail kiosk, you can exit at Main Street and lounge in a park found 1 block away. Continue straight on Main to head into South Cle Elum for food, lodging, and espresso.

Cle Elum was a lively town in railroading days—a crew-change town. When the train was electrified, the crew bunkhouse was moved to its present location on Sixth Street a few blocks east of the depot. It's now the Iron Horse B&B. If you call ahead to book a room or a caboose, you can enjoy the warmth of this establishment and the wealth of railroad history the proprietors have to share.

Cle Elum to Thorp, 18.6 miles

The trail from Cle Elum was resurfaced in 2005. Pass under I–90 at mile 3.16, leaving it south of the trail. The Yakima River (and Washington Highway 10) appears to your left at mile 5; look for rafters and anglers in the fast waters below the trail. The green of the foliage and the pine trees create a pleasant pathway, and the slight downhill grade eases your journey.

As you enter the Upper Yakima River Canyon, the river widens, trees become sparse, and hills are round and brown. Tall walls of basalt appear. The only shade you'll find is inside Tunnels 46 and 47. You'll be in the dark for a few seconds on a bike—a bit longer on foot—in the western tunnel. The eastern tunnel is short. Grasshoppers conduct their loud symphony of clicking. Tiny birds whisk about the trees, and striking black-and-yellow monarch butterflies disperse when you hit the wet potholes from which they drink. They'll escort you for a bit, then find another watering spot. Perhaps a muskrat will scurry by or a rabbit will bounce down the trail.

Active tracks and trail parallel the river between Cle Elum and Thorp.

As the last cliffs disappear, you emerge into an expanse of ranchland bordered by foothills in the distance. Cows stare from behind barbed wire. Pass through two gates. Be sure to resecure them behind you after you pass through.

Arrive at the Thorp Trailhead at mile 18.6. The kiosk reads, "Prairie grasslands dominate the landscape. Looking eastward it's all you can see for miles. Grasslands blend into sage-covered hills and the fertile farmland of the Columbia River basin." You have arrived at another transition zone.

You may want to make a stop at the Fruit and Antique Mall just across Thorp Prairie Highway and to your right, near the I-90 exit ramp. Piles of fresh fruit, jams, ice cream, beverages, and espresso await. Sample the feta and pink peppercorn dip or artichoke dip and view the antique carriages.

Thorp to Ellensburg East, 8.4 miles

Hop back on the trail to Ellensburg. You will cross two trestles that were decked in 2002.

Nearby Attractions

Take the time to explore the historic district of Ellensburg, the county fairgrounds, the rodeo, and the July jazz festival. And you might want to check out the Iron Horse Bed and Breakfast historic establishment in Cle Elum, (509) 674–5939.

Stay on the trail, leave the noise of I–90 behind, and enjoy the flat, open farmland and the occasional shade of a crab apple tree. Passage around several gates is narrow and sloping—they're tough to get around on a bike or a horse. You'll reach the first of two undecked trestles at mile 2.2. They cross WA 10 and the active railroad tracks. At 3 miles, use caution crossing U.S. Highway 97.

Reach the Ellensburg West Trailhead at Water Street at 6.8 miles. A kiosk displays the route you might want to use to take a 1.6-mile detour through town. Turn right on Water Street and left on 14th Avenue, which becomes Dean Nicholson Way as you pass through the college. Turn right at the T-intersection, Alder Street. Alder dead-ends at the Kittitas County Fairgrounds rodeo entrance after you cross 10th Avenue. The trail restarts here at the fairgrounds trailhead. There are restrooms, showers, and overnight camping for tents and RVs; available by reservation through the Kittitas County Events Center. While in town, cruise to the historic district and enjoy gourmet food.

Ellensburg East to Army East, 31.5 miles

From the fairgrounds, head through farm country on flat, open trail. If you like, take a side trip to view the 1875 log cabin and homestead of the Olmsteads at Olmstead Place State Park. At mile 6 and 1,674 feet, pull into Kittitas at the second of the two remaining depots. Built in 1909, it's listed

Washboard descent through rock cut near Army East. (Courtesy Richard Smith)

on the National Register of Historic Places. The town is smaller than it was in 1884, when it was built in a failed attempt to lure the Northern Pacific Railway. Twenty-four years later the Milwaukee Road built a right-of-way through town to transport the area's grains, fruits, vegetables, and live-stock. The railroad came in 1908 and gave the town a post office, as it did in Cle Elum. Once the arid lowlands were irrigated, the fertile soil could produce enough food to support residents. Check the kiosk to learn how long it took the *Olympian-Hiawatha* to reach Seattle from Chicago in 1945 on the Milwaukee Road.

Final approach to the Columbia River. (Courtesy Richard Smith)

There are amenities within 2 blocks of the trail. This is your last stop in civilization, and your last predictable water until the Army East Trailhead in 26.6 miles.

Back on the trail, at 8.6 miles, follow the sign to detour right on Prater Street to cross over I–90, then take an immediate left onto Boylston. Pass some cattle and climb until mile 12, where you'll cross under the trestle responsible for the detour. Turn right at the T-intersection just beyond. Find the Army West Trailhead on your left, complete with restrooms, water, an informational kiosk, and parking. Pump to start the water flowing, which is for horses—it is non-potable water.

The trail continues uphill to your right. Follow the sign through the gate and complete your entry permit. The next 22 miles are on sandy, rocky, unshaded, desert army property. You will get sucked into the soft surface for the first 4 miles. Rejoice when you enter the Boylston Tunnel. It's cool, shaded, and dark for a few seconds. Best of all, the surface improves, and you head downhill for much of the next 18 miles. Passages through the rock cuts are littered with rocks. The remainder of the surface is a bit rough and the grade is slight, but it's a great improvement over the sand.

Drink, drink, and drink again and slather the sunscreen. There's no exit from this area if you become dehydrated, overheated, or worn. At about mile 30, expect a mirage: a dirt road leading to restrooms, water, and a horse trough. Head left. Check the instructions for turning on the water. This would be a good time to engage your friends in a water fight, particularly if you've chosen a 100-degree day to traverse the desert. You'll find the Army East Trailhead beyond, along Huntzinger Road with parking. You can camp at Army East Trailhead by prior arrangement.

Continue straight on the trail. Enjoy views of the Columbia River and the old trestle in the distance. You can approach the trestle on the trail, but fences prevent access. Turn left at the gate at Huntzinger Road (paved) 2 miles beyond Army East, then turn left to reach the Wanapum Recreation Area, about 4 hilly miles down the road. Here you can camp, find amenities, cool off in the Columbia River, and congratulate yourself. The small town of Vantage, I–90, and the bridge across the river are 3 uphill miles ahead. The Gingko Petrified Forest is 1 mile north of Vantage. From here, grab a Greyhound bus or a motel room. Masochists may continue on the John Wayne Pioneer Trail on the east side of the Columbia. (See More Rail Trails for information on this eastern segment.)

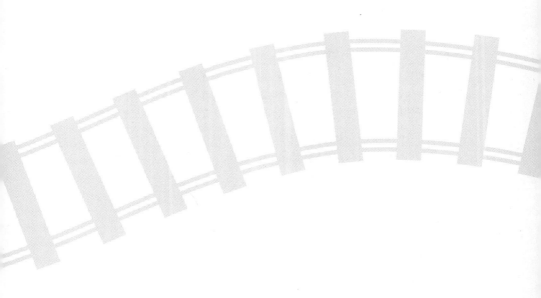

26 COWICHE CANYON TRAIL

The Cowiche Canyon Trail takes you through both geological and railroading history. Slicing through a canyon and crossing the creek repeatedly, this rail trail makes for a tour that's both dramatic and peaceful. You'll have many opportunities to observe plant and animal life.

Activities:

Location: Yakima, Yakima County

Length: 2.9 miles

Surface: Large gravel and dirt

Wheelchair access: The trail is not wheelchair accessible.

Difficulty: Easy

Food: No food is available along this trail.

Restrooms: You'll find restrooms at the Weikel Road Trailhead.

Seasons: The trail can be used year-round.

Access and parking: To reach the western trailhead from Yakima, exit U.S. Highway 12 on North 40th Avenue. Head south to Summitview Avenue. Turn right and drive 7 miles west to Weikel Road. Turn right, drive 0.25 mile, then turn right into the parking area. Continue along the road to the historical kiosk at the trailhead.

Rentals: Try Valley Cycling at 1802 West Nob Hill Boulevard in Yakima, (509) 453–6699, www.valleycycleandfitness.com.

Contact: The Cowiche Canyon Conservancy is a nonprofit organization dedicated to protecting the canyon as a natural resource area and ensuring its recreational use and enjoyment. Write P.O. Box 877, Yakima, WA 98907, or visit the Web site at www.cowichecanyon.org.

Bus routes: None

Cowiche Canyon is the result of geological activity that took place millions of years ago. From Pullman, lava flowed to form the Cowiche Canyon floor and the south wall 17.5 million years ago. This 6,000-foot-thick layer, called the Columbia River Basalts, covered eastern Washington. Then, one million years ago, Tieton Andesite flowed from the west to create the north wall.

In 1913 the North Yakima & Valley Railroad line of the Northern Pacific was built through the canyon to haul apples to Yakima from the productive orchards in Cowiche and Tieton. Workers blasted through vertical basalt cliffs to create the line, which crosses the Cowiche River eleven times. The constant curve of the canyon frames each rock formation ahead and paints a picture of the trains rumbling down the rails.

From the kiosk at the trailhead, travel a slight grade downhill to the first of nine bridges. Portions of the trail contain heavy gravel, making it tough going even for mountain bikes. Beware of a large step up to some of the bridges in addition to the absence of railings. Bikers should dismount if in question. Though sightings are rare, rattlesnakes may be present.

The contrast between the lush riparian vegetation along Cowiche Creek and the browns and yellows of the shrub-steppe on the hillsides

People and pets alike enjoy walking the Cowiche Canyon Trail.

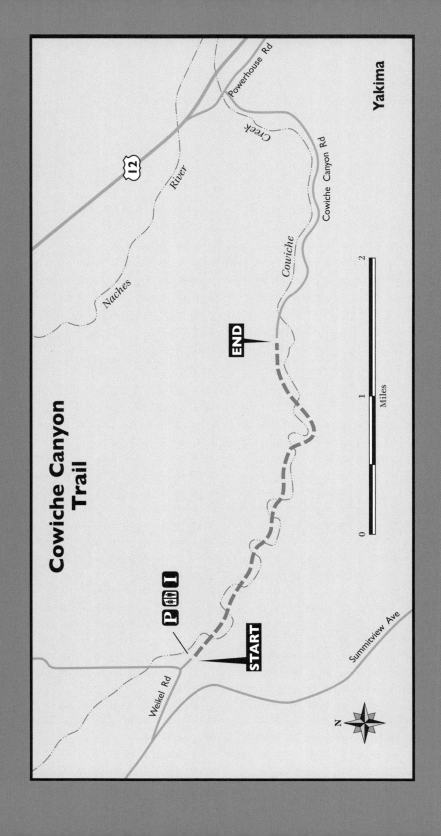

Cowiche Canyon
Trail

Yakima

12

Naches River

Powerhouse Rd

Creek

Cowiche Canyon Rd

Cowiche

END

P 🚻 ℹ

Weikel Rd

START

Summitview Ave

N

0   1   2
Miles

can be witnessed only in spring. The hot, dry summer months and cold winters put plant life to sleep.

The creek crossings give life to the still canyon. Look and listen for wildlife as you travel from bridge to bridge. The western meadowlark sings from March through June. Marmots and coyotes, canyon wrens, chickadees, and magpies may be seen or heard.

After bridge 8, the trail detours around two bridges that were destroyed during conflicts over trail development. Here you'll be following an old county road. This a poison ivy neighborhood.

When you emerge at Cowiche Canyon Road, turn around and return the way you came.

27 LOWER YAKIMA VALLEY PATHWAY

Wineries, sunshine, fresh fruit, and more wineries! This traverse of the world-renowned Yakima Valley wine country will take you past any number of gourmet delights—fine dining, farm stands, candy shops, and, of course, the area's many award-winning wine makers—all in a dusty, unshaded, desert environment.

Activities:

Location: The Yakima Valley towns of Sunnyside, Grandview, and Prosser, in Benton and Yakima Counties

Length: 14.5 miles

Surface: Asphalt, with occasional spots of dirt and gravel

Wheelchair access: The trail is wheelchair accessible in areas, but note rough spots mentioned below.

Difficulty: Easy; though it's moderate for skaters. The trail is narrow (8 to 8.5 feet) and has a bit of grade here and there, along with some rough pavement (noticeable for skaters). It runs on the roadside in Grandview for 1.5 miles. The Grandview parking area toward Prosser is smoothest for skating.

Food: There are grocery stores, fruit vendors, fast food, restaurants, and wineries along the way.

Restrooms: There are facilities 3.5 miles east of the western trailhead, and there's water at the East Grandview Trailhead.

Seasons: The trail can be used year-round, though it may be snowy or cold in winter.

Access and parking: Take Interstate 82 from Yakima or from the Tri-Cities of Pasco, Richland, and Kennewick to the exits for Sunnyside (exit 69), Grandview (exit 73), or Prosser (exit 82). The trail parallels U.S. Highway 12.

Parking areas are located in Sunnyside at North 16th Street, just west of an underpass at the western edge of Grandview, and east of the Grandview commercial district (where the trail restarts on the north side of US 12). You can also park on the street at the Yakima River crossing in Prosser.

Rentals: No rentals are available along this trail.

Contact:

- Yakima Valley Visitor and Information Center, (800) 221–0751, www.visit yakima.com

- Sunnyside Chamber of Commerce, (509) 837–5939, www.sunnyside chamber.com

- Prosser Chamber of Commerce, (800) 408–1517, www.prosserchamber .org

- Wine Yakima Valley, (800) 258–7270

- Washington Wine Commission, www.washingtonwine.org/tripp/yak map.asp

Bus routes: None

Cleverly sculpted garbage cans in the shape of animals line the trail.

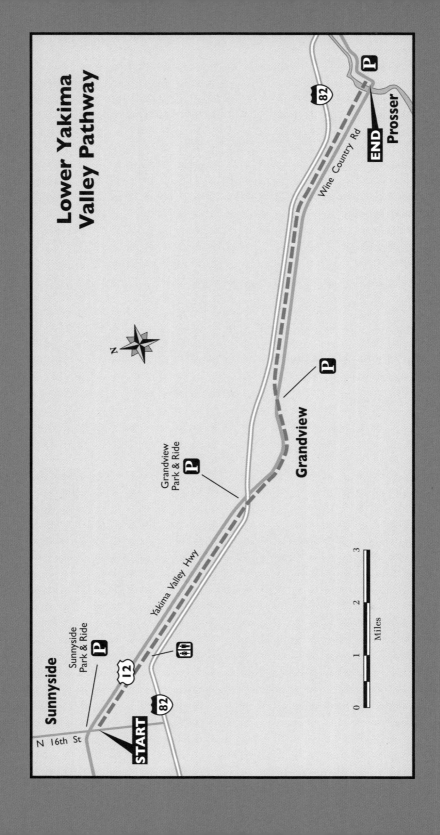

Lower Yakima Valley Pathway

Sunnyside

N 16th St

Sunnyside Park & Ride

P

82

12

START

Yakima Valley Hwy

P Grandview Park & Ride

N

P

Grandview

Wine Country Rd

82

END

P

Prosser

0 1 2 3

Miles

|||||||||||||||||||||||||||||||||||||||||||||||||||||||||||||||||||||||||||||||||||

The Lower Yakima Valley Pathway spans three desert towns between Yakima and the Tri-Cities. The desert clime is dry: hot in summer, cold in winter. It's also just right for producing the fine wines of Washington State. Vintners note its location on the forty-sixth parallel—the same as Burgundy and Bordeaux, the great wine-producing regions of France. The soil is twice as productive as most due to nutrients from rich volcanic ash.

Before the valley's fertile soil and climate were recognized in the 1950s, rail lines were built to transport the fruit and grains of the Lower Yakima Valley. The North Coast Railroad was incorporated in 1906, and merged with the Oregon-Washington Railroad and Navigation Company, beginning operations in 1910. The Attalia to North Yakima line was then leased to the Union Pacific on January 1, 1936. This line liberated the valley from the domination of the Northern Pacific Railway and their line from Kiona to Yakima City.

You'll be traveling in unshaded desert: Bring lots of sunscreen and water. The trail is narrow (about 8 feet wide)—cyclists and skaters should remember to be courteous to walkers. You can admire garbage cans disguised as cute animal sculptures while you relax on covered benches. The section between Grandview and Prosser has no services.

Although you can access the trail from several places, this description takes you from west to east. From Sunnyside to Grandview (6.5 miles), the trail is sandwiched between I–82 and US 12 (Yakima Valley Road), beside fast-food spots, gas stations, and the town's commercial districts. Tuckers Winery and Produce is across from the trail in Sunnyside. For other winery locations, call Wine Yakima Valley.

A 1.5-mile gap in the trail takes you between the two Grandview trailheads. Once you reach the trail's end at Grandview Park & Ride, continue east on US 12 to regain it. There's a shoulder most of the way. Look for an archway reading PALACIOS PARKWAY on the north side of the road at about mile 8. It's marked with a bench, water, and trailhead parking.

On your way through town, detour to the Dykstra House restaurant—a National Historic Site built in 1909—on Birch, 1 block off the highway. Grandview is a farm workers' town, easygoing and friendly, and a good choice for real Mexican food.

Nearby Attractions and Events

It's worth your while to visit the Lower Yakima Valley during a wine event. There's the Spring Barrel Tasting in April, Thanksgiving in the Wine Country (wines paired with appetizers), and Red Wine and Chocolate in February. Breweries offer tastings as well. Bring your bike booties or wool socks for fall and winter temperatures in the 30s.

Other amenities in the area include the golf course across from the trail at Sunnyside Park, the Columbia Gorge Discovery Center, and the Richland Educational Museum. The Umatilla County Lewis and Clark Commemorative Trail (Trail 35) is across the Columbia in Oregon, about thirty minutes away. The Cowiche Canyon Trail (Tail 26) is near Yakima.

The trail is newer and smoother much of the way from here to Prosser. Travel rural desert for almost 6 miles until Chukar Cherries appears. Do not pass go: Stop here for your gourmet sweet treat. Try wild Cascade blueberries coated with white chocolate, truffles, or Cabernet chocolate cherries. If you're lucky, you'll walk in on a tasting.

The trail has a touch of a grade here and there as you approach the desert mountains ahead. A section of trail dips down from the right-of-way to navigate an active trestle crossing at mile 11.5. Cross the Yakima River 3 miles farther on. The trail merges with the sidewalk east of the river and ends here in downtown Prosser. The Benton County Museum is down the road. Check your winery map to attend a tasting.

28 SPOKANE RIVER CENTENNIAL TRAIL

Welcome to 37 miles of paved riverfront trail in a region that receives a meager 11 inches of rain per year. The sun shines on the Spokane River, rapids rush downriver, and bridges crisscross the water. The Centennial Trail has three different personalities: the bustling and beautiful downtown Riverfront Park; the calm and gentle terrain to the east; and the hilly section high above the river, to the west. Both the eastern and western routes have sections on roadside shoulders. This is hot, desert country. Much of the trail is without services other than trailhead restrooms and water. Pack a snack and bring a water bottle to refill along the way. Benches and picnic tables offer rest stops beside the river.

Activities:

Location: Nine Mile Falls Dam to the Idaho border, Spokane County

Length: 37 miles

Surface: Asphalt, with some sections on roadside shoulders. Conducive to horseback riding from the trailer parking area at the state line to Barker Road between miles 6 and 7, and at trails near the Equestrian Center parking area between miles 28 and 29 in Riverside State Park.

Wheelchair access: Most of the trail is wheelchair accessible. The area west of downtown Spokane is quite hilly. Call the park for a list of accessible parking areas.

Difficulty: The trail ranges from easy to difficult; see the description of each section.

Food: You'll find things to eat in downtown Spokane, at the Spokane Valley Mall, and at the Idaho border.

Restrooms: There are many restrooms along the trail. See map for approximate locations.

Seasons: The trail is used year-round and closes at dusk. It is not plowed during the winter. Water is turned off and some restrooms are closed from October through March.

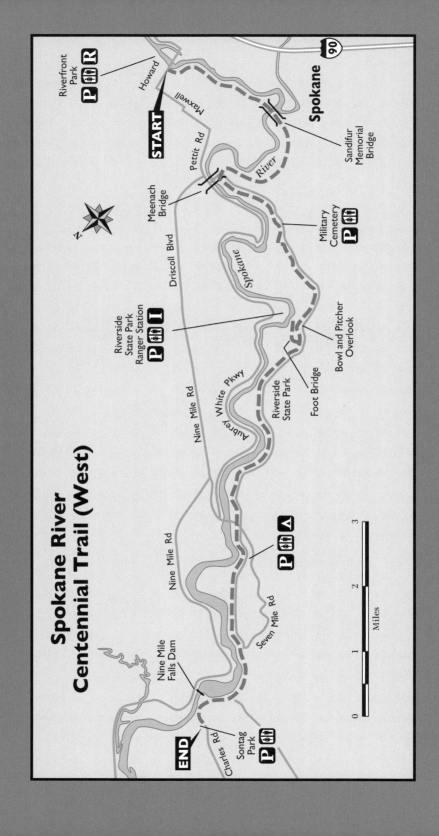

Spokane River
Centennial Trail (West)

Riverfront Park 🅿 🚻 🅁

Howard

START

Maxwell

90

Spokane

Pettit Rd

River

Sandifur Memorial Bridge

Meenach Bridge

N

Military Cemetery 🅿 🚻

Driscoll Blvd

Spokane

Riverside State Park Ranger Station 🅿 🚻 ℹ

Bowl and Pitcher Overlook

Nine Mile Rd

White Pkwy

Aubrey

Riverside State Park

Foot Bridge

Nine Mile Rd

🅿 🚻 ⛺

Seven Mile Rd

Nine Mile Falls Dam

END

Charles Rd

Sontag Park 🅿 🚻

0   1   2   3

Miles

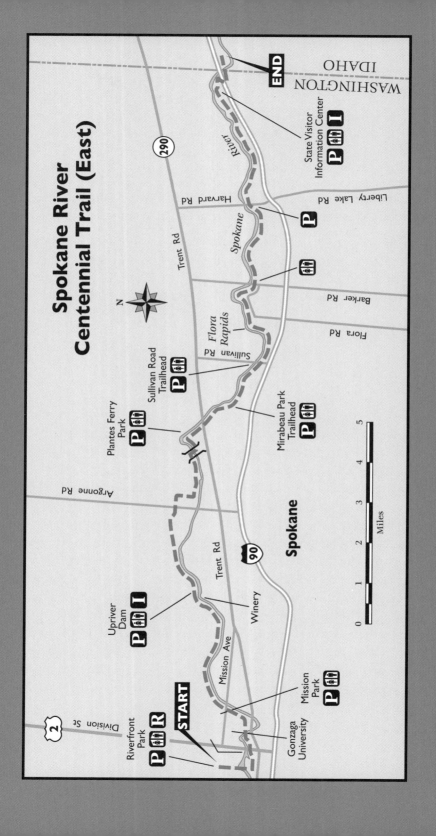

Spokane River
Centennial Trail (East)

N

290

Trent Rd

Argonne Rd

Harvard Rd

Spokane River

Flora Rapids

Sullivan Rd

Plantes Ferry Park
P 🚻

Sullivan Road Trailhead
P 🚻

Mirabeau Park Trailhead
P 🚻

Barker Rd

Flora Rd

Liberty Lake Rd

P

State Visitor Information Center
P 🚻 **I**

END

WASHINGTON
IDAHO

Upriver Dam
P 🚻 **I**

Trent Rd

90

Winery

Spokane

Mission Ave

Mission Park
P 🚻

Gonzaga University

START

Division St

2

Riverfront Park
P 🚻 **R**

Miles

0 1 2 3 4 5

Access and parking: You can access both the westbound and eastbound segments of the trail from Riverfront Park in downtown Spokane. Sontag Park on Charles Road and the Idaho border mark the western and eastern termini. Parking is available at most trailheads. The trail numbering starts at the Idaho state line at mile 1 and continues west, ending at mile 37.

Rentals: You can rent bicycles at bike shops on Division Street at the waterfront. Call the Spokane Regional Visitor Center for more information.

Contact: Riverside State Park, (509) 465–5064, www.riversidestatepark.org; or Spokane Regional Visitor Center, 888–SPOKANE, www.visitspokane.com; or Friends of the Centennial Trail, (509) 624–7188, www.spokanecentennial trail.org. Maps are avaiable.

Bus routes: For information, call (509) 328–RIDE, or visit www.spokane transit.com.

||||||||||||||||||||||||||||||||||||||||||||||||||||||||||||||||||||||||||||||||||||||

Walla Walla was the state's largest city in 1800, but that reign was short-lived. By 1883 a nationwide rail connection was established in Spokane, and the small town experienced a population explosion. In less than ten years, Spokane went from a city of 350 residents to a population of 19,222, quadrupling the size of Walla Walla.

The legacy of the rails is evident throughout the Spokane River Centennial Trail. Numerous railroads sketched a matrix of tracks in this area. The Inland Empire Paper Company, owned by the local newspaper company, completed a land exchange with the state parks from Argonne to the state line. Great Northern contributed the Don Kardong Bridge. Spokane's Great Northern Station sat on Havermade Island on the river.

Riverfront Park in downtown Spokane receives heavy use. This hundred-acre park blends a natural setting with a hearty history reflected in bridges, dams, and turn-of-the-twentieth-century buildings. Outdoor sculptures decorate the paths, from the amusement park and the Imax Theater to the century-old, hand-painted carousel. The rail trail tours downtown hotels and runs just blocks from pubs, coffeehouses, restaurants, and shopping. The city turned the abandoned railroad tracks into this unique park and outdoor amusement center for the 1974 Expo.

You can use Riverfront Park to begin an exploration of the Centennial Trail that travels either west or east. The eastern trip is gentle and dry; to the west, look for hilly terrain. If you're new to this area, you'll learn about boulder fields and basalt cliffs, ice floods and aquifers. You'll also see exquisite homes and parks created by the prosperous mining of silver and gold and nurtured by the railroad. Check with the visitors bureau to locate homes, restaurants, bed-and-breakfasts, parks, and gardens reminiscent of the mining era.

Riverfront Park to Nine Mile Falls Dam and Sontag Park, 14 miles westbound

The hilly route from the park west to Nine Mile Falls Dam passes through ponderosa pines, pastures, and Riverside State Park lands, all beside the Spokane River. It's a rural area with restrooms along the way. An equestrian area lies adjacent. To reach the equestrian parking area in Riverside State Park, take Seven Mile Road to Pine Bluff Road and park. You can ride the road back to the Centennial Trail and use the paved trail or the soft shoulder.

To park at the military cemetery, cross the TJ Meenach Bridge from Pettit Road, which becomes Fort George Wright Road on the south side of the bridge. Turn right (west) at Government Way. After about 1 mile, turn right on Houston Road to the lot. Farther down the road (0.5 mile) is the equestrian parking and trail access point. Horses can use the paved trail or the soft trail beside it.

To begin at Riverfront Park, exit the park on Howard Street near the Spokane Arena. Head 1 mile west on the north side of the river. Cross at the Sandifur Memorial Bridge and continue on trail alongside Government Way, a city street.

Trail view of Spokane and the suspension bridge in Riverside State Park.

Wander through young pines and horse pasture, up and down hills. Pass a trailhead parking area at the military cemetery. Turn right onto Riverside State Park Drive at the T-intersection at mile 29.5 (mile markers begin at the eastern terminus). The trail reaches a parking cul-de-sac and overlook above the Bowl and Pitcher rock formation and the suspension footbridge to Riverside State Park. The fun is yet to come. Head downhill 0.42 mile on the trail to a side trail on the right numbered 210. Take the side trail to the right to reach the footbridge in 0.3 mile. Take the narrow, dirt trail to a four-way intersection. A right turn will take you to a bridge and a picnic shelter; a left will let you hang out on the rocks above the river or choose a rocky trail to the bridge. Hug the cliffs to pass between them on this route. Once you're on the bridge, the river rapids under your feet are a rush. This is your starting point if you parked at the main entrance to Riverside State Park on Aubrey White Parkway.

Once you're back on the main trail, pass through a burned area with a basalt ridge above and river rapids below. Several trails drop to the river along the way. Near mile 34, explore the history of Seven Mile Camp, a Civilian Conservation Corps operation of the 1930s. The suspension footbridge is one of many accomplishments of this impressive group. Just beyond are the Wilbur Road Trailhead and a bit of trail on Aubrey White Parkway. Signs direct you to turn left onto Seven Mile Road, then make an immediate right onto Riverside State Park Drive. Enjoy the brief flat section before you cruise the hills to Nine Mile Falls Dam.

You'll drop down to Deep Creek Bridge and a picnic area just past mile 36. There are plenty of benches and overlooks along the way. The best view is that of the gushing water released at Nine Mile Falls Dam. From

The trail through downtown Spokane.

here the trail crosses Charles Road to quickly end at Sontag Park. Unless you've planned a shuttle trip, turn around and return the way you came.

Riverfront Park to Idaho, 23 miles eastbound

The eastern half of the Centennial Trail is nothing like the west, except that it runs by the river. Once you leave downtown at Upriver Drive, a calm river follows close beside a gentle grade most of the way to Idaho. Pines decorate the desert landscape; the sun warms you.

Leave Riverfront Park on the south side of the river by the Convention Center and the Doubletree Hotel. Wind around a quiet residential area to the Don Kardong Bridge. The unmarked left turn across the bridge is just beyond milepost 22. This teal-colored trestle paints a pretty exit from the city. Cross up and over Hamilton Street on a pedestrian overpass or remain beside it on the trail. The wheelchair-accessible trail turns left to cross the street at the light. Just beyond, cross Mission Avenue at Gonzaga University and follow signs to turn right onto the sidewalk and left onto the trail just before the river crossing. The trail has a bit of grade from here (noticeable for beginner skaters).

The city section gives way to the suburbs here. The trail lies on the generous roadside shoulder from mile 19.5 to mile 17.5 (Greene Street) and again from mile 16 to mile 13.5. The separated trail runs from mile 17 to mile 16 and again from the dead end of mile 13.5 (Maringo Drive) to Idaho. The dangerous roadside section is near Argonne Road (mile 16 to mile 14).

Pass the Arbor Crest Winery just past mile 18. The Upriver Dam is just ahead. A kiosk describes Spokane's search for clean water as the population grew in the early 1900s. The story of the aquifer that provides water to 300,000 residents is told here. Rock jocks and mountain bikers hang out at the Minnehaha Rocks at mile 17. This is one of the rock deposits dumped here from the collapse of the Purcell ice lobe, a 2,000-foot-high ice dam in Idaho. This glacial flood occurred at the tail end of the last ice age, 20,000 years ago.

Eastern section of the trail near Mirabeau Park.

Enjoy a wide, smoothly paved, scenic tour from Maringo to Mirabeau Park. Watch for deer, ospreys, and herons as you wander through the open pine forest. Cross the bridge at Plantes Ferry Park. Pause at the bench beside the secluded riverside. Skating is good from here all the way to Idaho. There are areas with some grade and one short, narrow hill as you approach Mirabeau Park.

Pass under Trent Road or take the side trail up to Fitness Fanatics for a retail break at this skate shop.

Reach Sullivan Road past milepost 10 and wake up to the traffic of the Spokane Valley Mall. Here you can grab some food and a bus to downtown Spokane (Interstate 90).

From Sullivan Road the trail returns to a rural riverside route with birds, boaters, and rapids. It opens up to to the prevailing winds 3 miles from the border. Cross under –90 and over the river. You can continue into Idaho, 4.5 miles to Post Falls and beyond. The falls here are spectacular. See the North Idaho Centennial Trail (Trail 39).

29 BILL CHIPMAN PALOUSE TRAIL— PULLMAN, WASHINGTON

Connecting one university town to another, this trail—spanning two states—is popular with commuters and visitors. It weaves along Paradise Creek and features extensive interpretive signs detailing rail history and local points of interest.

Activities:

Location: City of Pullman, Washington, in Whitman County, and city of Moscow, Idaho, in Latah County

Length: 6 miles in Washington and 1 mile in Idaho

Surface: Asphalt

Wheelchair access: Wheelchair access is available at the western terminus trailhead in Pullman and the eastern terminus trailhead in Moscow, Idaho.

Difficulty: Easy

Food: There are many restaurants and gas stations in Pullman near the western trailhead and in Moscow near the eastern trailhead.

Restrooms: Emergency phones and restrooms are located near miles 1.5, 4, and 5 as measured from the western terminus in Pullman.

Seasons: The trail can be used year-round.

Access and parking: To begin in Pullman, Washington, take Washington Highway 270 east or Washington Highway 27 south into Pullman and turn left onto Main Street. Continue on Main Street to Bishop Boulevard, then turn right onto Bishop Boulevard. If coming from Moscow, Idaho, take ID-WA 270 west for about 6 miles. When you reach the location where WA 270 turns into Main Street, continue another 2 miles by traveling on Main Street to the first stoplight and turning left onto Bishop Boulevard.

Bishop Boulevard winds toward the left, and within 1 block you turn left into the Quality Inn Hotel parking lot. The designated trailhead location for the western terminus starts at the northeast edge of the parking lot.

Or start in Moscow at the eastern terminus of the trailhead. To get there, take Main Street heading east out of Pullman, Washington. Main Street quickly turns into WA 270 (also called West Pullman Road). Travel about 7 miles to the intersection of Idaho Highway 270 and Perimeter Drive at the edge of the University of Idaho's campus in Moscow, Idaho. Park on the eastern edge of the Palouse Mall shopping center, at the intersection with Perimeter Drive. Cross WA 270 to get on the trail. The trailhead is clearly marked by a replica railroad station shelter. There are also some parking opportunities nearby on the University of Idaho's campus.

Rentals: In Pullman, you can rent bicycles at B & L Bicycles, 219 East Main Street, (509) 332–1703, www.bandlbicycles.com. See Appendix A for additional bicycle rentals in Moscow, Idaho, just across the Washington border.

Contact: The Pullman Civic Trust, www.pullmancivictrust.org/chipman.html

Bus routes: Contact Wheatland Express for Pullman-to-Moscow routes, (800) 334–2207 or (509) 334–2200, www.wheatlandexpress.com. For Pullman routes, contact Pullman Transit, (509) 332–6535, www.pullmantransit.com.

Local residents enjoy bringing their children to the Bill Chipman Palouse Trail near Pullman. (Courtesy Natalie Bartley)

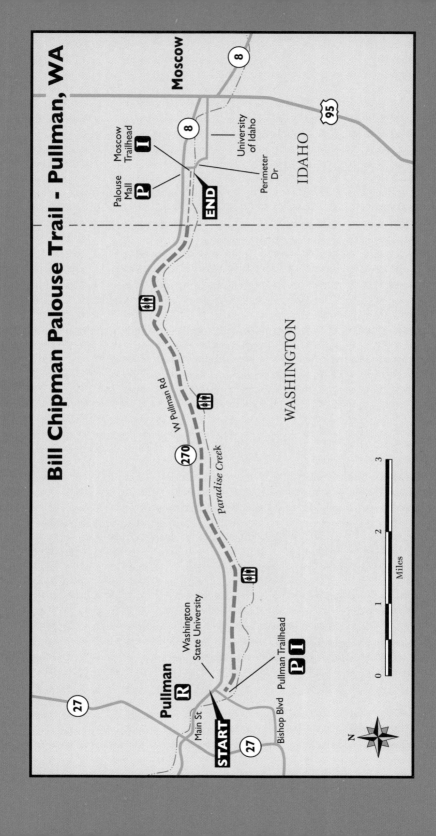

C leverly themed "All Aboard" and capturing the spirit of rail history, the trail is an adventure in learning. Discover commonly used rail terms and learn about the natural environment as you travel the route.

Opened in 1998, thanks to the work of the Pullman Civic Trust, the trail is jointly managed by Moscow, Pullman, the University of Idaho, Washington State University, and Whitman County. Since this smooth, easy trail is heavily used by bicycle commuters traveling between the two border cities of Pullman and Moscow, trail users need to be alert at all times and use proper trail etiquette.

Start at trail mile 0 on the east side of Pullman at the Pullman Trailhead on the edge of the Quality Inn parking lot, and end in Idaho at trail mile 7, just on the edge of the University of Idaho's campus in Moscow. Educational rest stops with detailed interpretive signs, frequent benches, restrooms, and emergency phones smooth the way for visitors. The trail runs parallel to WA-ID 270 as it wanders back and forth across Paradise Creek and over thirteen bridges.

Originally the first rail service to the area was the Oregon Railway and Navigation Company, which arrived in Pullman in 1885. It later became the Union Pacific Railroad. The trail follows a part of the line that eventually extended to Moscow. "Student Specials" carried students from various parts of Washington to school at Washington State University.

On the present-day trail you can learn loads of railroad lingo, such as the term jerkwater, which refers to a small town that has no water source. Train crews had to "jerk" buckets of water from a local source, like a creek, to provide the water to power their steam engines. Be sure to stop and enjoy the numerous educational signs along this well-documented rail trail.

After the first half mile out of the Pullman Trailhead, grain silos and a grain elevator loom large. They used to hold white wheat, a major crop of the region used for crackers, noodles, and cakes. A sign identifies the elevator spur as Lava Siding. A siding is a brief section of track that connects at both ends to the main tracks. The siding enables a train to wait on the side, where it can be loaded and unloaded—in this case with wheat. Interesting geological features are visible in the area. Note the basalt rocks, which indicate old lava flows that were 50 to 100 feet thick.

Farther down the trail, read about the Home Stead Flag Stop, at 3 miles. Near 5 miles the active track runs beside Paradise Creek and the

A bicycler and in-line skater travel the smooth, flat Bill Chipman Palouse Trail heading from Pullman, Washington, to Moscow, Idaho. (Courtesy Natalie Bartley)

trail. The small creek you are following originates in the Palouse Mountain Range to the south, ultimately traveling to Moscow, then Pullman, on to the Snake and Columbia Rivers, and then into the Pacific Ocean. Paradise Creek provides a habitat for local birds and wildlife. Western meadowlarks, killdeer, and tree swallows are but a few of the creatures supported by the creek ecosystem.

Beyond 6 miles you cross the Washington/Idaho border and enter the fringes of Moscow, Idaho. Continue the last mile to the eastern terminus, indicated by a train station replica and interpretive signs. After soaking up all the information offered at the kiosks, return the way you came.

Plans are in the making to build loop trails in Pullman and Moscow that would access the Bill Chipman Trail.

While you are in the area, consider visiting other Washington trails, including the Spokane River Centennial Trail (Trail 28), the Ben Burr Trail (Trail A), and the Colfax Trail (Trail B). You can also easily route onto the Latah Trail (Trail 40) in Idaho from the Bill Chipman Palouse Trail—Moscow, Idaho (Trail 41).

More Rail Trails

A BEN BURR TRAIL

The Ben Burr Trail is carved into a basalt rock outcropping above neighborhood homes. You'll find interesting geological formations here. The condominium building at Liberty Park is the old powerhouse for the electric railroad line.

Activities:

Location: City of Spokane, Spokane County

Length: 1.1 miles

Surface: Crushed stone, gravel, and dirt, rolled

Wheelchair access: The entire trail is wheelchair accessible.

Difficulty: Easy

Food: There are grocery stores several blocks from the trail.

Restrooms: You'll find restrooms and drinking water at both Liberty and Under Hill Parks during the summer months.

Seasons: The trail can be used year-round.

Access and parking: To reach Liberty Park, take exit 283A (Altamount) off Interstate 90 in Spokane. Turn right on Altamount and right on Fourth Street in 1 block. Turn left into Liberty Park; this lot is plowed when there's snow. You can also access the trail at Under Hill Park.

Rentals: You can rent bikes at Riverfront Park (800–336–PARK); skis and snowshoes at Mountain Gear, 2002 North Division Street in Spokane.

Contact: Spokane Parks and Recreation, (509) 625–6200; or Spokane Visitors Center, (888) SPOKANE, www.visitspokane.com.

Bus routes: None

B COLFAX TRAIL

The remote and woodsy Colfax Trail follows the Palouse River for 3 miles. Cattle are pastured across the trail in a couple of areas; one bridge is unimproved and taken at the user's risk.

Activities:

Location: City of Colfax, Whitman County

Length: 3 miles

Surface: Dirt

Wheelchair access: This trail is not wheelchair accessible.

Difficulty: Easy

Food: No food is available along the Colfax Trail.

Restrooms: There are no restrooms along the trail.

Seasons: The trail can be used year-round.

Access and parking: From Colfax, take Washington Highway 26 westbound for less than 1 mile, cross the bridge over the Palouse River, and take an immediate right onto Riverside Lane. Park just after the gravel pit on the right. The trail starts here, at the NO MOTORIZED VEHICLES sign. Please close all gates after passing through.

Rentals: No rentals are available near this trail.

Contact: Whitman County Parks, (509) 397–6238

Bus routes: None

C DRY CREEK TRAIL

The Dry Creek Trail parallels Dry Creek and passes through pockets of old-growth timber. It starts out flat, then climbs; your total elevation gain is nearly 500 feet.

Activities:

Location: Gifford Pinchot National Forest in Skamania County, 15 miles north of the Columbia Gorge

Length: 4 miles

Surface: Dirt—native surface

Wheelchair access: The trail is not wheelchair accessible.

Difficulty: Moderate

Food: No food is available along the trail.

Restrooms: There are restrooms at the Trapper Creek Wilderness Trailhead.

Seasons: You can enjoy the Dry Creek Trail from May through November.

Access and parking: Exit Washington Highway 14 at Wind River Highway in Carson. Drive 14 miles, past the Stabler Country Store. Turn right 1 mile after the Carson National Fish Hatchery, at a TRAPPER CREEK WILDERNESS sign. The road ends at the trailhead in approximately 1 mile. A pass is required; contact the U.S. Forest Service to purchase in advance.

Rentals: No rentals are available along this trail.

Contact: Mt. Adams Ranger Station for pass information, (509) 395–3400, www.fs.fed.us/gpnf

Bus routes: None

D DUWAMISH BIKEWAY

The north end of this trail sits at Alki Beach, the Venice (California) of Puget Sound, a beachfront with blades, bikes, and bronze volleyball bodies from here to there. Here the trail is wide, flat, and smooth. It extends south to an industrial area along the Duwamish River. The south end of the trail is near Kellogg Island, on West Marginal Way, south of Southwest Idaho Street.

Activities:

Location: West Seattle to South Seattle, in King County

Length: 5 miles

Surface: Asphalt, with brief sections along the roadside.

Wheelchair access: The trail is wheelchair accessible.

Difficulty: Easy

Food: You'll find things to eat in the town of Alki.

Restrooms: There are restrooms at Alki Beach.

Seasons: The trail can be used year-round.

Access and parking: To reach the trail, take the West Seattle Bridge to the Harbor Avenue exit. Turn right. The sidewalk on your right is the trail. Drive as far north as you like and park on the street. You can also access the trail from Kellogg Island Park.

Rentals: See Appendix A for a list of rentals in Puget Sound.

Contact: Bicycle Alliance of Washington, (206) 224–9252, www.bicycle alliance.org; or call Seattle Parks Department, (206) 684–4075.

Bus routes: #37 and #53. For information, call Metro Transit at (206) 553–3000, or visit transit.metrokc.gov.

E ISSAQUAH-PRESTON TRAIL

The scenic start on a wooden bridge over the East Fork of Issaquah Creek leads you down a wooded trail beside Interstate 90. This trail will eventually serve as a link between the Preston-Snoqualmie Trail and the East Lake Sammamish Trail.

Activities:

Location: Issaquah and Preston, King County

Length: 2 miles

Surface: Ballast

Wheelchair access: The trail is not wheelchair accessible.

Difficulty: Easy

Food: No food is available near the trail.

Restrooms: There are no restrooms along the trail.

Seasons: The trail can be used year-round.

Access and parking: Take exit 20 (High Point Road) off –90. Turn north and then left into the unmarked parking lot on the north edge of the I–90 on-ramp, westbound. This is the High Point Trailhead.

Rentals: See Appendix A for a list of rentals Puget Sound.

Contact: King County Parks Division, www.metrokc.gov/parks/trails

Bus routes: None

F JOHN WAYNE PIONEER TRAIL— MILWAUKEE ROAD CORRIDOR

This segment of the John Wayne Pioneer Trail is an adventure. It passes through several geological zones, some with dramatic scenery and varied wildlife. The trail is undeveloped, has some difficult surfaces, and is sometimes confusing to navigate. A 40-mile gap from Royal Junction to Warden takes you on detours over county roads. A permit is required. You may find snow for skiing and snowshoeing several weeks of the year—mostly from the Idaho border west about 20 miles. Fishing can be found on Department of Fish and Wildlife lands near the trail.

Activities:

Location: Beverly to Tekoa, in Grant, Adams, and Whitman Counties

Length: 145 miles

Surface: Crushed stone, ballast, and dirt; the surface is deep and sandy for long sections of the trail.

Wheelchair access: The trail is not wheelchair accessible.

Difficulty: Easy to moderate. Though the trail is mostly flat, the surface can make for tough travel.

Food: You'll find food in the towns of Othello, Beverly, Lind, Rosalia, Warden, and Tekoa.

Restrooms: There are no restrooms or drinking water along this trail.

Seasons: The trail can be used year-round.

Access and parking: To obtain information on the access points, present conditions, and permits, contact the DNR (see Contact). They will send a packet of information and maps.

Rentals: No rentals are available along this trail.

Contact: Washington Department of Natural Resources (DNR), Southeast Region Office, (509) 925–8510

Bus routes: None

G MIDDLE FORK TRAIL

The Middle Fork Trail is a narrow pathway through a dense forest of western hemlock, around pockets of old growth, across bridges over wetlands and streams, and occasionally beside the Middle Fork of the Snoqualmie River. Eventually you can reach the Alpine Lakes Wilderness. The terrain becomes more rugged in the upper reaches of the trail. The privately owned Goldmyer Hot Springs Conservancy is in the area. Reservations are required; call in advance.

Activities:

Location: North Bend, King County

Length: 14.5 miles

Surface: Gravel, dirt, and clay

Wheelchair access: The trail is not wheelchair accessible.

Difficulty: Moderate; there are some narrow, steep sections.

Food: No food is available along the trail.

Restrooms: You'll find restrooms at the Middle Fork Trailhead.

Seasons: Although the trail can be used year-round, it's not maintained in winter.

Access and parking: Take exit 34 off Interstate 90 (468 Avenue Southeast). Turn north, drive 0.4 mile, then turn right onto Southeast Middle Fork Road. Go 2.25 miles to the end of the pavement. The dirt Forest Road 5600 takes you to the trailheads. You'll find the Middle Fork Trailhead 12.3 miles from I–90, and Dingford Creek 5.5 miles farther at the end of the road. Cross the river on foot bridges to the trail. Cross-country skiing is not recommended, but you can snowshoe from any point you can reach by car. A trailhead parking pass is required. Purchase information is available at Forest Service offices.

Rentals: No rentals are available along the trail.

Contact: U.S. Forest Service, North Bend, (425) 888–1421; or Goldmyer Hot Springs Conservancy, (206) 789–5631, www.goldmyer.org

Bus routes: None

H NECKLACE VALLEY TRAIL

The Necklace Valley Trail is named for the loop of lakes it travels, which look like a jeweled necklace. It's a very steep trail; the railroad right-of-way portion of the trail extends for 1.5 miles. This portion was logged in the 1920s. Continue for 3.5 miles on a flat trail through old-growth forest, then climb steeply for the last 2.5 miles.

Activities:

Location: Mount Baker–Snoqualmie National Forest, King County

Length: 7.5 miles, 1.5 miles of which travel on the railroad right-of-way

Surface: Dirt

Wheelchair access: The trail is not wheelchair accessible.

Difficulty: Easy for 5 miles; very difficult for 2.5 miles

Food: No food is available along the trail.

Restrooms: There are no restrooms along the trail.

Seasons: The trail can be used year-round.

Access and parking: From U.S. Highway 2, turn south on Foss River Road. Drive 4.1 miles to the Necklace Valley Trailhead on the left, signed TRAIL #1062. In winter the road is plowed up to the trestle, 1.5 miles from the highway. Snow is in the area six months of the year.

Rentals: No rentals are available along the trail.

Contact: U.S. Forest Service, Skykomish Ranger Station, (360) 677–2414

Bus routes: None

PACIFIC CREST NATIONAL SCENIC TRAIL: STEVENS PASS RIGHT-OF-WAY SECTION

The Pacific Crest National Scenic Trail spans 2,000 miles. A 1.5-mile railroad right-of-way begins at Stevens Pass and follows the path of the upper switchback of the rail line. The trail then leaves the right-of-way and enters the Henry M. Jackson Wilderness Area.

Activities:

Location: U.S. Highway 2, Stevens Pass, Chelan County

Length: 1.5 miles

Surface: Dirt

Wheelchair access: The trail is not wheelchair accessible.

Difficulty: Easy. Avalanche danger on the trail during winter months.

Food: No food is available along the trail.

Restrooms: There are no restrooms along this trail.

Seasons: The trail can be used year-round.

Access and parking: The trail begins at Stevens Pass, the lot directly across from Stevens Pass Ski Area. It takes off from the north corner of the lot.

Rentals: No rentals are available along the trail.

Contact: U.S. Forest Service, Leavenworth Ranger Station, (509) 548–6977

Bus routes: None

J RAINIER MULTIUSE TRAIL

The paved trail begins on Rainier Avenue Southeast at Gilman Boulevard, 1 block west of Front Street. It passes the community center, the historic railroad depot, the logging railroad display, the Skateboard Park, and the brewery and eateries of downtown Issaquah. After crossing Second Avenue, it becomes a narrow, undeveloped dirt-and-gravel trail that heads uphill behind the high school. At 1 mile you'll reach a three-way intersection. The Rainier Trail drops down to the left onto Sunset Way and crosses the Sunset interchange. It then connects to the Issaquah–High Point Regional Trail.

Activities:

Location: Issaquah, King County

Length: 2.54 miles

Surface: 1.54 miles of the trail is paved; 1 mile is dirt and ballast.

Wheelchair access: The paved portion of the trail is wheelchair accessible .

Difficulty: Easy to difficult

Food: You'll find groceries and restaurants in the town of Issaquah.

Restrooms: There are restrooms at the community center.

Seasons: The trail can be used year-round.

Access and parking: Take exit 17 off Interstate 90 and head south to Gilman Boulevard. Turn right on Gilman. Take the first left, onto Rainier Avenue Southeast, just past the chamber.

Rentals: See Appendix A for a list of rentals in Puget Sound.

Contact: City of Issaquah, (425) 837–3322

Bus routes: #200, #209, #271. Information at (206) 553–3000 or King County Metro Transit at transit.metrokc.gov.

K SHIP CANAL TRAIL

This flat, paved trail lies in a peaceful park setting between the Fremont Bridge and Seattle Pacific University on the south side of the ship canal. The benches on the grassy waterfront, the shade of the willow trees, the boats slowly passing by, and the occasional rising of the bridge provide a relaxing stroll or skate. Cyclists use the trail as a connection between city bike routes. There are plans to extend the trail westward.

Activities:

Location: Seattle, King County

Length: 0.8 mile

Surface: Asphalt

Wheelchair access: The entire trail is wheelchair accessible.

Difficulty: Easy

Food: Try the Fremont eateries and breweries across the bridge.

Restrooms: There are no restrooms along this trail.

Seasons: The trail can be used year-round.

Access and parking: Park at Ewing Ming Park on Third Avenue West, 1 block north of West Nickerson Street, or on Nickerson. The trail runs from Sixth Avenue west to the Fremont Bridge.

Rentals: See Appendix A for a list of rentals in Puget Sound.

Contact: Bicycle Alliance of Washington, (206) 224–9252, www.bicycle alliance.org

Bus routes: #13, #17. For more information, check out the Metro Transit Web site at transit.metrokc.gov, or call them at (206) 553–3000.

L SNOQUALMIE CENTENNIAL TRAIL

The Northwest Railroad Museum is the highlight of this trail. Pass old steam engines on the tracks, visit the museum, and take a train ride to the ledge above the famous Snoqualmie Falls in summer or during the Christmas holidays. Visit the elegant Salish Lodge just beyond the trail.

Activities:

Location: Snoqualmie, King County

Length: 0.6 mile

Surface: Asphalt, dirt

Wheelchair access: The entire trail is wheelchair accessible.

Difficulty: Easy

Food: You'll find restaurants in the town of Snoqualmie.

Restrooms: There are restrooms in town and at the museum.

Seasons: The trail can be used year-round.

Access and parking: Take Interstate 90 to exit 31. Head north and follow Washington Highway 202 through North Bend and on to the town of Snoqualmie. You can park on the street near the Northwest Railroad Museum.

Rentals: See Appendix A for a list of rentals in Puget Sound.

Contact: City of Snoqualmie, (425) 831–5784

Bus routes: #209, #214, #929. For more information, check out Metro Transit at transit.metrokc.gov, or call them at (206) 553–3000.

M WEST TIGER RAILROAD GRADE

The West Tiger Railroad Grade lies deep within the boundaries of the Tiger Mountain Natural Resources Conservation Area. All trails in this half of Tiger Mountain are for hiking only. You can reach this one only after hiking other trails that begin from the street; the access trails are steeper than the West Tiger Railroad Grade itself. From the trailhead, take the main trail 0.25 mile to the first trail to the right (High School Trail). Then take the right fork to reach an old gate. Reach the Tradition Plateau in about 1 mile;fork right at the power-line corridor. Turn right again, to another trail intersection (signed) to the Poo Poo Point Trail; this intersects the West Tiger Railroad Grade in about 2 miles.

Activities:

Location: Tiger Mountain State Forest, West Tiger Mountain Natural Resources Conservation Area, Issaquah, King County

Length: 5.5 miles

Surface: Dirt

Wheelchair access: The trail is not wheelchair accessible.

Difficulty: Moderate, with one steep area

Food: No food is available along the trail.

Restrooms: There are no restrooms along the trail.

Seasons: The trail can be used year-round. Seasonal closure for horses runs October 15 to April 15.

Access and parking: Take exit 17 (Front Street) off Interstate 90 from either direction. Head south 0.7 mile to Sunset (stoplight) and take a left. After 0.2 mile, turn right onto Second Avenue. Pull into the dirt lot on the left just beyond the high school in 0.8 mile.

Rentals: No local rentals are available.

Contact: Washington State Department of Natural Resources, South Puget Sound Region Office, (360) 825–1631, www.dnr.wa.gov

Bus routes: Contact King County Metro Transit, (206) 553–3000.

Rail Trails
OREGON

OVERVIEW

Though Oregon has only a few developed rail trails, they run the gamut of terrain, scenery, and travel options. Some draw you to the state's most stunning sites; others combine with impressive light-rail and bus service to provide a commuter pathway. Tour forested foothills, riverside farmland, covered bridges, dams, and 100 miles of trail through mountains and river valleys. Pick a rural desert perch above the Columbia River, enjoy an oceanfront town, or follow the Deschutes River into a desert canyon. Travel beside towns buried under water when dams were built.

Lewis and Clark reached Astoria in 1805, making this town the oldest settlement in the West. This beach resort town of the early 1900s sits on the northwestern tip of Oregon, where the Columbia River empties into the Pacific. The very civilized trail here entices you to stroll, ride, dine, and explore history. The Banks-Vernonia State Trail, also west of Portland, is quite a contrast: It's a forested trek in the hills near tall trestles and railroad remnants between the tiny towns of Banks and Vernonia.

The Springwater Corridor is part of a 40-mile loop around Portland and outlying areas. Combined with light-rail and bus service, this route provides a great leisure trip to Gresham and a commuter route with convenient, more passive options for the return trip. Botanical gardens and wildlife refuges near the trail replace the amusement parks that rallied railroad riders in the early 1900s.

The rich agriculture of the Willamette River Valley, from Portland south, drew the railroads up from California as early as 1870. The Row River Trail is the only rail trail in this region. Enjoy the wildlife, wildflowers, and covered bridges as you travel alongside the river and the lake created by the dam.

The desert trails of eastern Oregon traverse above rivers and beside basalt rock walls. The trails in the Malheur National Forest hide you down in a draw and raise you to the highest point of the Sumpter Valley Railway. The rural Umatilla County Lewis and Clarke Commemorative Trail sits high above the Columbia River, near the McNary Dam, and ends in riverfront parks. The Deschutes River Trail starts near the Columbia River Gorge and penetrates 18 miles into a desert canyon with ever-changing rock formations, high above the Deschutes River.

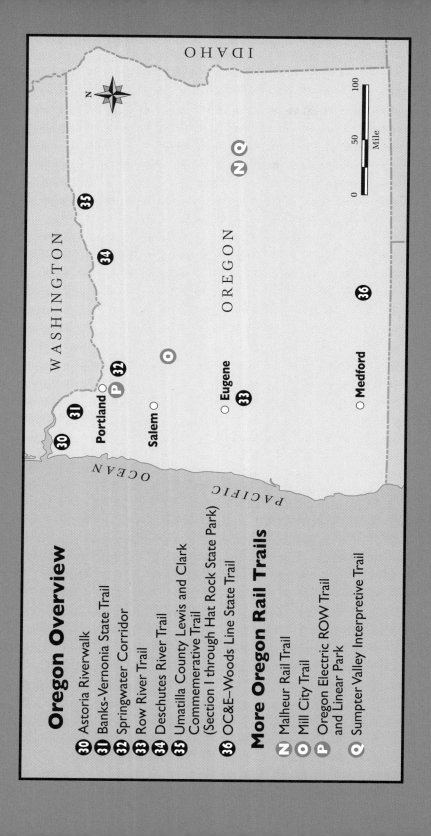

Oregon Overview

30 Astoria Riverwalk
31 Banks–Vernonia State Trail
32 Springwater Corridor
33 Row River Trail
34 Deschutes River Trail
35 Umatilla County Lewis and Clark
Commemerative Trail
(Section I through Hat Rock State Park)
36 OC&E–Woods Line State Trail

More Oregon Rail Trails

N Malheur Rail Trail
O Mill City Trail
P Oregon Electric ROW Trail
and Linear Park
Q Sumpter Valley Interpretive Trail

WASHINGTON

IDAHO

OREGON

PACIFIC OCEAN

N

Portland

Salem

Eugene

Medford

0   50   100
Mile

The OC&E–Woods Line State Trail, near the border of California, passes through small towns and climbs the old railroad switchbacks as it traverses nearly 100 miles of diverse scenery and terrain.

Travel through history, natural beauty, and urban amenities on the rail trails of Oregon. These trails are gifts that allow us to tour the state while we walk, skate, ski, or ride bikes and horses. Take advantage of them!

30 ASTORIA RIVERWALK

Portland's beach resort town of the early 1900s sits on the north-western tip of Oregon where the Columbia River empties into the Pacific Ocean. Lewis and Clark's 8,000-mile trek in search of the Northwest Passage brought them here in 1805, making this town the West's oldest American settlement and a National Historic District. Later the Spokane, Portland & Seattle Railway brought cityfolk to the beach on Friday night for a weekend on the coast. Today bridges and boardwalks, canneries and cafes, docks and decks, galleries and espresso shops decorate the riverfront with history, views, and yuppie delights.

Activities:

Location: Smith Point to 41st Street, Astoria, in Clatsop County

Length: 3.5 miles, 3 of which are fully developed (from Portway Street to 41st Street)

Surface: The developed portion is paved or planked trestles. The trestles are filled with bollards east of 41st.

Wheelchair access: The developed section of the trail is wheelchair accessible.

Difficulty: Easy from Portway Street to 41st Street. Use caution on other parts of the trail.

Food: You'll find things to eat in downtown Astoria.

Restrooms: Facilities are at the foot of 39th Street, the Dough Boy Monument, and city public buildings.

Seasons: The trail can be used year-round.

Access and parking: To reach the trail, drive U.S. Highway 101 to Astoria. From Interstate 5 in Washington, exit at Longview, cross the Columbia River, and head west on U.S. Highway 30. From Portland, take US 30 west. From the south, take US 101 north. The trail is easily accessed anywhere along its length: Any numbered street from Sixth to 39th ends at the river's edge and the trail. Park on the street.

Rentals: To rent bicycles, check out Hauer's Cyclery Shop at the foot of 16th Street (1606 Marine Drive in Astoria), or Bikes and Beyond at 11th Street and Marine Drive.

Contacts: City of Astoria, (503) 325–5821; Chamber of Commerce, (503) 325–6311

Bus routes: A restored city trolley runs from the western trail terminus at Smith Point to 39th Street daily in summer, and on Friday, Saturday, and Sunday, noon to 3:00 p.m. in winter. You can flag it down at any point. The trolley cannot take bicycles; however, the City Bus allows bicycles.

A restored trolley runs along the trail from the western trail terminus to 39th Street.

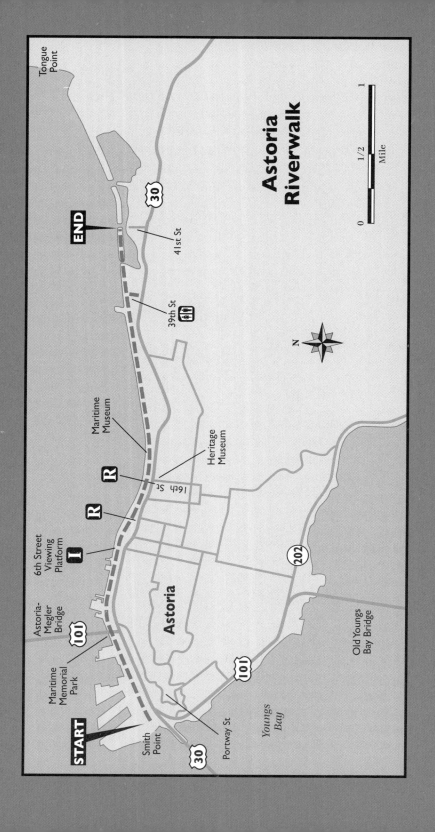

Astoria
Riverwalk

0   1/2   1
Mile

N

START

END

Astoria

Tongue Point

Smith Point

30

Portway St

Youngs Bay

Old Youngs
Bay Bridge

101

202

101

Astoria-
Megler
Bridge

Maritime
Memorial
Park

6th Street
Viewing
Platform

I

R

R

Maritime
Museum

16th St

Heritage
Museum

39th St

41st St

30

Nearby Attractions

Climb the 164 steps to the observation deck of the Astoria Column for a panoramic view of the region. The neighboring town of Warrenton has a waterfront trail and an eagle sanctuary. Nearby scenic locations include Long Beach Peninsula (famous for cranberries) and Seaside on the Oregon coast. Nearby rail trails include the Raymond to South Bend Riverfront Trail to the north (Trail 23) and the Banks-Vernonia State Trail toward Portland (Trail 31). Call the chamber (see Contact) for its guide to the city and events.

The Astoria Riverwalk Trail invites you to savor the sights, sounds, and tastes of a fun town while the historic buildings, fort, and monuments paint a picture of the earliest days of pioneering on the West Coast. US 101, the coastal highway, is a busy street loaded with commercial activity. The Riverwalk lets you avoid this main drag and explore on foot, on a bike, or quite easily in a wheelchair. You can access this trail from almost anywhere and design a tour of your own.

The downtown section from Sixth Street to 17th Street is more formal with benches, lighting, and interpretive kiosks. It meanders along the riverfront with easy access to shops, restaurants, and museums. From 17th Street to 41st Street, you'll find a 10-foot-wide asphalt trail with fewer amenities. Use extreme caution on the trestles; the open ties here can capture a foot or bike tire.

Though Astoria has an impressive list of claims to fame, its most amazing may be the sight of the Columbia River disappearing into the ocean. The 4.1-mile drive to Washington over the Astoria-Megler Bridge offers great views from the longest continuous three-span through-truss bridge in the world. The shore is one of ten locations between Alaska and Mexico where more than 100,000 birds may gather at one time. Try a visit during fall migration.

For a unique tourist attraction, watch a "bar pilot" leap from a tug onto a freighter to be guided in to Astoria. This is the only city on the

West Coast where you'll see this. The river bar that separates the Columbia from the Pacific is considered one of the most dangerous in the world. It is said to have claimed 233 shipwrecks at the bottom of the "Graveyard of the Pacific."

If you hear a chorus of sea lions, look down to see them below the trestles. The city offers kayaking, canoeing, surfing, waterskiing, fishing, clamming, boat tours, and rail-bike tours. When you're done recreating, stop at the Wet Dog Cafe and Brew Club on 11th Street or the Rogue Ale House on 39th Street.

31 BANKS-VERNONIA STATE TRAIL

The Banks-Vernonia Trail stretches through the hills east of the Coast Mountains. It's 35 miles west of Portland and 52 miles east of the coastal town of Seaside. Both trail endpoints—at Banks and at Vernonia—are paved for several miles, mostly along the highway. As you approach the middle third of the trail, it leaves the road and climbs into the forested hills on a gravel-and-ballast surface. Here you enter a different world. Miles of side trails create an oudoor museum of railroad relics, including an old section cabin. Look up at two 90-foot-high, 680-foot-long trestles. Enjoy views of the Coastal Range. Listen for an owl. You might see a fox, an elk, a deer, or a great blue heron.

Activities:

Location: The towns of Banks and Vernonia, in Columbia and Washington Counties

Length: 21 miles

Surface: 12 miles of the trail is asphalt, 9 miles is gravel.

Wheelchair access: Wheelchair access is available on the trail's paved portions and at parks.

Difficulty: Easy to moderate, with difficult sections. The steep, potentially muddy descent to the highway at the Tophill Trailhead can be tough, and some areas have heavy gravel that's challenging even on a mountain bike. The trail has a 2 to 5 percent grade.

Food: The small town of Vernonia has a bar with food. Minors are not allowed. The area just west of the junction of U.S. Highway 26 and Oregon Highway 47 has a market, a restaurant, and gas station mini marts, scheduled to be demolished for a highway overpass.

Restrooms: There are vault and chemical toilets at all the trailheads except Manning.

Seasons: The trail can be used year-round.

Access and parking: To start in Vernonia, take US 26 from Seaside or Portland to OR 47. If you're coming from Portland, head north 15 miles on OR 47; from Seaside, drive 11 miles north on a small unmarked road west of OR 47 signed TO VERNONIA. Stop at City Hall for a map. Turn south at the railroad engine on Adams Street in town. Park in Anderson Park; there's an interpretive kiosk here, as well as hitching posts.

The Beaver Creek Trailhead is found on OR 47 just over 4 miles south of Anderson Park; the Tophill Trailhead (with hitching posts), also on OR 47, is about 8 miles south. You'll have to make a steep uphill climb whether you start here or just pass through this part of the trail. For accessing the trail at the L. L. Stub Stewart State Park, continue south on OR 47 past Tophill Trailhead. Turn left into the park. The trail crosses over the entrance road. Look for trail access signs. To reach the Buxton Trailhead, turn north on Fisher Road from US 26, 0.5 mile east of the intersection with OR 47. Follow signs to the park. The Manning Trailhead is also on US 26, 1 mile east of OR 47. This is the southernmost trailhead, 3.3 miles from the trail's end.

Rentals: None closer than Portland (see information for Springwater Corridor, Trail 32).

Contact: L. L. Stub Stewart State Park, (503) 324–0606

Bus routes: None

|||||||||||||||||||||||||||||||||||||||||||||||||||||||||||||||||||||||||||||||||||||||||

The Spokane, Portland & Seattle Railway built the Gales Creek & Wilson River line in 1922. Other railroads refused to build a line expressly for hauling lumber, so this one was created to move timber products from northwestern Oregon, and in particular from the Oregon-American lumber mill in Vernonia. The trains also carried freight and passengers from Keasey to Portland. The line ceased operation when the mill closed in 1957. The Vernonia South Park & Sunset Railroad leased the line and operated a steam sight-seeing train from 1960 to 1965. Abandoned in 1973, the rails were salvaged and the right-of-way sold to the state highway department. In 1990 it became the first linear state park in Oregon.

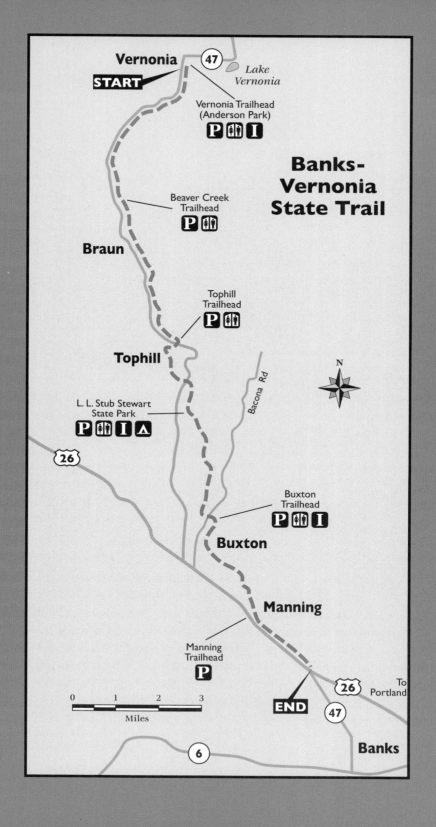

**Banks-
Vernonia
State Trail**

Vernonia
START
47
*Lake
Vernonia*

Vernonia Trailhead
(Anderson Park)
P 👫 I

Beaver Creek
Trailhead
P 👫

Braun

Tophill
Trailhead
P 👫

Tophill

Bacona Rd

N

L. L. Stub Stewart
State Park
P 👫 I ⛰

26

Buxton
Trailhead
P 👫 I

Buxton

Manning

Manning
Trailhead
P

26
To
Portland

0   1   2   3
Miles

END
47

Banks

6

Five trailheads allow for easy access and trips of various lengths on paved or gravel surfaces. When you choose your starting point, keep in mind that the trail runs downhill from Vernonia on a 2 to 5 percent grade. Cyclists are asked to ride on one side, equestrians on the other. The grade may tempt you to cruise downhill on a bike; if so, pay attention to avoid collisions. Cyclists must yield to all users, and hikers must yield to horses. The paved areas of the trail are not ideal for skating; on the unpaved portions, a mountain bike works best.

This description takes you from Anderson Park in Vernonia southward. In Vernonia, the Banks-Vernonia Trail will eventually connect to the paved loop around Lake Vernonia, creating a lakeside trailhead. After you leave the park, the trail is paved for 7 miles. It parallels OR 47 and Beaver Creek until the shrubs and fir separate you from the highway. Good access to the Newhalem River for fishing can be found about 1 mile south of Vernonia.

The trail leaves open areas lined with blackberry bushes and deciduous trees at mile 7, becomes dirt and gravel, and climbs into a forest of Douglas fir. As you approach the Tophill Trailhead, prepare for a steep descent to OR 47, where the burned Horseshoe Trestle forces trail users to cross the highway. Use caution.

The Banks-Vernonia State Trail passes through the forested hills east of the Coast Mountains.

Take a side trip to see this burned-out trestle.

A short climb returns you to the original grade. Detour left where the trail levels out to stand at the edge of the 90-foot-high Horseshoe Trestle. It was 680 feet long before the other end fell victim to a fire. Indeed, fires plagued the construction of this portion of railway from the very start.

Turn right to follow the trail into deep forest. Cross the highway at milepost 10. Shortly you will come to the entrance of the new L. L. Stub Stewart State Park, located on the left side of the trail. The large campground opened in 2007. The trail crosses the entrance road to the park at milepost 10.5. Campsites, RV sites, hike-in campsites, a horse camp, rustic cabin rentals, and a day-use area provide a convenient overnight spot for trail users. Reservations are highly recommended.

Continuing south on the main trail, you will encounter a group of historic side trips. At milepost 12, hitch your horse or park your bike and walk to the old section cabin. Picture the railroad crew cooking on the woodstove inside. At milepost 12.5, find another side trail, which crosses the main trail after 0.5 mile and crosses it again to become a short, fun single-track. These short, historic side trails built by the state park ranger and volunteers total 10 additional miles. Due to irregular maintenance, trail conditions may vary.

Just past mile 13, you'll find an open area with picnic tables and hitching posts, built by the Oregon Youth Conservation Corps. Arrive at Buxton Trailhead to enjoy the grassy area and the pond stocked with newts, turtles, and frogs. Here 5,000 children learn about the ecosystem each year.

At milepost 15, Pongratz Road, detour onto 1.5 miles of dirt county road. At the T-intersection with Pihl Road, a right turn takes you to the Manning Trailhead. Heading east, the trail dead-ends in the brush 0.25 mile from Banks.

When you've explored the trail to your heart's content, turn around and return the way you came. If your trip home takes you westward, visit the largest sitka spruce in the United States, on display on US 26. If you're returning to Portland, check out the Northwest 23rd District off Burnside Straat and Northwest 23rd Avenue for funky cafes and trendy shops. If you're on a rail trail roll, check out the Astoria Riverwalk (Trail 30) or Portland's Springwater Corridor (Trail 32).

32 SPRINGWATER CORRIDOR

The Springwater Corridor is the major southeast section of a system of nature trails encircling Portland. Ride, walk, or skate the trail to enjoy parks, botanical gardens, and wetlands—not to mention herons, coyotes, and deer—as you travel through industrial, suburban, and rural areas. August is blackberry month; don't hesitate to savor your way down the trail.

Activities:

Location: Portland to Boring, in Multnomah and Clackamas Counties

Length: 20 miles

Surface: Mostly asphalt, although 3 miles from Hogan to Boring are dirt

Wheelchair access: The paved portion of the trail is wheelchair accessible.

Difficulty: Easy

Food: You'll find things to eat at several spots along the trail and in downtown Gresham.

Restrooms: There are restrooms at Gresham Main City Park, at Tideman Johnson Park, and along the trail east of milepost 13.

Seasons: The trail can be used year-round.

Access and parking: To start at the northern terminus of the trail, park at Southeast Ivon Street and Southeast Caruthers Street just east of the Willamette River near the Ross Island Bridge in Portland. Or start at the six-acre Tideman Johnson Park and park in the lot at Southeast Johnson Creek Boulevard near Southeast 45th Street. The trail numbering starts in the north and increases as you head southeast.

At the trail's southeastern terminus, you can leave your car 3 miles from the east end of the trail by parking near Gresham Main City Park on U.S. Highway 26 and South Main Avenue, or at the trailhead at Hogan Avenue, south of 19th Street in Gresham.

Rentals: You can rent bikes from Fat Tire Farm at 2714 Northwest Thurman in Portland, (503–222–3276).

Contact:

- Portland Parks and Recreation, (503) 823–PLAY, www.portlandonline
  .com/parks/

- Portland Visitor Center, (877) 678–5263, www.travelportland.com

- Gresham Visitor Center, (503) 665–1131

Bus routes: See sidebar in this chapter for information on the light rail system and bus routes.

The Springwater Corridor consists of 20 miles of the 40-mile loop around the greater Portland area, a path first conceived of in 1903 to serve as a nature trail encircling the city. Though our forefathers lived in a city of woodlands and meadows, they had the foresight to plan this park and trail system, now slated to ultimately extend for 240 miles. This trail loop will

Tideman Johnson Park provides a lovely backdrop for a leisurely ride on the Springwater Corridor. (Courtesy Portland Parks and Recreation)

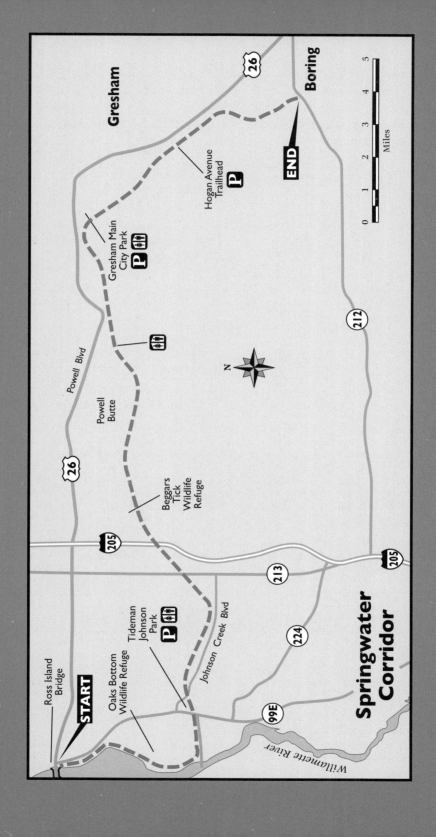

Gresham

US 26

Boring

Hogan Avenue
Trailhead

P

END

Gresham Main
City Park

P 🚻

🚻

Powell Blvd

Powell
Butte

N

212

Beggars
Tick
Wildlife
Refuge

205

213

205

Ross Island
Bridge

START

Oaks Bottom
Wildlife Refuge

Tideman
Johnson
Park

P 🚻

Johnson Creek Blvd

224

99E

Willamette River

US 26

**Springwater
Corridor**

0   1   2   3   4   5

Miles

connect three rivers and thirty parks, including 5 miles of the Columbia Slough suitable for canoeing, and an equestrian loop. A 10.8-mile section from south of Boring to Estacada may link the trail to the Pacific Crest Trail (a route from Mexico to Canada).

The Springwater Division Line of 1903 reached peak usage in 1906. Portland General Electric and the Portland Railway Light & Power Companies had six electric plants and 161 miles of rail, carrying 16,000 passengers each year and hauling farm produce to Portland markets. Towns popped up along the line; the railroad rallied ridership further by building amusement parks. Thousands of weekend passengers rode the rail to destinations such as the Oaks Amusement Park on the Willamette River. Passenger service continued until 1958; the city took over in 1990. In 1996 the Portland trail segment opened.

> ## Taking the Max
>
> Another result of Portland's prowess for planning is the city's light rail system, the MAX. This system allows you to bike, roll, or stroll the Springwater Corridor as far east as Gresham and Boring, then return easily via bus or rail. You must buy a Trimet pass to board your bike on MAX or a bus. There is no extra fee; bikes can ride on the regular fare. There are only two spaces per bus for bicycles.
>
> For more information on the light rail system and buses, visit www.trimet.org or call (503) 238–RIDE.

There are several spots from which to access the trail; this description takes you from the trail's starting point at Southeast Ivon and Southeast Caruthers Street, just east of the Willamette River near the Ross Island Bridge. Trail numbering increases as you head south and east. Shortly you will pass alongside the Oaks Bottom Wildlife Refuge, a 170-acre preserve of wetlands, meadows, and woodlands. Residential and migrating birds frequent the area. Take a detour on the three hiking trails, one of which is also for biking.

After passing the southern end of the refuge at mile 4, you will come to a 0.25-mile detour at Southeast. 7th Avenue. Directions are posted on

> "Parks should be connected and approached by boulevards and parkways. . . . The system of scenic reservations, parks and parkways and connecting boulevards would . . . form an admirable park system for such an important city as Portland is bound to become."
> —The Olmstead brothers, landscape architects, 1904 (the same family designed Spokane's original parks)

the trail to guide you through the detour and back onto the trail. Watch for the new bridges over Johnson Creek, McLoughlin Boulevard, and the railroad tracks as you head to Tideman Johnson Park. Take the new trail down to the creek; it loops back to the main trail. From the park, the trail runs east beside roads in a mildly industrial neighborhood. Cross to the north side of Johnson Creek Boulevard at Southeast Bell Avenue for a brief respite from road noise.

Find Beggars Tick Wildlife Refuge on the left at milepost 11, at Southeast 111th Avenue. Take a break to wander the wetlands and watch the wood ducks, teals, and mergansers. Find one of several sheltered benches just beyond the refuge. These shelters suit the Northwest, where drizzle can set in at any time.

Take a right at Southeast 122nd Avenue for several blocks to explore five acres and 1,500 species of native plants at the Leach Botanical Garden. Mile 12.5 places you adjacent to a 630-foot-high volcanic rise called Powell Butte Nature Park, with an access trail to the butte. Stop for views of the city and the mountains; a hike among the orchards, meadows, and forest; or a picnic. There are restrooms on the opposite side of the hill.

Hills begin to appear and civilization disappears (for a while) as you head toward the mountains. Cross a peaceful creek at mile 13.5 and find those great covered benches just beyond. If you've been waiting for a restroom, here's your chance. If you're tired, consider this: The former Linneman Rail Station was named for a pioneer couple who navigated the Oregon Trail by oxcart in 1852. Bikes, walking shoes, and pavement seem quite the luxury compared to dirt, rocks, and oxen.

Pass beside Powell Boulevard and under Southwest Eastman Parkway on your way to Main City Park in Gresham. Exit at the park to explore the eateries of Gresham on a pedestrian walkway and catch the bus or MAX back to Portland. It's fun to arrive for an evening out. Exit the trail through the park to Main Avenue. Cross US 26/Powell Boulevard and continue on Main to 10th. Cross the tracks to the transit center. Check out the restaurants on Main Avenue. Then relax on your bus ride home.

To complete the trail, continue for another 2 miles on pavement, then 3 miles on dirt, to reach Boring. Boring Junction is the last remaining ticketing station of the Springwater Corridor. From Boring, take a bus back to Gresham.

Portland is a great city blessed with amenities such as a rose garden, a paved waterfront trail, and great food. Explore.

33 ROW RIVER TRAIL

This abandoned railroad line left us five Howe truss bridges and twenty-three pile trestles to cross. Ospreys and eagles, a small town, covered bridges, and prairie wildflowers will delight you as you tour the scenic right-of-way. With more than twenty covered bridges, Lane County has more of these scenic spans than any other county west of the Appalachians.

Activities:

Location: Cottage Grove, 25 miles south of Eugene, in Lane County

Length: 16 miles

Surface: Asphalt and quarter-inch gravel for horses

Wheelchair access: This trail is wheelchair accessible.

Difficulty: Easy, although there's 1 mile of hills that may be tough for beginner skaters.

Food: You'll find things to eat in the towns of Dorena and Cottage Grove.

Restrooms: There are vault toilets at the Mosby Creek Trailhead and at Dorena Dam, Harms Park, Bake Stewart Park, Dorena, and Culp Creek. Mosby Creek and Schwarz Park have drinking water.

Seasons: The trail can be used year-round.

Access and parking: To reach the western trailhead, Cottage Grove, take exit 174 off Interstate 5 at Row River Road in Cottage Grove. Park downtown on Main Street. To reach Mosby Creek, remain on Row River Road and drive 2.5 miles southeast to Layng Road and the Currin Covered Bridge. Turn right, crossing Mosby Creek. Turn into the trailhead at 200 yards. The Mosby Creek Covered Bridge, built in 1920, is the oldest remaining covered bridge in Lane County.

Other trailheads are all found on Row River Road. These include Dorena Dam, Harms Park, Bake Stewart Park, Dorena, and Culp Creek.

Rentals: No local rentals are available. Eugene and Springfield, 25 miles away, have bike shops.

Contact: Bureau of Land Management, Eugene, (541) 683–6600

Bus routes: None

|||||||||||||||||||||||||||||||||||||||||||||||||||||||||||||||||||||||||||||||||||||||||||

The Row River Trail passes by the Dorena Dam and runs beside Dorena Lake as it follows the Row River. The river (pronounced to rhyme with *cow*) was named for a fatal brawl over grazing rights in the 1850s. The Willamette Valley was one of the great farming areas in the 1880s, along with the Palouse and Walla Walla Valleys. These eastern areas of the state were already building railroads for their farm products. The West needed to move its goods.

In 1883 the Oregon & California Railroad constructed a line through Salem, and in 1902 the "Old Slow and Easy" main line of the Oregon & South Eastern Railroad Company was built. It ran ore from the Bohemia mining district as well as logs, supplies, mail, and passengers from Cottage Grove to Disston, in the Umpqua National Forest. In 1914 the Oregon Pacific & Eastern took over. Though regular passenger service ended in July 1930, the *Goose* hauled summer tourists in the 1970s. A handful of runs served the Culp Creek lumber mill into the late 1980s. The Bureau of Land Management (BLM) acquired the right-of-way in 1993 and paved it in 1996. The remaining 3 miles, through the city of Cottage Grove, were paved in the early 2000s.

Although you can access the trail from several points, this description takes you from the Mosby Creek Trailhead eastward. The trail parallels the Row River Road most of the way. You'll arrive at Dorena Dam and the lake it created at 3.5 miles. Before the dam was built, the river repeatedly flooded towns downstream. In addition to flood control, the dam provides irrigation, recreation, and improved navigation.

Look for a spring shout of color from the delicate plants at Row Point, remnants of the native prairie community. Please leave them protected so they can survive. At mile 5.3, see if you recognize the trestle at Harms Park, immortalized in the movies of Ernest Borgnine and Buster Keaton.

Smith Creek is an area of streams, marshes, and canary grass fields. Ospreys, herons, ducks, and geese are commonly seen. A keen eye may

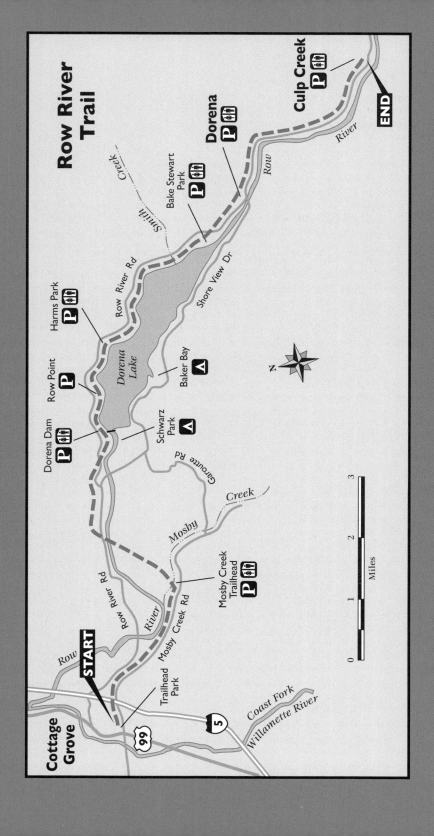

Row River Trail

Cottage Grove

START

Row River Rd

Row River

99

5

Trailhead Park

Mosby Creek Rd

Mosby Creek Trailhead
P 🚻

Mosby Creek

Garoutte Rd

Coast Fork
Willamette River

Dorena Dam
P 🚻

Row Point
P

Harms Park
P 🚻

Dorena Lake

Row River Rd

Schwarz Park
🏕

Baker Bay
🏕

Shore View Dr

Smith Creek

Bake Stewart Park
P 🚻

Dorena
P 🚻

Row River

Culp Creek
P 🚻

END

N

Miles
0   1   2   3

The trail runs beside the Dorena Reservoir. (Courtesy Bureau of Land Management (BLM) Eugene, Oregon)

also catch a bald eagle, a deer, or the occasional black bear. You can also see the remains of an early settler's orchard below Smith Creek Bridge.

Bake Stewart Park is named for two lilies: a poisonous one and an edible one. The bulb of the blue flowering lily was once dug up in early spring and baked in earth ovens for winter storage, while the white or "death" camas lilies were carefully avoided.

Arrive at the postdam town of Dorena at mile 12.5. Established in 1899, the original townsite included a church, dance hall, post office, store, blacksmith shop, and grocery, all located near the center of the present reservoir. To prepare for the dam, a portion of the railway and some buildings were moved. Others were burned prior to the filling of the reservoir in the 1940s. The old railroad route can be seen along the lake bottom during winter drawdown.

The eastern terminus of the trail, Culp Creek, was one of twenty mill towns along the railway. Before the railroad, logs went to mill via "river rats." These fellows made quite a wage riding the logs downriver to the mills. The railroad put an end to these wild and risky rides. The last mill disappeared a decade ago.

Whenever you're ready, turn around and return the way you came.

34 DESCHUTES RIVER TRAIL

Take a scenic desert tour in a canyon above the Deschutes River. Visit the Columbia Gorge, Hood River, Goldendale, and the Dalles, and you've got an aesthetic, tasty, and interesting weekend. The canyon is hot, somewhat rocky, and occasionally sandy. It's a pretty flat trail that offers a slight downhill grade on the return. There are some nifty features along the way, including a constant view of the river.

Activities:

Location: Deschutes River State Park at the Columbia River, Wasco, in Sherman County

Length: 18 miles

Surface: Dirt and gravel

Wheelchair access: The trail is not wheelchair accessible.

Difficulty: Easy, although in several spots the gravel may be difficult to ride on a bike.

Food: There are vending machines in the park.

Restrooms: Public restrooms and drinking water are available at the park.

Seasons: The trail is open year-round for hikers and bikers; it's open from March 1 through June 30 for equestrians by reservation only.

Access and parking: Take exit 104 off Interstate 84. Park signs point you south of the highway. Turn right (west) at the stop sign at the frontage road in the corner town of Biggs. Turn left into Deschutes River State Park at just under 5 miles. You can park here at the park entrance and head through the gate from the parking area. Or drive to the end of the park road and travel across the grassy area that extends from the parking strip. Follow the sign up a steep, narrow trail to the upper trail. This is the main trail.

Rentals: There are no rentals available near the trail.

Contact: Deschutes River State Park, (541) 739–2322; or Oregon State Parks, (800) 551–6949, www.prd.state.or.us; camping reservations at Reservations Northwest, 1 (800) 452–5687

Bus routes: None

O n the Deschutes River Trail, you're in the desert. You'll have hot, dry weather and little shade most of the year. There are no roads and no water beyond the park (except, of course, the river). The Department of Fish and Wildlife provides a few outhouses and two horse troughs, and some old boxcars have been renovated for shade. Still, to have a great day here, bring a hefty supply of water in insulated containers, heavy-duty sunscreen, and snacks. Try the trail in spring when lupine and other wildflowers are out, the weather is moderate, the pale hair of the big-horned sheep stands out against the green, and folks from west of the Cascades are ready for relief from the winter soak.

The desert canyon walls along the Deschutes River Trail.

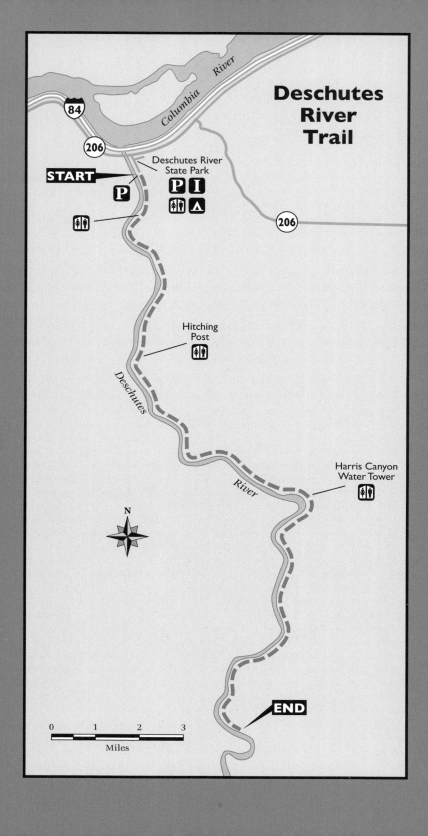

Deschutes
River
Trail

Columbia River

84

206

Deschutes River
State Park

START

P

P I

I

206

Hitching
Post

Deschutes

River

Harris Canyon
Water Tower

N

END

0   1   2   3
Miles

Also note that the trail is dotted with nefarious plants called punctured vine or goat heads, which are excellent at flattening bike tires. Bring an extra tube and a patch kit. If you get a flat, check your tire carefully for other three-thorned vines waiting to flatten you down the road. The Department of Fish and Wildlife sprays the area and removes huge bags of them for the safety of cyclists. The department also does a great job of providing habitat for birds, deer, and big-horned sheep along the trail and on the ridgetops. You may see western meadowlarks, doves, ospreys, and golden eagles.

In addition to the main, upper trail that you'll be on, two lower walking trails run closer to the river for 2 miles. Anglers bike out or walk the lower trail to fish for steelhead from the banks of the Deschutes. Several paths along the main trail lead down to the river. The first 3 miles of the Deschutes River Trail are in the state park; the next 15 are in Fish and Wildlife lands. The trail ends at a washout, which marks the start of Bureau of Land Management land.

From your perch on the trail, the canyon displays changing rock formations and views of the river. Magpies fly by, showing their striking black on white. Small birds and butterflies disperse as you disrupt the occasional drinking puddle.

You may see a train heading for Bend on the active line across the river. This western line, and the right-of-way you'll travel, were built by fierce competition. After receiving approval in 1906, two railroad companies—Hill's Oregon Trunk (OT) and Harriman's Des Chutes Railroad Company—went head to head in 1908 in a violent and political battle. The Oregon Trunk was a subsidiary of the Seattle, Portland & Spokane Railway, which was itself a subsidiary of the Northern Pacific and the Great Northern. Harriman's project was a subsidiary of the Oregon-Washington Railroad & Navigation Company, a Union Pacific company. The battle ended October 5, 1911, in Bend when seventy-three-year-old James Hill drove home the golden spike in two blows. The Des Chutes Railroad, where the trail runs, built 95 miles of track, into Metolius. It used the Oregon Trunk trackage for routes from Metolius to Bend. The 156 miles of OT track is still used.

Trail mileage is well marked. The terrain drops into the river from the trail, presenting a dramatic view. At mile 3.5, near Colorado Rapid, a dirt road provides access to the river and an outhouse. Also located at 3.5 miles is a rock wall built by Chinese railroad workers. Uphill from the trail, natural springs irrigate a cluster of shade trees. Cross a bridge built over a wash-out and find a horse trough at mile 4.5. Though a trail meanders down-hill, it does not reach the riverside outhouse for boaters or anglers. Wait until mile 5.5, where a hitching post marks a trail to another outhouse. A renovated boxcar just beyond provides shade, a bit of history, and even a campsite. At mile 7 the old pilings of "Free Bridge," a non-toll bridge, can be viewed. For a swim, some shade, or a visit to an outhouse, drop down to the river at mile 8. A small, old wooden trestle, called Bed Springs—the last trestle standing along the trail—can be seen, as well as another box-car. Climb the steps to pass through the open gate.

From here the canyon widens and flattens. You might see a lonely cow grazing across the river. At 10 miles the trail approaches the Deschutes at a spot where towering rock formations jut out across the water. At mile 11, out of the barren hills emerge golden wheat and barley fields, followed by the old Harris homestead and a wooden water tower. The Department of Fish and Wildlife plants grains here to provide upland bird habitat (pheas-ant, quail, chukar) and deer and elk foraging. It also plants cottonwood trees for shade and for the birds—but no sooner are they planted than the beavers arrive in herds of twenty or more to chow down. Beware: The grasses hide rattlers, bull snakes, and nestling fawns.

Find some shade and a resting place on the deck of an old building, and a trough for horses. At the water tower, a trail to Harris Canyon merges with other trails.

Most travelers turn around at the Harris Ranch, because the trail beyond it is more remote. Washouts from the floods of 1995, 1996, and New Year's Eve 2005 have been repaired with bridges covered by heavy gravel. Most of these are beyond mile 11.

If you continue, you'll find another old boxcar at mile 16, still sporting its original stove. You are also likely to see clusters of whitewater rafters. To allow rafters a quieter float, powerboats are allowed on the river only on alternating weekends during the summer, though they can travel the river during all weekdays.

Washouts make the trail impassable beyond mile 18.5. When you're ready, turn around and return the way you came.

35 UMATILLA COUNTY LEWIS AND CLARK COMMEMORATIVE TRAIL (SECTION 1 THROUGH HAT ROCK STATE PARK)

Umatilla, Oregon, is a rural desert community at the southern tip of the Interstate 82 bridge across the Columbia River. It connects the Yakima Valley wine country of Washington to Oregon. The historic trail begins and ends at riverside parks.

Activities:

Location: Umatilla County, 3 miles from the town of Umatilla

Length: 7.6 miles

Surface: Gravel

Wheelchair access: The trail is not wheelchair accessible.

Difficulty: Easy to difficult. Most of the trail is easy; its middle section has some hills.

Food: You'll find convenience stores and a cafe at Hat Rock State Park; there are mini marts 1.1 miles west of McNary Beach Park. The town of Umatilla is 3 miles from McNary Beach Park.

Restrooms: There are flush toilets and drinking water at McNary Beach Park, Hat Rock State Park, and Warehouse Beach Recreation Area from May through September; a chemical toilet is available year-round at McNary.

Seasons: The trail can be used year-round.

Access and parking: To begin at the western trailhead, drive 3 miles east of Umatilla on U.S. Highway 730 to the MCNARY PARK sign. Turn left (north) onto Port of Umatilla Road and drive 1 mile to the McNary Beach Park Recreation Area entrance.

The entrance to Hat Rock State Park is 8.2 miles east of Umatilla on US 730. The eastern starting point is at Warehouse Beach Recreation Area. This is the primary staging area for equestrians, accessed by turning north off US 730, 1 mile east of Hat Rock State Park; follow the Warehouse Beach signs.

Rentals: No rentals are available along this trail.

Contact:

· McNary Dam Natural Resources, (541) 922–2268, www.nww.usace.army
  .mil/corpsoutdoors/

· Hat Rock State Park, (541) 567–5032 or 567–4188

Bus routes: None

|||||||||||||||||||||||||||||||||||||||||||||||||||||||||||||||||||||||||||||||||

S ection One of the Umatilla County Lewis and Clark Commemorative
Trail is a nonmotorized diverse-use trail. The Commemorative Trail in-
cludes a total of four sections, with equestrian access on Sections One and
Four.

This trail description covers the area from McNary Beach Recreation
Area Park east through Hat Rock State Park, ending at the trailhead at
Warehouse Beach Recreation Area. Previously known as the Lake Wallula
River Hiking Trail–Hat Rock Corridor, it has now been absorbed into a lon-
ger trail system developed to celebrate the Lewis and Clark expedition's
travels through the area more than 200 years ago.

Located along the Columbia River in the Oregon desert, the rugged
terrain is stunningly beautiful in its simplicity. Ride or walk this trail on
a sunny day—and most days here are sunny—and you'll know you're in
heaven. The trail is hot and unshaded, so bring water, serious sunscreen,
and a hat.

McNary Beach, on the western end of Section One, lies adjacent to
the dam that in 1953 flooded miles of Oregon-Washington Railroad and
Navigation Company (OWR&N) line and several towns upriver. The McNary
Dam was built to produce hydroelectric power and to relieve the problems of navigating the Columbia. Inland waterways were critical to trade,
and the Umatilla rapids caused more grief and delay to barge lines than
any other obstacle on the Columbia River. The dam flooded the main-line
railroad from Cold Springs to Attalia and Wallula. The 35-mile backflow,
along the Yakima line to the Kalan Bridge, was called Lake Wallula.

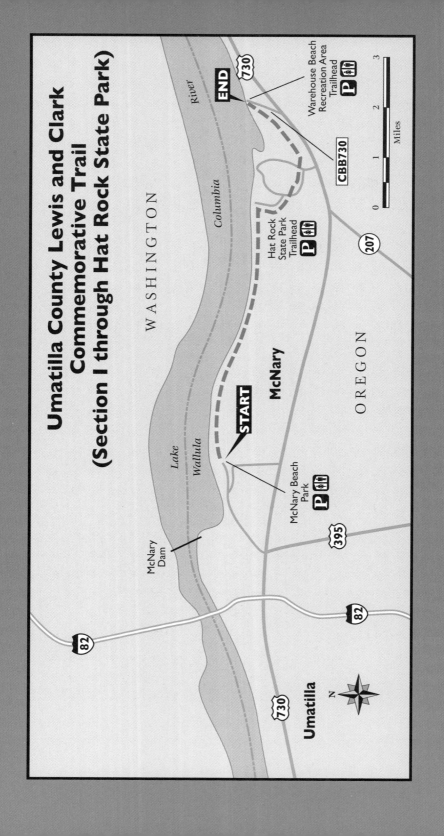

Umatilla County Lewis and Clark Commemorative Trail (Section I through Hat Rock State Park)

WASHINGTON

OREGON

Columbia

River

Lake

Wallula

McNary Dam

McNary

Umatilla

END

730

CBB730

Warehouse Beach Recreation Area Trailhead

P

207

Hat Rock State Park Trailhead

P

START

McNary Beach Park

P

395

82

82

730

N

Miles

0   1   2   3

Hat Rock looms over the trail.

Following dam construction, the towns and railyards were moved to their new location and the railroad rebuilt. This boosted the success of the OWR&N, an operating segment of the Union Pacific Railroad. Though the waterways could now compete with the rails, government funding allowed the railroad to improve the tracks that had been so hastily blasted through basalt cliffs in 1880. Sharp curves, rockfall, and avalanches had for decades caused delays and derailments, shoving engines over the banks and into the river.

The last steam-powered train ran these tracks in 1955. Now you can walk 7.6 miles of the route beside the chunk of history that lies under Lake Wallula.

The paved access to the trail starts to the left off the McNary Beach park road before you reach the parking lot. It quickly becomes dirt and gravel as it cuts into the basalt cliffs and through the sagebrush.

The grassy riverfront at McNary Beach Park has a fishing dock and picnic tables. Look for the trail at the east end of the parking lot. The first mile is easy. Then the trail climbs up onto a steeper riverbank with great views. Choose the uphill fork where a side trail heads down to a pump plant. The path seems to end at a washout 2 miles down the trail; however, it was improved in 2005 and is passable. Still, use caution. If you find it too risky, explore the east end of the trail from Hat Rock State Park to Warehouse Beach Recreation Area, a 2-mile stretch.

As you approach Hat Rock State Park from the west, the trail becomes relatively flat. The view becomes more interesting, as homes, inlets, and rock formations appear. The scenery changes as the land creeps into the river and the basalt cliffs change shape. The river is wide and blue, the sagebrush a faded yellow. Boats cruise by and locals walk their dogs and themselves down the trail. Listen for the metallic rustle of the cheatgrass and bunchgrass in the wind.

Arriving at Hat Rock State Park is like entering the Emerald City. The desert browns and yellows turn into bright green. Everything takes on color and texture and life. Green grass, green willow trees, and flowers encircle the pond, where ducks and geese create ripples as they fetch gifts of food. Anglers wait on the banks of the inlet and pond for steelhead, bass, or catfish. A little bridge across the inlet leads you to the open desert trails. The Hat Rock towers above the park looking like . . . you guessed it, a huge hat.

Nearby Attractions

- **Pacific Salmon Visitors Information Center, (541) 922–4388**

- **The town of McNary, (541) 922–3211**

- **Umatilla Marina Park, (541) 567–5032**

- **McNary Wildlife Nature Area, (541) 922–3211**

The donors of the parkland, the Jewett family, maintain this lovely park and pond and the trails out of appreciation for its special beauty.

Continue through Hat Rock State Park on the trail until it rejoins the river's shoreline. Hat Rock was a land feature sighted by Lewis and Clark and recorded in personal journals written during their expedition. Travelers today can pass the rock and follow the old railroad bed for 2 miles to Warehouse Beach Recreation Area, a day-use area with restrooms, picnic shelters, and a swimming beach. This is the primary access point for equestrians as well as mountain bikers and hikers. Future plans include a trail between Warehouse Beach and Sand Station Recreation Area, 2 miles east.

To experience other sections of the Commemorative Trail, head west from the western side of Section One. The trail drops down to the McNary Lock and Dam, passes by the McNary Wildlife Nature Area, enters the city of Umatilla for 3.5 miles, and then returns to the Columbia River. Contact McNary Dam Natural Resources or Hat Rock State Park for current information on the trail west of McNary Beach Park.

36 OC&E–WOODS LINE STATE TRAIL

Explore the 94-mile OC&E–Woods Line State Trail for its solitude and panoramic views. Walkers, joggers, cyclists, equestrians, skateboarders, and other nonmotorized travelers have one thing in common on this great pathway—they're all welcome!

Activities:

Location: OC&E Main Line: Klamath Falls to Bly, in Klamath County. Woods Line: Beatty to the Sycan Marsh, in Klamath County.

Length: 94 miles (63 miles on the OC&E Main Line Trail; 31 miles on the Woods Line Trail)

Surface: The trail is paved for 7 miles out of Klamath Falls. On the remainder of the trail, all the heavy ballast has been graded off and compacted with a vibrating roller to create a smooth surface.

Wheelchair access: Only the paved section is wheelchair accessible.

Difficulty: Easy to moderate

Food: Klamath Falls has all services. There are convenience stores in Olene, Dairy, Sprague River, Beatty, and Bly; cafes in Dairy, Sprague River, Beatty, and Bly.

Restrooms: There are restrooms at the Wiard Junction Trailhead, the Route 39 Trailhead, Switchback Trailhead, and Horse Glade Trailhead.

Seasons: The trail can be used year-round. The paved section is plowed in the winter to clear the trail for bicycling; however, the trailheads are not plowed.

Access and parking:

- Oregon Highway 140 (four trailheads): Four trailheads off OR 140 access the paved section of the OC&E portion of the trail. Reach Klamath Falls from Interstate 97 or Oregon Highway 39 to OR 140. For the Main Trailhead (formerly called Crosby Trailhead), drive 0.25 mile east of Washburn Way on Crosby Avenue. Turn left between the self-storage facility and Circle DE Lumber. To enter at the Wiard Junction Trailhead, go 1.5 miles east of Washburn Way on South Sixth Street. Turn right on Hope Street, go 0.4 mile, and turn left into the trailhead. For the Route 39 Trailhead, go 0.4 mile south of South Sixth Street. The trailhead is on the right. A fourth trailhead, Pine Grove, is the last trailhead on the paved section of the trail. It is accessed from Klamath Falls by starting from the intersection of OR 140 and South Sixth Street. Head east 1.6 miles on OR 140 to Reeder Road. Turn right on Reeder Road and go 0.58 mile south. Parking is on the left.

- Egert Road Trailhead: Go to the Hildebrand old town site area, located 1.27 miles east of Dairy on OR 140E. Turn left onto Hildebrand Road and travel 3.64 miles. Turn left on Egret Road and follow for 1.5 miles until the pavement ends. The trailhead is on the left.

- Switchback Trailhead: From Klamath Falls, take OR 140 eastward to Dairy (14 miles). Continue 3 miles past Dairy to Yonna Valley Store. Turn left onto Bliss Road. Approximately 12 miles up Bliss Road, turn left onto Forest Road 22 (Switchback Road). Park when you turn onto FR 22. This is the trailhead to use for cross-country skiing.

- Bly Mill Trailhead: Take OR 140 east from the intersection of OR 140 and South Sixth Street. Travel approximately 35 miles to Beatty. From Beatty, continue 12 miles to a small stone block building located on the left. The trailhead entrance is on the left just past the building.

- Sycan Shops Trailhead: This trailhead lies at the intersection of the OC&E Trail and the Woods Line Trail. Take OR 140 east to Beatty. For Sycan Shops, turn left on Godowa Springs Road. After 2.1 miles, turn right on Sycan Road. Turn right when the paved road turns to dirt. Park at the big yellow railroad snowplow.

- Horse Glade Trailhead: Take OR 140 east from Beatty for 15 miles to Ivory Pine Road. Turn north and drive 12.5 miles. Turn left onto Forest Road 27 toward Thompson Reservoir and continue 1.3 miles.

- Forest Road 3207 Trailhead: This is the last trailhead on the trail, and it places you at the north terminus. Continue 9.7 miles farther on FR 27, then turn right onto FR 3207. Continue for 5 miles until the trail crosses the road. Park on the left along the railbed.

Rentals: Yankee Peddler Bicycles, 2616 Altamont Drive, Klamath Falls, (541) 850–2453

Contact:

- Collier Memorial State Park, (541) 783–2471, www.oregonstateparks .org/park_230.php

- Klamath Rails-to-Trails Group, (541) 884–3050, www.klamath-trails.org

Bus routes: None

||||||||||||||||||||||||||||||||||||||||||||||||||||||||||||||||||||||||||||||||||

At the turn of the twentieth century, railroads were leading the growth of the West. Robert Strahorn had a dream of connecting central and eastern Oregon with rail lines by linking Klamath Falls to Lakeview via Sprague River, and Bend and Burns via Sprague River and Silver Lake. The first step in this grand plan was the OC&E, also known as the Klamath Municipal Railway. Groundbreaking occurred near Third Street and Klamath Avenue in Klamath Falls on July 3, 1917.

Quickly a ribbon of steel stretched out toward Sprague River. Soon mills and branch lines sprang up along this new railway. The line was declared open on September 16, 1923. In 1927 the line was extended to Bly, but that would be the end of the line for Strahorn's dream.

Southern Pacific and Great Northern (later Burlington Northern) jointly operated the OC&E from 1925 until 1974. One railroad would manage the line for five years, then pass responsibility to the other for five years. Weyerhauser took over the entire line in 1974, but by the end of the 1980s, the line was no longer a cost-effective way to move logs. The line was railbanked and handed over to Oregon Parks and Recreation in 1992.

The trail is actually two trails—the original OC&E, and the old Weyerhauser Woods Line that heads from Beatty to just north of the Sycan Marsh. The Woods Line heads uphill from south to north and is forested with

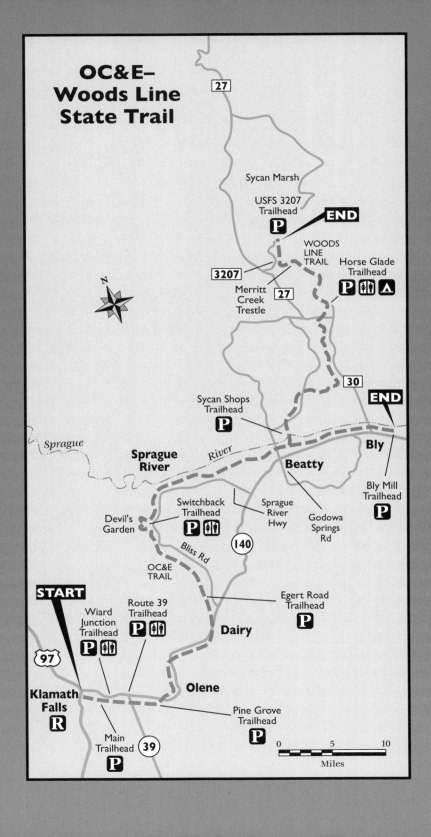

OC&E–
Woods Line
State Trail

sagebrush meadows. On the main-line trail, you'll travel through ranchland and desert, with one hilly section. Future plans are to upgrade the trail surface and add 0.5 mile of paving on the western end of the trail.

If you're a cross-country ski enthusiast, snow can be found in the switchback area and on miles 10 through 30.5 of the Woods Line, though trailheads are not cleared of snow for parking.

OC&E Main Line Trail, 63 miles

The first 7 miles of the OC&E Trail are paved, starting at Washburn Way in Klamath Falls and ending at Olene. Pass by local shopping areas and through residential neighborhoods. This section receives the most use, but there's much more to explore as the trail heads east.

The trail passes through agricultural areas with wonderful views of surrounding mountains, including Mount Shasta to the south. The trail crosses OR 140 and pushes on through juniper and sagebrush to the town of Olene and then the Poe Valley. To your right spreads a panoramic view of the Poe Valley and the Lost River.

The trail continues on to Swede's Cut, the spot where Swedish workers carved a pass through solid rock to gain access to Pine Flat. The job required great skill at using drills and black powder and more than a bit of bravado.

Emerge from Pine Flat at the town of Dairy at mile 18. To visit the small tavern, cafe, or convenience store in town, continue to the Dairy Siding just east of town. Bear right. Continue to the T-intersection with OR 140 and turn right; Dairy is 0.8 mile away. This is your last chance for food or water until the town of Sprague River at mile 35. The valleys around Dairy and Bonanza saw violent conflicts between Native Americans and settlers during the Modoc Indian War in 1872.

The trail heads north from Dairy to skirt around Bly Mountain via Switchback Hill. Just past Hildebrand the forested trail gains 600 feet in 9 miles at a 2 percent grade. Climb up Switchback Hill on a large horseshoe turn, so sharp that the end of the train saw the lead cars passing directly above. The switchback allowed the heavy trains laden with timber

The Merritt Creek Trestle. (Courtesy Art Sevigny)

and some cattle to make the 600-foot climb. Passengers rode the line only in the 1920s. The tracks zigzag over the steep hillside, forming a double switchback. There were once plans to cut a tunnel through Bly Mountain to replace the switchbacks, but they never materialized.

From the top, look to the southeast for a great view of the Devil's Garden. Take a 7-mile (round trip) side trip to this extinct volcano on old logging roads.

The trail descends to the river and the town of Sprague River at mile 38.5. Here in the Sprague River Valley, you'll find country stores and small cafes, vistas of surrounding mountains, forests, and ranches. Your next stop is Beatty, at mile 51.5. To reach this town, take Godowa Springs Road about a mile south to OR 140.

Just east of Beatty, the Woods Line branches north. To continue on the main trail, head east through pastures of grazing cattle and marshy and open-water areas. Sandhill cranes, eagles, red-tailed hawks, egrets, great blue herons, ducks and geese, swarms of red-winged blackbirds, beavers, deer, and other wildlife can be seen along the Sprague River. The trail ends in Bly near the South Fork of the Sprague River and just southwest of the Gearhart Wilderness Area (America's least used wilderness), at mile 63.25.

Woods Line Trail, 31 miles

To take the Woods Line Trail, head northeast from Beatty on a steady uphill climb. The trail crosses over the Sprague River and passes by the Sycan Shops (former maintenance yard for the Woods Line). Keep an eye out for an old tipple hidden in the woods. The trestle at mile 9 was abandoned once the ravine was filled in. At mile 10 you'll reach Five-Mile Creek and trout fishing; for the next 6 miles, this creek will be your companion. Arrive at Horse Glade Trailhead at mile 19. Here you'll find a restroom and camping. Pass through second-growth forest; at mile 27 you'll cross the most spectacular structure on the trail: the Merritt Creek Trestle, which spans 400 feet and rises 50 feet above the ground.

At present the trail ends at about 5 miles to the north at the Sycan Marsh. For a one-way shuttle trip that's all downhill, park one car at one of the northern trailheads and another at Sycan Shops.

Five-Mile Creek. (Courtesy Art Sevigny)

More Rail Trails

N MALHEUR RAIL TRAIL

The Malheur National Forest sits in the Blue Mountains of eastern Oregon. It's hot in summer and snowy in winter. The Malheur Rail Trail is a somewhat rugged trail that travels through a draw. The Forest Service has rated it difficult due to its surface; its grade is mostly moderate.

Activities:

Location: Malheur National Forest, John Day, Grant County

Length: 17.2 miles out and back

Surface: Gravel

Wheelchair access: The trail is not wheelchair accessible.

Difficulty: Difficult

Food: No food is available along this trail.

Restrooms: There are restrooms and drinking water at the trailhead at Big Creek Campground on Forest Road 815.

Seasons: The trail can be used year-round. It serves as a groomed snow-mobile trail from December to April.

Access and parking: From Prairie City, take County Road 62 for 19 miles to Summit Prairie. From here, travel west on Forest Road 16 for approximately 6 miles. Turn right on Forest Road 815. Travel 1 mile to Big Creek Campground, where the trailhead starts.

Rentals: No rentals are available along this trail.

Contact: U.S. Forest Service, Prairie City Ranger District, (541) 820–3800, www.fs.fed.us/r6/malheur/index/shtml

Bus routes: None

MILL CITY TRAIL

The trail begins on a refurbished railroad bridge that crosses the salmon-filled pool created by Mill City Falls. It parallels the river for a while and offers several scenic points.

Activities:

Location: Mill City, Linn County

Length: 1.5 miles

Surface: Asphalt

Wheelchair access: The trail is wheelchair accessible.

Difficulty: Easy

Food: There are restaurants near the start of the trail in Mill City.

Restrooms: There are no restrooms along the trail.

Seasons: The trail can be used year-round.

Access and parking: Go east on Oregon Highway 22 to Mill City. Turn right onto Northeast Second Avenue, then turn left at the T-intersection with Wall Street to reach the Sennium River. You'll see the railroad bridge on your right beyond the parking area. Park and cross the street to the river.

Rentals: No rentals are available along this trail.

Contact: City of Mill City, (503) 897–2302

Bus routes: Take the Canyon Connector Route through the CARTS (Chemeketa Area Regional Transportation System), (800) 422–7723.

P OREGON ELECTRIC ROW TRAIL AND LINEAR PARK

This short trail connects two parks in a rural section of Beaverton. It's part of a master plan to link Beaverton's 55 square miles of parks with a pedestrian and recreation path.

Activities:

Location: Beaverton, Washington County

Length: 1 mile

Surface: Asphalt

Wheelchair access: The entire trail is wheelchair accessible.

Difficulty: Easy

Food: Near the trailhead across the street from Garden Home Recreation Center

Restrooms: There is a portable toilet at Garden Home Recreation Center.

Seasons: The trail can be used year-round.

Access and parking: Take Sunset Highway (U.S. Highway 26) west to Oregon Highway 217. Turn south, drive to Allen Boulevard, then turn east and cross over Scholls Ferry Road. Turn south on 92nd Avenue. Follow 92nd until it turns into Garden Home Road. Follow this road 1 mile to Oleson Road; turn left into Garden Home Recreation Center. Park at the north end of the parking lot.

Rentals: No rentals are available along this trail.

Contact: Tualatin Hills Park and Recreation Department, (503) 645–6433

Bus routes: Information at www.trimet.org, or call (503) 238–RIDE

Q SUMPTER VALLEY RAILROAD INTERPRETIVE TRAIL

This interpretive trail marks the highest point of the Sumpter Valley Railway: 5,277 feet. It overlooks switchbacks into the John Day Valley. Learn about the historic railway and why the route was abandoned.

Activities:

Location: Malheur National Forest, John Day, Grant County

Length: 0.25 mile

Surface: Asphalt

Wheelchair access: The entire trail is wheelchair accessible, but watch areas with steep terrain.

Difficulty: Moderate

Food: No food is available along this trail.

Restrooms: There are no restrooms along the trail.

Seasons: While the trail can be used year-round, the lot adjacent to the highway isn't plowed; expect snow from November through April.

Access and parking: From Prairie City, take U.S. Highway 26 east for 8 miles. The trail is located before Dixie Summit on the right.

Rentals: No rentals are available along this trail.

Contact: Malheur National Forest, (541) 820–3863, www.fs.fed.us/r6/malheur/index/shtml

Bus routes: None

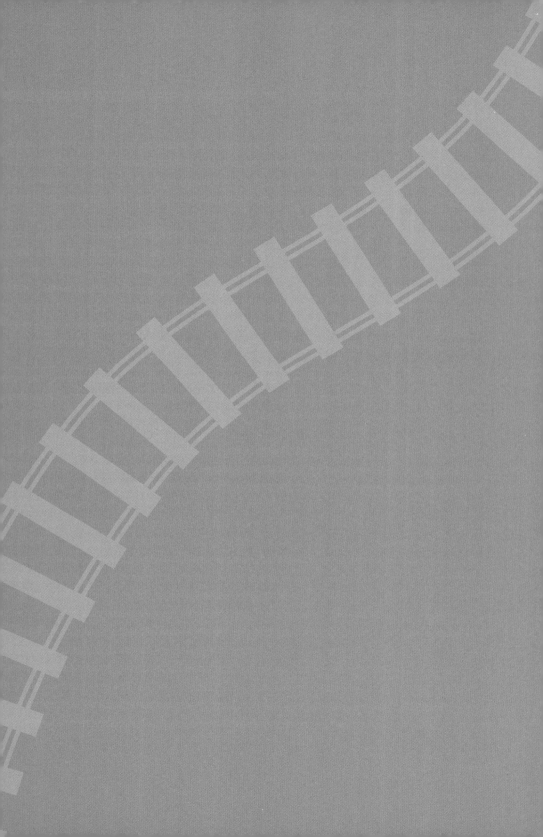

Rail Trails
IDAHO

OVERVIEW

Rail trails in Idaho are constantly emerging as part of a statewide and regional effort to expand and interconnect trails. Current trails are on, or near, past railroad main lines and spurs that carried timber, silver, copper, gold, grains, fruits, and passengers through the region.

Northern Idaho rail trails go into rural timber and mining towns, through remote forests, and along clean rivers and lakes. In southern Idaho, rail trails run past rural farms, basalt rock canyons, forested passages, and through park-studded greenbelts along creeks and rivers.

If you're looking for long, nonmotorized, paved rail trails, head to northern Idaho. The Trail of the Coeur d'Alenes runs for 72 smooth miles, while the North Idaho Centennial Trail boasts 23 miles. For a ride through timbered wilderness on a compacted gravel rail trail that heads downhill through tunnels and across trestles, try the Route of the Hiawatha, also in northern Idaho.

Spring is an ideal time to visit rail trails in Latah County in northern Idaho. Shamrock green grain fields glisten in the sunshine, meadowlarks chirp, and a cool breeze blows. Three paved trails, each unique in its own way, are within a short drive of Moscow. The Ed Corkill Memorial River Trail runs from Juliaetta to Kendrick and is a stroll through railroad history in rural towns, while the Latah Trail from Troy to Moscow is a rigorous rolling pathway through forest and farms. The latter connects directly with the Idaho section of the Bill Chipman Palouse Trail, which starts at the University of Idaho campus in Moscow and runs to Pullman, Washington, featuring detailed interpretive signs on railroad tidbits and local history.

In the southern part of the state, the short Crown Point Trail attracts winter sports enthusiasts. For the longest rail trail in the state, visit the Weiser River Trail, which runs for 85.7 miles. Urban trails in southern Idaho with nearby attractions and amenities include the Boise River Greenbelt, the Nampa Rails Trails, and the Indian Creek Greenbelt. Or travel on the Wood River Trail, where the railroad helped to build the famous Sun Valley Resort.

Wherever you travel in Idaho, enjoy the diversity that the state's rail trails offer.

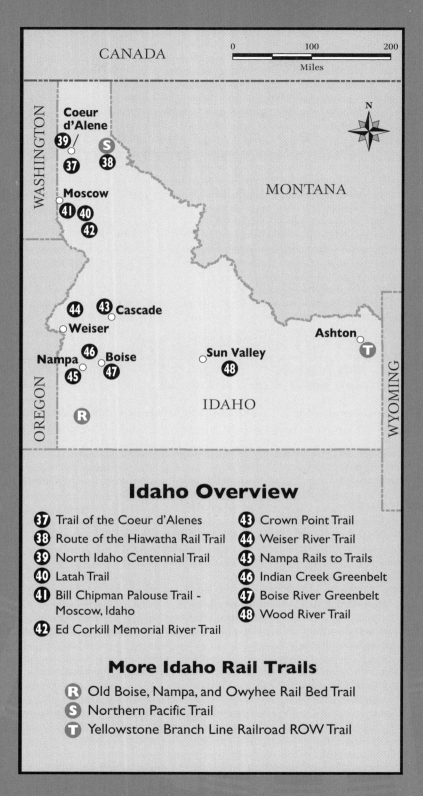

CANADA

0   100   200
Miles

WASHINGTON

Coeur
d'Alene
39
37   **38**   **S**

Moscow
41 **40**
42

MONTANA

44   **43** Cascade
Weiser

Nampa   **46** Boise
45   **47**

Sun Valley
48

Ashton
T

WYOMING

IDAHO

OREGON

R

Idaho Overview

37 Trail of the Coeur d'Alenes

38 Route of the Hiawatha Rail Trail

39 North Idaho Centennial Trail

40 Latah Trail

41 Bill Chipman Palouse Trail -
Moscow, Idaho

42 Ed Corkill Memorial River Trail

43 Crown Point Trail

44 Weiser River Trail

45 Nampa Rails to Trails

46 Indian Creek Greenbelt

47 Boise River Greenbelt

48 Wood River Trail

More Idaho Rail Trails

R Old Boise, Nampa, and Owyhee Rail Bed Trail

S Northern Pacific Trail

T Yellowstone Branch Line Railroad ROW Trail

Idaho's
Top Trail Trails

37 TRAIL OF THE COEUR D'ALENES

If you're looking for the longest paved trail in the country, visit the Trail of the Coeur d'Alenes, located in the northern panhandle of Idaho. It runs for 72 smooth, flat miles, offering a diverse mixture of timber and mining towns against a backdrop of wetlands, rivers, lakes, and mountains. Toss in wildlife viewing and food stops. The result is an endless opportunity for admiring the region's lush scenery and rail history.

Activities:

Location: Coeur d'Alene tribal lands, the towns of Plummer, Harrison, Enaville, Pinehurst, Kellogg, Osburn, Wallace, and Mullan, in the counties of Benewah, Kootenai, and Shoshone

Length: 72 miles

Surface: Asphalt

Wheelchair access: The entire trail is wheelchair accessible.

Difficulty: Easy, with a moderate uphill grade heading into Plummer

Food: Restaurants are located in the small towns along the trail, such as the Snake Pit Bar and Restaurant in Enaville.

Restrooms: Public facilities are available at numerous trailheads and along remote sections of the trail at rest stop waysides. Trailhead restrooms include Plummer, Chatcolet, Harrison, Springston, Medimont, Bull Run Lake, Cataldo, Enaville, Smelterville, and Mullan.

Seasons: The trail can be used year-round. Snow is often on the northern reaches between November and May.

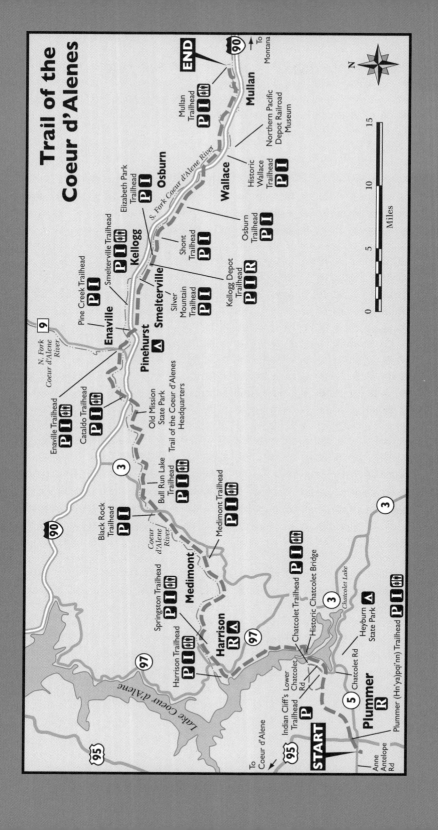

Trail of the Coeur d'Alenes

Access and parking: There are nineteen trailheads with parking and, in some cases, restrooms. Here are the easily accessible trailheads:

- Plummer Trailhead: The western terminus, also called Hn'ya)pqi'nn (The Gathering Place), is reached by taking U.S. Highway 95 north from Moscow, or south from the town of Coeur d'Alene. Turn west onto Anne Antelope Road and then immediately left into the well-marked, large parking lot on the west side of the highway on the north side of the town of Plummer. Pick up the trail just beyond the kiosk and restrooms.

- Indian Cliffs Trailhead: Access by taking Idaho Highway 5 east from the town of Plummer. Drive about 5 miles and turn left into Heyburn State Park on Chatcolet Road. Go 1.2 miles and turn left to the Indian Cliffs Trailhead, which also says NATURE TRAIL. A $4 per vehicle day-use fee is required.

- Chatcolet Trailhead: Continue past Indian Cliffs Trailhead for 0.8 mile to the V in the road. Take the right onto Chatcolet Lower Road and go 0.4 mile into the Chatcolet Trailhead parking lot on the right. A $4 per vehicle day-use fee is required.

- Harrison Trailhead: Take Idaho Highway 97 south from Coeur d'Alene, or ID 97 north from its junction with Idaho Highway 3, to the town of Harrison. Turn west off ID 97 into Harrison on Harrison Street. Go 1 block to Lakefront Avenue. Turn left on Lakefront Avenue, then immediately right into the small trailhead parking area next to One Shot Charlies. Walk or bike downhill 1 block to the official trailhead next to the city beach.

- Medimont Trailhead: Follow ID 3 north from the junction of ID 97 and ID 3. After 9.3 miles, turn left off ID 3 and follow the road for about a mile to the trailhead.

- Black Rock Trailhead: Travel 15.6 miles north on ID 3 from the junction of ID 97 and ID 3. Turn left to the trailhead parking area.

- Bull Run Lake Trailhead: Drive 18.7 miles north on ID 3 from the junction of ID 97 and ID 3. Turn right and go less than 0.25 mile to the trailhead.

- Cataldo Trailhead: ID 3 North arrives at Interstate 90 at 21.9 miles from the junction of ID 97 and ID 3. Take I-90 east for 6.1 miles to exit 40, turn right off the exit toward Cataldo, and go 0.7 mile to the trailhead.

- Enaville Trailhead: Head east on I-90 from Cataldo. After 2.3 miles, take exit 43 (Kingston). Turn left off the ramp and drive north on Forest Road 9 for 1.8 miles through Kingston and on to Enaville. Park in Enaville at the trailside dirt lot on the left off FR 9.

- Pine Creek Trailhead: Travel I-90 east. Take exit 45 at Pinehurst, turning left off the ramp. Drive 0.3 mile and turn left into the paved trailhead lot.

- Smelterville Trailhead: Drive I-90 east from Pinehurst, then take exit 48 into Smelterville, turning right off the exit. In less than 0.1 mile, turn left, then immediately right into the trailhead parking area.

- Silver Mountain Trailhead: Continue east on I-90 to exit 49. Turn right off the exit ramp onto Bunker Avenue, then after 0.4 mile turn right to the trailhead, parking at the Silver Mountain parking lot. Pick up the trail on the south side of the lot, though you may see signs saying SILVER VALLEY TRAIL ROUTE and KELLOGG GREENBELT.

- Kellogg Depot Trailhead: Take exit 51, the Kellogg exit, off I-90. Turn right off the exit onto Division Street. Go about 0.1 mile and turn right onto Railroad Avenue, then left into the parking area next to Excelsior Cycle, which is near the Kellogg Depot Trailhead. Pick up the trail just off the parking lot. Or, after turning right off the exit onto Division Street, turn left off Division Street onto Station Avenue, then left again into the east- or west-side parking lot of the Passenger Depot Building, which serves as the Historic Silver Valley Chamber of Commerce. Pick up the trail on the north end of the parking lot.

- Shont Trailhead: Use exit 54 off I-90. Turn right off the exit and drive less than 0.1 mile, turning left into the trailhead parking area.

- Osburn Trailhead: Take I-90 to exit 57. Turn right off the ramp, then left at the stop sign onto Canyon Avenue. Drive 0.1 mile toward Osburn. Turn left on Mullan Avenue, then right on South Sixth Street. Cross the trail and turn right and into the trailhead parking area.

- Historic Wallace Sixth Street Trailhead: Take the second Wallace exit, number 62, off I–90. Turn left off the ramp at the stop sign onto Canyon Avenue. Canyon Avenue shortly turns into Bank Street. At 0.3 mile after turning from the stop sign onto Canyon Avenue, turn right on Sixth Street. Go past the Northern Pacific Depot Railroad Museum on the right. Continue under the interstate overpass for 0.1 mile to the trailhead. Parking is on the right.

- Mullan Trailhead: Take exit 68 off I–90. The off-ramp becomes River Street and practically puts you at the trailhead. Travel on River Street, driving toward the town of Mullan, which is visible from the exit. Take a left off River Street onto Second Street, then turn left immediately into the trail's eastern terminus parking lot.

Rentals: For bicycle rentals in Plummer, try Great Cycles Touring Company, 643 C Street, (208) 686–1568. In Harrison, try Pedal Pushers Bike Rental & Repair, 101 North Coeur d'Alene Avenue, (208) 689–3436, www .bikenorthidaho.com. In Kellogg, try Excelsior Cycle, 21 Railroad Avenue, (208) 786–3751. Near the eastern terminus off I–90 at exit 0, try Lookout Pass Ski and Recreation Area, (208) 744–1301, www.skilookout.com.

Contact: For trail information on the Plummer to Harrison section, contact the Coeur d'Alene Tribe Natural Resources Division, (208) 686–7045, www .cdatribe-nsn.gov. For information on the Harrison to Mullan section contact trail headquarters at Old Mission State Park, (208) 682–3814, www .parksandrecreation.idaho.gov.

For other trails in the region, visit the Friends of the Coeur d'Alene Trails Web site, friendsofcdatrails.org. For information about the Cataldo to Mullan area, contact Historic Silver Valley Chamber of Commerce, (208) 784–0821, www.historicsilvervalleychamberofcommerce.com.

For shuttles, contact Pedal Pushers Bike Rental & Repair, (208) 689–3436 or Silver Valley Transportation, (208) 682–3550.

Bus routes: City Link runs a free bus service between Coeur d'Alene and Plummer; call (877) 941–RIDE, or visit www.idahocitylink.com. For reaching the eastern portion of the trail, try North Idaho Public Transportation, (866) 440–RIDE.

||||||||||||||||||||||||||||||||||||||||||||||||||||||||||||||||||||||||||||||||||||||||||||||||

Traveling the trail from the western starting point in the town of Plummer to the eastern terminus in rural Mullan near the Idaho/Montana border is an adventure not to be missed. You will travel on the original rail route for much of the trip. You can also camp at one of the many campgrounds near the trail.

Along the way you travel beside vacation homes, lakes, streams, rivers, wetlands, interstate highways, mining towns, and timber towns. Frequent interpretive signs along the trail keep visitors informed about nature, history, and nearby attractions. Colorful wildflowers grace the trail in the spring and summer, while deciduous trees show their many colors during the autumn against the deep green backdrop of the coniferous trees. En route it is common to spot moose, deer, ospreys, bald eagles, and other wildlife.

Winds usually move up the rivers and valleys by midday and calm down in the evenings. Some days they reach a speed of 10 to 15 miles per hour. Bicyclists may want to factor winds into their departure time and their direction of travel.

Taking the trail from the east to the west, starting at the eastern terminus in Mullan and heading to Plummer, gives one a sensation of gradually descending downhill. Along the trail, waterfalls and creeks flow into the south fork of the Coeur d'Alene River, then into the main stem of the river, which passes through the lake district and finally into Coeur d'Alene Lake. The route crosses over thirty-six bridges and trestles.

This long trail is an environmental cleanup effort that has resulted in a smooth, seamless trail. In the late 1880s mining was growing in popularity in the Silver Valley near Kellogg. Rails were constructed to assist the mining and timber industry. Waste rocks and tailings from the mines were used to create the railbed. Unfortunately, they contain high levels of lead and heavy metals that leach into the soil and water sources.

General awareness of contamination hazards from lead increased during the last couple of decades. Cleanup activities in recent years consisted of a joint effort between the Union Pacific Railroad, numerous government agencies, and the Tribe of the Coeur d'Alenes. The rail tracks were removed, asphalt was put down, and gravel barriers were installed to restrain contaminants.

Today recreationists enjoy a smooth-as-silk surface that is the longest paved trail in the United States and guaranteed to stay intact forever. Due to the environmental cleanup resolution, the trail has to be seal-coated every five years and asphalted every twenty to twenty-five years. The most recent seal-coating was completed during the summer of 2007.

Each segment of the trail has its own character. There are nineteen developed trailheads accessing the trail. You could break your trip into sections as small as you desire and do an out-and-back. Or you could increase the distance for a one-way trip by hiring a shuttle from Pedal Pushers Bike Rental & Repair (Harrison) or Silver Valley Transportation (Coeur d'Alene). Bicycle rentals and repair services can be found close to the trailheads in Plummer, Harrison, and Kellogg. Be sure to pick up a free detailed trail map, available at the major trailheads.

Plummer to Harrison, 16 Miles

Water dominates the scenery in this segment. From the trail's start at the Plummer Trailhead to the Harrison Trailhead, the route takes visitors along the Plummer Creek canyon, by Chatcolet Lake, across a 3,100-foot-long bridge trestle, and beside the wide-open Lake Coeur d'Alene.

After leaving the hustle and bustle of the large, paved western trailhead on US 95, called Hn'ya)pqi'nn (The Gathering Place) in the language of the Coeur d'Alene tribe, you will pass by a gravel pit and the backyards of Plummer residents. At about 1 mile from the trailhead, you travel through forested areas along the trail. The trail marker mileage is a bit off at the start of the trail, but it equalizes toward Chatcolet Lake.

Get ready for a roly-poly ride. Ponderosa pines along this section provide food and shelter for local birds like pileated woodpeckers and warblers. Between mile 2 and mile 5, there are two rest stops, one at a rail trestle crossing over Plummer Creek.

At about 5.2 miles the trail enters Heyburn State Park, the oldest park in Idaho. This spot also serves as a trailhead, with limited parking and no

Bicyclists head toward Chatcolet Trailhead on the Trail of the Coeur d'Alenes. (Courtesy Natalie Bartley)

restrooms. For spectacular views of the area, take a quick hike on the dirt Nature Trail and Indian Cliffs Trail just off the paved trail. Horses are allowed on the Indian Cliffs Trail.

Return to the asphalt trail and continue to the larger Chatcolet Trailhead at 7 miles. Vistas open up, and the famous Historic Chatcolet Bridge appears in the distance, as does the marina located at the trailhead. This and the Indian Cliffs Trailhead are the only fee-based parking sites along the trail, requiring a $4 per vehicle day-use payment to the state park. As you travel along Chatcolet Lake toward the trailhead, forested mountains blanket the scenery while ducks bob on the water and ospreys soar above.

Pass the Chatcolet Trailhead and proceed to the long bridge trestle. Mile 8 puts you at the east end of the bridge, where you will pass near lakeside cabins and many interpretive signs. Two more trailside restrooms and picnic sites dot the trail between 8 miles and the Harrison Trailhead at 15.3 miles. O Gara Bay and Shingle Bay lie between the Chatcolet and Harrison Trailheads. Be sure to wear sunscreen. You travel close enough to the lake to be exposed to reflected sunlight as well as the direct rays of the sun.

The Historic Chatcolet Bridge is located on the western segment of the Trail of the Coeur d'Alenes near the Chatcolet Trailhead. (Courtesy Natalie Bartley)

The area you are traveling through was once important for commerce. Mining started in the Silver Valley in the mid-1880s. Lumber, ore, and passengers were transported via boats on the waterways between 1880 and the 1920s. Rail lines started in 1888 to move timber and ore. After the rails arrived, boat use dropped off.

When you enter the Harrison area, you will receive your first exposure (pardon the pun) to information regarding the soil and sediments in this area and beyond. As previously stated, these materials still contain high levels of lead and other heavy metals. Mining activity in prior years produced these by-products. Information signs, starting at the Harrison Trailhead, provide guidance and advice on how to avoid contact with the soil. Children and pregnant women are at higher risk. Basically, do not drink lake, stream, or river water. Refrain from eating plants from the trailside, like those tempting wild berries. Wash your hands before eating, and avoid contact with the soil. Stay on the paved trail and in designated safe areas, such as picnic sites and restroom waysides. These guidelines will apply for the rest of your journey eastward.

That doesn't mean you can't venture into the trailside towns. At the Harrison Trailhead you can tent or RV camp or enjoy a meal at the Gateway Marina. Or go a block into this small town for a meal at any of a number of local restaurants, and an espresso at the Pedal Pushers Bike Rental & Repair.

Harrison to Pine Creek Trailhead at Pinehurst, 33 miles

The water theme continues as the trail leaves the Harrison Trailhead and glides along a glacial valley, past lakes and wetlands, and along the Coeur d'Alene River toward Pinehurst. The trail first heads north, then east, along Anderson Lake, which branches off from Lake Coeur d'Alene. Visitors are now entering the lake region, where a chain of twelve lakes along the Coeur d'Alene River blanket the area in glistening wetness, supporting wildlife in a moist environment. Sightings of deer, otters, beavers, ospreys, nesting eagles, and other wildlife are common to the alert observer, especially during the mornings and evenings.

Backwater Bay Wayside, located west of Enaville at mile marker 45.5, is a scenic rest stop along the Trail of the Coeur d'Alenes. (Courtesy Natalie Bartley)

A trestle crossing on the Trail of the Coeur d'Alenes between Pine Creek Trailhead and Enaville Trailhead. (Courtesy Natalie Bartley)

After leaving the marina, you will pass by Anderson Lake Wayside at 16.6 miles and cross over a rail trestle. Nesting bald eagles are in this area in the spring, as well as osprey nests. The Springston Trailhead appears at 18.4 miles, near the northeast edge of Anderson Lake. Beyond, the Cottonwood picnic site and Gray's Meadow Wayside enhance the next 2 miles with rest stop options. On the way you are enveloped in the vibrant green of the nearby hills, the distant mountains, and the wetlands. Beyond lies a 3.5-mile stretch of trail with the potential for sighting Canada geese, great blue herons, and even moose. After Cave Lake Picnic Spot at 24.2 miles is the Medimont Trailhead on Cave Lake at 25.8 miles.

Continue on the trail toward the next picnic and restroom area at Lane at 29.6 miles. Beyond is Black Rock Trailhead at 31.2 miles, with a parking area and interpretive signs at the Coeur d'Alene River Wildlife Management Area. The Idaho Department of Fish and Game oversees about 5,000 acres in the area. The agency has identified more than 200 bird species and 300-plus species of wildlife on the management area.

Beyond there, the trail passes marshlands. The highway traffic becomes audible as you travel toward the Bull Run Lake Trailhead and restrooms at 33.5 miles. Even the restrooms are educational along the trail. Inside this vault facility, read about the differences between soft and hard pines. After this trailhead users can access picnic areas at 34.9, 36.4, 38.6, and 40.1 miles. Along the way, read about local floods and the river ecosystems that support trout and whitefish.

Be sure to take a break near the Latour Creek picnic area at 40.1 miles and look across the gently flowing Coeur d'Alene River between 40 and 42 miles for a view of the yellow, historic mission building at Old Mission State Park. Built during 1850 to 1853, it is acknowledged as one of the oldest buildings still standing in Idaho. The park houses the trail's headquarters, though it is not accessible from the trail. The Cataldo Trailhead at 42 miles has no services, though I–90 crosses over the trail near this point. There is an RV campground along the trail near 42 miles, accessed off I–90. Plus there are two eateries just off the trail on Latour Creek Drive.

Leave Cataldo, cross the bridge built over the river in 1902, and continue northeast away from I–90. Pass along the river through a forested stretch where you might be able to see muddy animal prints on the trail. Beyond are picnic waysides at Pine Meadows at 43.6 miles, Gap Rock at 44.3 miles, and Backwater Bay at 45.5 miles. Meadows grace the trailside with yellow and white flowers in the spring, while snow-topped mountains tower in the distance, adding color to the scenery along the trail.

After 45.5 miles the trail crosses the river via another bridge trestle, built in 1924. Shortly the trail moves into the outskirts of the small town of Enaville; the Enaville Trailhead is at 47.1 miles. Carefully cross the trail and highway, since this is your first trail encounter with heavy motor vehicle traffic.

If you are hungry, hop off the trail for a bite to eat at the historic Snake Pit Bar and Restaurant in Enaville, off FR 9. They have been in business since 1880. Dine in the rustic timber building or out on the front porch.

Near Enaville, the south fork and the north fork of the Coeur d'Alene River join to form the main stem of the Coeur d'Alene, which you have been following for many miles. Leaving Enaville, head up the south fork of the river toward the Pine Creek Trailhead at Pinehurst at 48.7 miles. Though this paved trailhead does not have a restroom, the town of Pinehurst, a short 0.25 mile away, offers eateries, grocery stores, and a campground, all easily accessed off I–90.

Pine Creek Trailhead at Pinehurst to Mullan, 23 miles

Once the trail departs from Pine Creek Trailhead, the character of the Trail of the Coeur d'Alenes changes dramatically. It morphs from a nature, water-based trail experience to a history-based journey that moves through numerous old timber and mining towns as it travels near, and right beside, busy I–90. This is not to say that it feels urban. Timbered mountains still surround visitors in a deep green cloak of color. While on the trail, the distance between restrooms increases in length, though you can jump off the trail and go into town for restaurants and bathrooms.

Heading east out of the Pine Creek Trailhead at 48.7 miles, you can keep an eye on I–90 as you approach the Smelterville Trailhead at 51.1 miles. Once there, the most convenient drive-through espresso hut sits right beside the trail, at the trailhead parking lot. A latte and a bagel with cream cheese is a perfect way to launch the forthcoming gentle uphill journey from the local elevation at about 2,100 feet to 3,300 feet in Mullan.

Continue through the industrial area along the trail to the Silver Mountain Trailhead at 53.1 miles, where a pub and grill is trailside. This is a busy recreation area year-round. In the winter the ski area is in full swing. You can see the gondola passing overhead. Come summer, mountain recreation pursuits are popular, including hiking and bicycling.

The interstate shifts across the river at Silver Mountain, and the trail picks up along the river. Stay on the trail as it passes through the town of Kellogg and by the Kellogg Depot Trailhead at 53.8 miles. There is a lot of mining history in the area, depicted on the interpretive signs. The best place to learn more about the area is at the Historic Silver Valley Chamber of Commerce visitor center, trailside in Kellogg. Just up the hill the historic district of the town of Kellogg offers stores, eateries, and a hotel.

Silver Valley, in the Coeur d'Alene region, is about 4 miles wide and 20 miles long. For many years this area produced more silver than anywhere else in the world. Mining materials were carried by rails from the mines to Plummer.

The Trail of the Coeur d'Alenes passes through the town of Osburn in the Silver Valley.
(Courtesy Natalie Bartley)

While on this part of the trail, you will find that the Trail of the Coeur d'Alenes signage looks a bit different than elsewhere on the route. The trail is merged here with the Silver Valley Trail Route and Kellogg Greenway. Keep following the trail eastward along the mild whitewater of the south fork of the Coeur d'Alene River as it rushes west toward the lake region.

Elizabeth Park Trailhead is ahead at 55.2 miles. Beyond is a pretty stretch of trail along wooded hillsides near the river, with numerous side creeks contributing water. Milo Creek enters from the south, followed by Big Creek near Shont Trailhead at 57.4 miles. On this segment you pass by forested mountains and abandoned lumber smelters and into small towns that were once active in lumber and mining industries. All are now within easy access to I–90.

Emerging from the forest, the trail enters the fringes of Osburn and the Osburn Trailhead at 60.4 miles. After leaving the outskirts of Osburn, the trail passes under I–90 and follows directly beside the interstate through another industrial area.

The town of Wallace is ahead, with a trailhead at Sixth Street in downtown Wallace at 64.6 miles. Visit the Northern Pacific Depot Railroad

Nearby Attractions

A visit to the following sites will round out your visit to the trail:

- Heyburn State Park, (208) 686–1308, www.parksand recreation.idaho.gov. Located near Plummer at the western terminus, this is a great park to enjoy hiking, camping, boating, and fishing.

- Old Mission State Park, (208) 682–3814, www.parksand recreation.idaho.gov. This is a day-use park of historical significance located off I–90, Cataldo exit 39.

- Northern Pacific Depot Railroad Museum, 219 Sixth Street, (208) 752–0111. Located in the eastern portion of the trail next to the Wallace Trailhead. Enjoy learning about the railroad and mining history of the area.

- Sierra Silver Mine Tour, (208) 752–5151, www.silvermine tour.org. Located in Wallace, this unique mining tour is led by actual miners who demonstrate operating mining equipment, giving the tour a realistic feel.

Museum just off the trail near the trailhead. In Wallace the trail literally travels under I–90 and along the south fork of the Coeur d'Alene River, where local residents can walk on the trail out of the weather during rainy season.

Railroads played an important role in this area by supporting the mining and timber industry. The first railroad built in Coeur d'Alene was the Coeur d'Alene Railroad and Navigation Company, which ran from the Old Mission to Wallace in the late 1880s.

Busting out of town and into the woods again, the trail passes by Restless Rapid Wayside at 65.9 miles, where a restroom is located near a scenic rapid. Golconda Wayside is just ahead at 67.7 miles. You will pass by a restricted area where mining waste cleanup is currently under way. Continue to the eastern terminus at Mullan at 71.4 miles, an old mining town that has a hotel and cafe.

At Mullan you can return the way you came. While in the area, consider visiting the Northern Pacific Trail (Trail S), the Route of the Hiawatha (Trail 38), and the North Idaho Centennial Trail (Trail 39).

Future Plans

There are plans to create a large network of trails by joining existing rail trails. The Trail of the Coeur d'Alenes presently links with the Northern Pacific Trail in Mullan. Ultimately the Northern Pacific Trail will join the Route of the Hiawatha, which will then hook up with the Old Milwaukee Road, and then the Trail of the Coeur d'Alenes near St. Maries.

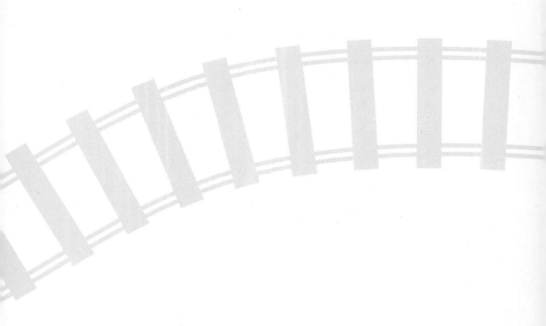

38 ROUTE OF THE HIAWATHA RAIL TRAIL

Opened to the public in 1998, the Route of the Hiawatha Rail Trail offers a spectacular amount of variety. It is famous for its tunnels, achieving the status of having the most rail trail tunnels in the state and the longest tunnel in Idaho (1.8 miles long). Waterfalls, wildlife, seven high rail trestles, and ten tunnels—some in total darkness—await the 23,000 visitors who use the trail each year. There are ten tunnels but visitors can only go through nine of them. Informative interpretive signs enhance the experience by describing local mining, timber, and rail history.

Activities:

Location: Near the towns of Wallace, Mullan, and Avery, in Shoshone County

Length: 14.4 miles

Surface: Compacted gravel

Wheelchair access: Motorized electric wheelchairs are allowed on the trail, with access points at all trailheads

Difficulty: Moderate

Food: At Lookout Pass Ski and Recreation Area

Restrooms: There are restrooms at Lookout Pass Ski and Recreation Area, East Portal Trailhead, the halfway point at Adair, and Pearson Trailhead.

Seasons: The trail is open for bicycling and hiking seven days a week from late May until the first weekend in October, 8:30 a.m. to 6:00 p.m. Opening and closing dates vary depending on snowpack. Peak season is July and August. Snowmobile use dominates the trail during the winter months.

Access and parking: There are two main commonly used access points, the northeast and southwest terminuses. Three other access points are also described. A trail-use fee is charged. You can purchase the passes at the trailheads and at Lookout Pass Ski and Recreation Area.

To access the downhill gradient from the northeast terminus, take Interstate 90 east from Mullan toward Lookout Pass Ski and Recreation Area and into Montana toward Missoula. Take exit 5 (the Taft exit) in Montana. It is 2 miles from the Taft exit on a gravel road. Turn right off the ramp, then drive past large gravel piles. Turn right over a small white bridge onto Rainey Creek Road. Continue to the East Portal Trailhead on the left at the St. Paul Pass (Taft) Tunnel 20. Watch for signs guiding you to the trailhead.

The southwest terminus at the Pearson Trailhead is accessed about 20 miles from Wallace. Travel on I–90 and take exit 62 on the east side of Wallace. Turn onto Bank Street, heading south into the town of Wallace. Take Bank Street to King Street and turn left. King Street becomes Forest Road 456, also called Moon Pass Road. Follow the dirt road past the intersection with Forest Road 326 on the left, also called Loop Creek Road. The Pearson Trailhead is just ahead, located south of the intersection with FR 326, on the east side of FR 456.

Or, to access the Pearson Trailhead from the east end of the town of Avery, drive about 9 miles north on FR 456. The trailhead is on the right just before the intersection with FR 326.

There are two approaches to access the smaller, less-used trailheads at Moss Creek and Roland, located between the East Portal and Pearson Trailheads. From the south, starting at the intersection of FR 456 and FR 326 (the latter of which is also called Loop Creek Road), drive about 3.5 miles on FR 326 to Forest Road 506; turn left. Follow the dirt road for about 1.5 miles to the small parking lot at Moss Creek Trailhead. The next section of road is also the route of the Hiawatha Trail. Follow it for about 2.3 miles to the Roland Trailhead, which is near the west portal of the St. Paul Pass (Taft) Tunnel. From Roland Trailhead, you can access the East Portal Trailhead by continuing on FR 506. It departs from the Hiawatha Trail at the Roland Trailhead. Drive for about 3.5 miles on FR 506, going up and over the St. Paul Tunnel, then turning right to get to the East Portal Trailhead in Montana. Watch for signs indicating the trailhead.

To access the southern trailheads from the East Portal Trailhead, leave the parking lot and turn left onto FR 506. Follow FR 506 for about 3.5 miles and turn left into the Roland Trailhead parking lot. For the three-vehicle parking lot at the Moss Creek Trailhead, continue about 2.3 miles on FR 506 and park on the left. There is additional parking at a third, lesser-used site at Adair, between tunnels 25 and 26. Access Adair by taking FR 326 east from the intersection with FR 506. Go about 3 miles into the parking lot.

Last, for the southwest terminus at the Pearson Trailhead, continue on FR 506 to the intersection with FR 326 and turn right. Continue on FR 326, also called Loop Creek Road, to the intersection with FR 456. Turn left; go about 0.5 mile and turn left. Go 0.25 mile to the Pearson Trailhead.

Rentals: Mountain bikes, headlamps, and helmets can be rented near the northeastern terminus at Lookout Pass Ski and Recreation Area, (208) 744–1301, www.skilookout.com. See Appendix A for additional bicycle rental options in northern Idaho.

Contacts: Lookout Pass Ski and Recreation Area, (208) 744–1301, www.ski lookout.com; U.S. Forest Service, Avery office, (208) 245–4517, www.fs.fed .us/ipnf/rec/activities/biking/hiawatha

Bus routes: Every 1.5 hours a bus carries riders and their bicycles from the Pearson Trailhead to the Roland Trailhead, at the west portal of the St. Paul Pass (Taft) Tunnel. Check on the departure time of the last shuttle, generally between 4:15 p.m. and 5:45 p.m. If you parked your vehicle at the East Portal Trailhead, you will need to ride back through the tunnel to get to your vehicle. Or you can drive your own vehicle to the trailhead of your choice, perhaps riding the trail round-trip instead of one-way. For shuttle information, contact Lookout Pass Ski and Recreation Area, (208) 744–1301, www .skilookout.com.

Travelers come from as far as New Zealand, Australia, and Japan to enjoy this trail. If you want to take the quick, scenic route to the Pearson Trailhead and enjoy the downhill grade, allow two to four hours to complete the route if on a bicycle and a half hour for the shuttle ride back to the Roland Trailhead. For the bicyclist desiring more of a physical challenge or wanting to avoid a shuttle, start at Pearson Trailhead and ride the uphill 2 percent grade to East Portal. Stop to read the interpretive signs along the way and catch your breath. At the trailhead at East Portal, turn around and relax during the downhill ride back to Pearson. You will have completed a 28.8-mile round trip.

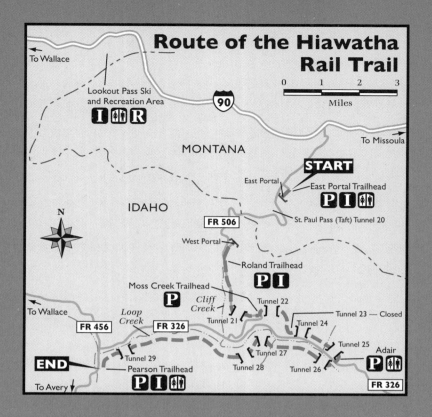

A mountain biker reads an interpretive sign beside the St. Paul Pass (Taft) Tunnel 20 at the West Portal in Idaho. It is the longest tunnel on the trail, at 8,771 feet. (Courtesy Natalie Bartley)

When you buy your trail pass at Lookout Pass Ski and Recreation Area or at a trailhead from a trail marshal, you will get a briefing. It is mandatory that each rider and walker use a quality headlight. Each cyclist must also have a front-mounted bike light. Helmets are mandatory for walkers and bicyclists. You can rent bicycles, helmets, and lights from Lookout Pass Ski and Recreation Area.

The railroad bed that you will be traveling on was originally built between 1906 and 1911. Known as the Pacific extension of the Chicago, Milwaukee & St. Paul Railroad, it ran until it went bankrupt in 1977. It is a section of the abandoned Milwaukee Road, which went from Chicago to Seattle, crossing northern Idaho. Volunteers and government agencies converted the rails to a compacted recreation trail for bicyclists, hikers, and wheelchair users. No pets are allowed on the trail.

Along the length of the route, you pass a variety of plants such as Douglas fir, white pine, maple, white ash, and huckleberries. Wildlife, including mule deer, roam freely on and off the trail. En route, water, bathrooms, and picnic tables are provided for riders' comfort.

Starting at mile 0 at the East Portal Trailhead, you encounter the 1.8-mile-long St. Paul Pass (Taft) Tunnel, which crosses between Montana and Idaho. This cold, wet, and totally dark ride is one of the many highlights on the route. Be sure to have a good headlamp with you, and not just any headlamp. Rent a bright light from the Lookout Pass Ski and Recreation Area if you need one. When you get deeper into this tunnel, all the light disappears, and you rely on your tiny light to see while moving on your bike or walking. The bigger the light, the better you will be able to see. It can be very disorienting in complete darkness. Also, the average temperature in the various tunnels ranges from 34 to 40 degrees Fahrenheit, so you might need an extra layer of clothing, especially for this tunnel. You can tell how fast your bicycling buddies went through the tunnel by the size of the mud splatter on their back—the faster the ride, the bigger the mud splatter.

As you pass through the tunnel, watch for the interpretive sign on the wall indicating the Montana/Idaho border. At the end of the tunnel, you emerge into what seems like the intensely bright light of day. You are now in Idaho and approaching the Roland Trailhead at 1.8 miles. If using the shuttle service, you will start your journey at this trailhead.

Bicyclists exit tunnel 24 and move on to trestle 216 at Small Creek on the Route of the Hiawatha. (Courtesy Natalie Bartley)

Along the route you will encounter many interpretive signs describing the history, culture, geology, and biology of the area. You will traverse nine tunnels, ranging from the 8,771-foot-long tunnel at the start to shorter, brighter tunnels of 178 feet. Additionally, you will pass over seven expansive, high trestles that afford wide-open views of the surrounding forests and valley.

Leave the Roland Trailhead, where FR 506 joins the trail for the next 2.3 miles, and head south toward tunnel 21, located at 3.2 miles. Motor vehicles use tunnel 21, so be sure your light is on and proceed cautiously. It is the only tunnel you will share with vehicles. After you exit tunnel 21, stop at the scenic viewpoint on the west side to look down at the green panoramas of the Bitterroot Mountains in Idaho and Montana. You can see the route you are following and the steel trestles you will cross, nestled in the Idaho Panhandle National Forest.

The trail departs from the road at Moss Creek Trailhead before tunnel 22. To avoid confusion between tunnels 21 and 22, think as if you were a train. Head straight toward tunnel 22 so you do not inadvertently follow FR 506 as it turns sharply downhill. At 4.1 miles you'll enter tunnel 22. This is the second-longest tunnel on the route. It is 1,516 feet long, and you can see some daylight at the end of the tunnel. Within a mile you will encounter a closed tunnel, number 23. Take the brief bypass around it and head into a short tunnel, number 24, which runs for 377 feet.

When you arrive at 5.3 miles, you cross trestle 216 at Small Creek. It is 515 feet long and 120 feet high. Immediately after this trestle you travel over trestle 218 at Barnes Creek, which is slightly smaller at 507 feet long and 117 feet high.

After negotiating the first two trestles, take a break at 5.8 miles and read about the forest fire of 1910. Just ahead is trestle 220 over Kelly Creek, at 6.1 miles. Enjoy the passage; it is the longest and tallest trestle on the trail, measuring 850 feet long and 230 feet high. Continue downhill toward the halfway point at Adair, at 6.9 miles and 3,707 feet elevation. Trail users have moved steadily downhill from the 4,147-foot elevation at the East Portal Trailhead.

At 7 miles you will encounter the 966-foot-long tunnel 25, immediately followed by the 683-foot-long tunnel 26. Between the two tunnels you pass the Adair Trailhead, wth the last restroom on the trail until the Pearson Trailhead, and cross over the dirt road FR 326.

Riders encounter a deer on the Route of the Hiawatha Trail. (Courtesy Natalie Bartley)

Beyond Tunnel 26 are four trestles. They are spread over 1.4 miles. If you are not used to the heights yet, you will be soon. Cross over Turkey Creek, Russell/No Name, Bear Creek, and Clear Creek; identified as trestles number 224, 226, 228, and 230. They range from 281 feet to 760 feet long and from 96 feet to 220 feet high. They provide a contrast to the back-to-back tunnels.

Trestles on the route have an interesting history. After the forest fire of 1910, smaller wooden trestles were converted into earth-filled trestles that could withstand a fire. Thus there are many trestles that trail users ride over that do not appear to be trestles. There are an estimated thirty trestles of this nature on the trail.

Between 9.8 and 14.4 miles, the trail passes through three short tunnels. They range in length from 178 to 470 feet long. At 10.6 miles the trail passes near the historic mining towns of Falcon and Grand Forks. Take a path off the main trail to visit the old building remnants.

At mile 14.4 you will pull in to the final trailhead at Pearson. Trail marshals supply water at Pearson, East Portal, and Adair. If it is a hot day, they may have run out of water, so carry your own just in case. From the Pearson Trailhead you can pick up the shuttle back to the Roland Trailhead or return up the trail to the trailhead where you parked.

Nearby Attractions

- Lookout Pass Ski and Recreation Area (208) 744–1301, www.skilookout.com. Located just off I–90 at exit 0, the area serves as headquarters for the Route of the Hiawatha. Trail passes, shuttles, rentals, and food services are available.

- Trail Pass: Adults $9; children three to thirteen years $5. On Saturday and Sunday you can purchase passes at trailheads from the trail marshals. Shuttle fee: Adults $9; children $6. Boxed lunch: $7. Bike Rentals: Ranges from $18 to $32, depending on whether you are renting children's bikes, adult bikes, or attachable bike trailers. Helmets rent for $6 each, and lights for $4 each.

- Get wet by whitewater rafting on the St. Joe, Moyie, and Lochsa Rivers with ROW Adventures, (800) 451–6034, www.rowadventures.com.

Future Plans

Reflective materials may be installed in some of the longer tunnels to help guide visitors. Additionally, plans are under way to extend the trail 31 miles on the Montana side. The Route of the Hiawatha is also one the trails identified for inclusion in a connected loop of trails in the Idaho Panhandle.

While in the northern Panhandle, take in the Northern Pacific Trail (Trail S), the Trail of the Coeur d'Alenes (Trail 37), and the North Idaho Centennial Trail (Trail 39).

39 NORTH IDAHO CENTENNIAL TRAIL

A highlight of this trail is that it runs primarily along the Spokane River and Lake Coeur d'Alene. Trail users journey near Interstate 90, pass through the conifers of northern Idaho, and go through the towns of Post Falls and Coeur d' Alene, ultimately finishing along the scenic Coeur d'Alene Lake Drive.

Activities:

Location: Post Falls and Coeur d'Alene, in Kootenai County in the northern Idaho Panhandle

Length: 23 miles

Surface: Asphalt and public roads

Wheelchair access: The trail is wheelchair accessible and slopes steeply near the Huetter Reststop Trailhead, with 10 percent grades uphill and downhill.

Difficulty: Easy, with a few grades on the western and eastern ends

Food: There are many eateries just off the trail in Post Falls and Coeur d'Alene.

Restrooms: You'll find restrooms along the trail at the western trailhead (the Stateline Visitor Information Center in Washington), Huetter Reststop Trailhead, Seltice Way Trailhead, Rutledge Trailhead, and Higgens Point Trailhead. Additional restrooms and water are at parks just off the trail on the western segment, including Stateline Park, Corbin Park, Falls Park, and Coeur d'Alene City Park Beach. The eastern section along Coeur d'Alene Lake Drive between Rutledge Trailhead and Higgens Point has five wayside restrooms in a 4.5-mile stretch. All sites are wheelchair accessible.

Seasons: The trail can be used year-round.

Access and parking: There are many places to access the trail. The following are the larger and more easily accessible sites that put you directly on

Overlook at Falls Park on the Spokane River near the town of Post Falls on the North Idaho Centennial Trail. (Courtesy Natalie Bartley)

the trail when coming by vehicle from I–90. Watch for CENTENNIAL TRAIL signs on I–90, indicating these quick-access locations.

- Western terminus at the border of Idaho and Washington, in Washington: If coming from the east on I–90 from Post Falls, take exit 299 (Stateline) off I–90, just over the Idaho/Washington border in Washington. Turn right off the exit, cross over the trail, then turn left into the Stateline Visitor Information Center, traveling a total of 0.2 mile from the exit. When coming from Washington, take exit 299 off I–90, turn left, then turn left again into the visitor information center. Access the trail on the east side of the visitor center and head east.

- Trailheads along I-90 heading east: Get on I–90 at Washington exit 299 and head east into Idaho.

- Spokane Street Trailhead: Take exit 5 off I–90. Turn right off the ramp onto Spokane Street. Go 1 block, turn right on Fourth Avenue, then go another block to the stop sign at the rail crossing. Turn right into a dirt Centennial Trail parking lot beside the trail, a total of 0.2 mile from the exit.

- **Huetter Reststop Trailhead:** This is accessible only by vehicles that are eastbound on I–90. Exit at I–90 mile marker 8 and drive into the rest stop. Pick up the trail at the south side of the rest area.

- **Seltice Way Trailhead:** Take exit 11 off I–90, which leads to three local colleges. Turn right off the ramp and onto Northwest Boulevard. Go 1 block and turn right onto Seltice Way, then immediately right into the trailhead parking lot beside the trail.

- **City Park Beach trail access in downtown Coeur d'Alene:** Take exit 13 off I–90. Turn right off the ramp onto Third Street, a one-way road. Go 1.7 miles on Third Street, directly into a Public Pay-to-Park lot. Pick up the trail on Front Avenue.

- **Rutledge Trailhead:** To get to the lakeshore portion along the eastern side of the trail, take exit 15 off I–90. At the end of the ramp, cross over Sherman Avenue and drive 0.8 mile on Coeur d'Alene Lake Drive. Turn right into the Rutledge Trailhead, a large paved lot on the lakefront. The trail is on the south side of the lot, along the lake.

- **Steamers Wayside, Beacon Point, Osprey Point, and unnamed parking sites:** Access these locations by continuing east along Coeur d'Alene Lake Drive toward Higgens Point.

- **Higgens Point Trailhead:** This is the eastern terminus of the trail. From Rutledge Trailhead, continue east for 4.5 miles on Coeur d'Alene Lake Drive to the large parking areas at the end of the road.

Rentals: In Post Falls, bicycles can be rented at Mountain View Cyclery and Fitness, 306 Spokane Street, (208) 457–8439, www.mountainviewcyclery .com. In Coeur d'Alene, bicycles, cross-country skis, and snowshoes are available to rent at Vertical Earth, 308 Coeur d'Alene Avenue, (208) 667–5503, www.verticalearth.com.

Contact:

- North Idaho Centennial Trail, www.northidahocentennialtrail.org

- Idaho Department of Parks and Recreation (208) 769–1511. Or try the Post Falls/Coeur d'Alene Chamber of Commerce, (800) 292–2553, www .visitpostfalls.org.

Bus routes: For information, call City Link at (877) 941– RIDE, or visit www .idahocitylink.com.

||||||||||||||||||||||||||||||||||||||||||||||||||||||||||||||||||||||||||||||||||

S elected as Idaho's Millennium Legacy Trail, this route symbolizes a piece of Idaho's heritage. It offers a pleasing mix of urban settings against the backdrop of the Spokane River and Lake Coeur d'Alene. The trail allows for visits to local parks and an array of convenient food stops. Open year-round, the trail is nonmotorized, though parts of it are bike lanes or local roads. The trail is managed by a partnership between Kootenai County, the Idaho Department of Transportation, and the cities of Post Falls and Coeur d'Alene. Frequent signage keeps trail users oriented. Be sure to pick up a free trail map at any of the major trailheads.

North Idaho Centennial Trail's western terminus is accessed at the interstate visitor center in Washington just off I–90, where the North Idaho Centennial Trail joins the Spokane River Centennial Trail. You travel east along the Spokane River, through the towns of Post Falls and Coeur d' Alene, and along the shoreline of Lake Coeur d'Alene.

Pick up the trail on the east side of the visitor center, near the entrance from the highway. Cross the busy road and head east. The trail passes briefly along the Spokane River, beside I–90, and then turns left at a small trail junction. At about a mile you will pass the Washington/Idaho border and cross a bridge over the Spokane River. The trail mile markers begin at the border and ascend toward the east. Shortly, in about 0.2 mile from the border, you will be at Idaho's Stateline Park, accessible only by trail.

Continue east with I–90 to your left. The Greyhound Park and Events Center comes into view, and just beyond, the North Idaho Factory Stores. After 2 miles there is a busy road intersection. At this point the trail crosses diagonally to the left, resuming beside the Sleep Inn. An educational sign trailside describes the Pleasant View Road Railroad Trestle and Pleasant View Bridge. After you pass this area, the trail becomes a bit more rural and crosses small streets.

At about 3.2 miles, read about McGuires Junction, which served as a major intersection on the Milwaukee Road rail line. Two rails formed the

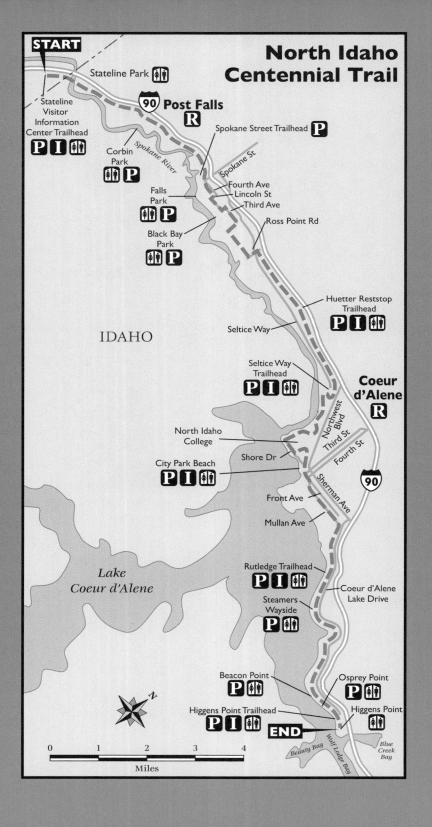

Look for the North Idaho Centennial Trail markers as you pass through the towns of Post Falls and Coeur d'Alene. *(Courtesy Natalie Bartley)*

junction. The Coeur d'Alene branch, formerly called the Coeur d'Alene Electric Line, headed east. The Metaline Falls branch traveled north and was previously the Idaho & Washington Northern Railroad.

The scenery gets even better at trail mile marker 4, where the river comes into view again and you can see the waterfalls in the distance. An interpretive sign describes a community member, D. C. Corbin, who built many of the railroads in this area.

Beyond the viewpoint the trail crosses a small road and runs along an active rail track. At this location Post Falls is easily accessed, as are restaurants just off the trail. Just before 5 miles, trail users cross the five-lane

Spokane Street. If you want to take in a close-up view of the falls, turn right on Spokane Street and go about 0.2 mile into Falls Park. Refill your water bottles, stroll near the top of the waterfalls, and enjoy the mist of the Spokane River as it plunges 40 feet over rocks. Return to the intersection of the trail and Spokane Street.

To continue east on the trail, cross the rail tracks and follow the well-signed path along the tracks. The trail turns right onto a bike lane on Lincoln Street. Continue to a stop sign and turn left onto Third Avenue. Continue along the bike lane for 0.5 mile, still following the encouraging Centennial Trail signs. At about 6 miles the trail starts again on the left. Black Bay Park is to the right on a side trail. It offers restrooms, nature trails, shade trees, and a beach.

After 6 miles the trail moves more deeply into Post Falls, a city that was founded by Frederick Post. It's easy to jump off the trail and grab a bite to eat at one of the many nearby eateries. Between mile 7 and mile 8, the trail becomes a road path through a residential area. It resumes as a trail at the intersection of Ross Point Road and Seltice Way, at about 8.5 miles.

Cross the big intersection and join the trail as it climbs to run parallel with I–90 again, through a tree-shaded area. Grades in the range of 6, 8, and 10 percent greet trail users as they approach a major trailhead at the Huetter Reststop at 10 miles. Take in the shade, the visitor center, and the restrooms before heading east on the trail.

After you leave the rest stop, you travel above the Spokane River valley and along I–90. Mountains that serve as a backdrop harbor native conifers including Douglas fir, Engelmann spruce, western red cedar, ponderosa pine, western larch, and many other species.

Near 12 miles, enjoy the downhill grade as you approach the valley. The Lewis and Clark College, the University of Idaho, and North Idaho College are located nearby. A few street detours, following Centennial Trail signs, will take you past the Seltice Way Trailhead at 13 miles, then across a big intersection and through an industrial area. Watch for the educational signs describing the extensive timber and rail history in this area. Between mile 14 and mile 16, the trail winds along the Spokane River, through the North Idaho College campus, and onto Shore Drive. Once on Shore Drive, the trail is along the lake. Soon you'll pass through the Coeur d'Alene City Park Beach, by the Coeur d'Alene Plaza, and past the city's marina facilities.

Trail users near the Coeur d'Alene City Park Beach. (Courtesy Natalie Bartley)

A quick visit to downtown Coeur d'Alene and its restaurants is convenient at this point. The paid parking lot is at 16 miles. Watch for Centennial Trail signs as the trail winds through residential areas after mile 16.

The trail follows Mullan Avenue and turns right at about 17.25 miles, hooking up with the Coeur d'Alene Lake Drive and a distinct road bike route. At this point the trail changes out of its city mode and switches into a linear state park, managed by the Idaho Department of Parks and Recreation. The park offers 1,000 feet of shoreline, a mile-long fitness trail, scenic overlooks, wide-open views of the lake, and glimpses of wildlife.

Rutledge Trailhead, at about 18.5 miles, is the formal start of this pleasant section. Even though the trail runs parallel to Coeur d'Alene Lake Drive, it feels relaxed and rural. Bird sightings are common in the area. Watch for great blue herons, ospreys, bald eagles, common mergansers, and American tree sparrows.

As you head to Higgens Point, the eastern terminus, ponder the fact that Lake Coeur d'Alene is 23 miles long and offers 109 miles of shoreline. The Spokane River is the western outlet of the lake.

Heading east there are plenty of waysides at which you can picnic, rest, use the bathroom, and enjoy the peaceful scenery. You will pass

Steamers Wayside at about 19.25 miles. Booth Park is just past 21 miles. Beacon Point, Osprey Point, and finally the eastern terminus trailhead are between mile 22 and mile 23.

Marina parking is at the end of the road and requires a $4 day-use fee. The paved trail continues about 0.25 mile more, uphill to Higgens Point, where a park sits at the top of the knoll. On the side of the trail before you climb up the final hill, there are two viewing scopes. These are great for bird-watching and gazing at the boating activity on the lake. At the flat top of Higgens Point, take in the panoramic view of Blue Creek Bay, Wolf Lodge Bay, and Beauty Bay. Foot trails lead off the point, down to the beach, and back to the paved trail.

When you are done, return the way you came. Along the trail between Higgens Point and Rutledge Trailhead are restaurants, including Tony's Supper Club and the Beach House Ribs and Crab Shack, offering views of the lake as well as food and beverages.

While in the area, consider visiting the Spokane River Centennial Trail (Trail 28), the Trail of the Coeur d'Alenes (Trail 37), or the Route of the Hiawatha Rail Trail (Trail 38).

Higgens Point scenic overlook and the eastern terminus of the North Idaho Centennial Trail. (Courtesy Natalie Bartley)

40 LATAH TRAIL

This is a rail trail with an adventurous feel to it. Visitors pass through forested areas and open grain fields and travel near Idaho Highway 8 as it heads from the rural town of Troy to the university town of Moscow in the Palouse region of north-central Idaho.

Activities:

Location: Troy and Moscow, in Latah County

Length: 11 miles plus 3.3-mile optional extension on area trails

Surface: Asphalt, except for a 1.7-mile gravel section between 2 and 3.7 miles

Wheelchair access: This trail is wheelchair accessible.

Difficulty: Easy to moderate

Food: Restaurants, grocery stores, and gas stations are in each town.

Restrooms: Public restrooms are located at the Troy City Park, the trail-head located 4 miles from Troy on ID 8, and the Berman Creekside Park in Moscow.

Seasons: The trail can be used year-round.

Access and parking: To reach the eastern terminus in Troy, take ID 8 east from the intersection of U.S. Highway 95 and ID 8 in Moscow. Drive 12.1 miles to Troy, turning left into the Troy City Park. The trailhead begins on the west side of the parking lot.

There is also a trailhead located 4 miles out of Troy on the left side of ID 8. It is 8.1 miles from the intersection of US 95 and ID 8 in Moscow. Another option is to use the trailhead for the Paradise Path, located at Berman Creekside Park in Moscow, by turning left on Styner Avenue off ID 8 just as you enter Moscow from Troy. Or, from the intersection of US 95 and ID 8 in Moscow, go 0.5 mile to Styner Avenue and turn right. Go 0.2 mile into the parking lot of the Berman Creekside Park Trailhead. To pick up the trail, head east on the Paradise Path on the east side of the park. It transitions into the Latah Trail in about 1.5 miles. You can also get on the trail at a variety of informal locations as the trail passes eastward through Moscow and the University of Idaho campus on the way to the Bill Chipman Palouse Trail.

There are other small, dirt trailside parking spots along ID 8 that you can use to access the Latah Trail. Coming from Troy, a gravel parking lot is at 9.1 miles on Mill Road on the south side, across from the golf course. There is another one 11.8 miles out of Troy at the junction of US 95 and ID 8.

Rentals: For bicycle rentals and repairs in Moscow, try Paradise Creek Bicycles, 513 South Main Street, (208) 882–0703; or Follett's Mountain Sports, 407 South Washington Street, (208) 882–6735. You can rent snowshoes and cross-country skis in Moscow from the University of Idaho's Outdoor Program at their Outdoor Rental Center in the Student Recreation Center, 1000 Paradise Creek Street, (208) 885–6170, www.campusrec.uidaho.edu/outdoor.

Contact:

- The Latah Trail Foundation, www.latahtrailfoundation.org

- The Moscow Parks and Recreation Department, (208) 883–7085, www.moscow.id.us

- Outdoor Program, University of Idaho, (208) 885–6810, www.campusrec.uidaho.edu/outdoor

- Bike Moscow, www.bikemoscow.org

- Moscow Chamber of Commerce, (800) 380–1801, www.moscowchamber.com

- Troy Chamber of Commerce, (208) 835–2041 (Sterling Bank)

Bus routes: Valley Transit runs Monday through Friday. Call (208) 883–7747, or visit users.lewiston.com/valleytransit.

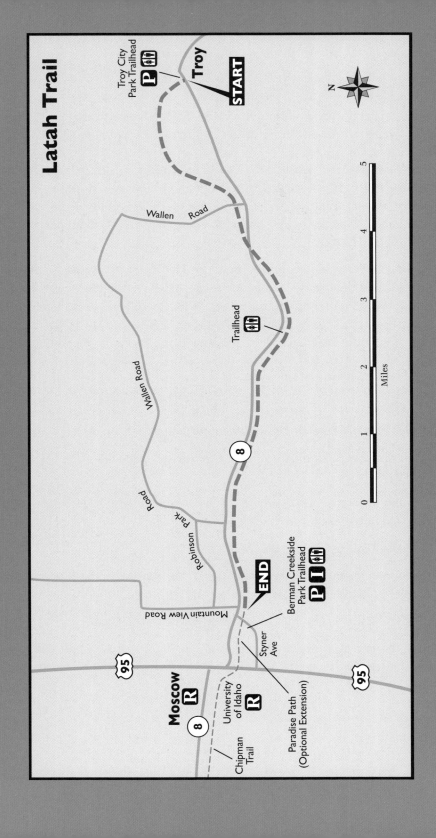

Troy to Moscow, 11 miles

Whatever season you visit the Latah Trail, you are in for a treat. During the spring, grain fields the color of shamrock green glisten in the sunshine while meadowlarks chirp and a cool breeze blows. In the late summer and autumn, miles of ripe yellow fields of grain ripple in the wind. When winter arrives, snow-covered trails encourage snowshoers and cross-country skiers to journey between Troy and Moscow.

The Latah Trail is a rolling pathway along the former Moscow–Arrow Rail Line. It passes through stands of timber, between farmland, and along ID 8. Ultimately it connects with the Bill Chipman Palouse Trail, which travels from Moscow to the Idaho/Washington border and to Pullman, Washington.

The overpass tunnel under ID 8 serves as a place to get out of the sun, wind, or rain while traveling the Latah Trail between Troy and Moscow. (Courtesy Natalie Bartley)

Start in a forested area in the small town of Troy at the trailhead at Troy City Park, at trail mile marker 0. The first 2 miles swing away from the highway and up an incline, with glimpses of open meadows and distant forested hilltops. At 2 miles the smooth asphalt trail turns to gravel, indicated by the placement of bollards. By 2.2 miles you will see a trail sign declaring SUMMIT. Take a break at the bench for a well-earned rest.

Continue through farmland on the gravel railbed to 3.5 miles, where ID 8 comes back into view. At 3.6 miles you reach an abrupt steep hill indicating a downed railroad trestle that crossed over Wallen Road. Carefully navigate down the steep incline, cross the road, and go up the other side to rejoin the original railbed. The paved trail resumes just beyond the steep incline.

An alternative for road bicyclists is to pedal 2.5 miles on busy ID 8, turn right on Wallen Road, and pick up the trail heading west, missing the gravel start. There is no established parking on the road, so other trail users should consider starting at the Troy City Park.

At 3.7 miles you will be traveling near the highway, a bit of a surprise after the remote portion at the start of the trail. From 4.4 miles the trail moves smoothly through an underpass, keeping trail users safe from the rigors of ID 8. It's a good place to stop and get out of the sun, wind, or rain for a break. Note the parts of the old stone overpass bridge repurposed into benches.

Given the rural nature of the trail, bird-watchers are usually in luck. Meadowlarks, ospreys, and Canada geese are not strangers to this trail. At 4.9 miles you will come to a trailhead with paved parking and restrooms, located on ID 8. From that point the trail moves downhill for over a mile to Katsam Crossing at 6.1 miles. Grain silos and elevators soon loom into view. Continue heading through the rural countryside toward Moscow.

Between mile 9 and mile 9.2, the trail takes a sharp left turn and traverses uphill through cultivated fields until it reaches a knoll. The trail levels out a bit, with intermittent roads crossing over the trail as you approach the urban area of Moscow.

Strong winds blow along this stretch and can help or hinder you. The posted suggested speed limit is 15 mph on all the trails, and you are wise to follow it due to the intermittent farm and construction equipment crossings on the western end of the trail.

A bicyclist travels east from Moscow on the Latah Trail. (Courtesy Natalie Bartley)

At about 10 miles you'll see the Moscow Elks Lodge Golf Course along the highway. A WELCOME TO MOSCOW HOME OF THE UNIVERSITY OF IDAHO sign turns up at 10.6 miles. If you continue on the trail, a cemetery can be spotted across the highway. By 12 miles you will find restaurants, a grocery store, and shops at the Eastside Mall, just off the trail.

The end of the Latah Trail is considered to be the intersection of ID 8 and Mountain View Road east of the intersection of US 95 and ID 8. For an additional 3.3-mile ride, take the Paradise Path west to the eastern edge of the University of Idaho campus, then continue through campus and to the eastern terminus of the Bill Chipman Palouse Trail.

Optional Extension—Latah Trail to Paradise Path to Bill Chipman Palouse Trail, 3.3 miles

To pick up the Bill Chipman Palouse Trail, continue past Mountain View Road. The trail connects smoothly with the Paradise Path, which in turn connects with the Chipman Trail. It is a slightly confusing route that winds through parts of Moscow and the University of Idaho's campus before hooking up with the well-marked Chipman Trail.

If you are continuing, at about 12.5 miles the trail briefly sweeps off the original railbed for a detour into a neighborhood park, the Berman Creekside Park. It's an excellent place to use as a trailhead, with a wheelchair-accessible toilet, water fountains, and paved parking. Additionally, interpretive signs describe butterflies, wetlands, and riparian zones. Continue toward the right along the creek when the trail splits, and meet up with the original railbed again. The trail becomes "chip coat," which is basically oiled gravel.

At 12.8 miles grain elevators come into sight, and shortly after, the University of Idaho campus. Take the left branch off the rail trail and cross US 95 to get on the Paradise Path paved trail at the university. Once on the edge of campus, take a sharp right behind the water fountains. Follow the signs for the Paradise Path along the creek on the edge of campus and across an assortment of campus roads. On the way, at about 13.4 miles, you'll cross over another campus entrance at Sixth Street. Continue on the campus trail past soccer and baseball fields, and finally onto the Bill Chipman Palouse Trail on the west side of campus at the intersection of ID 8 and Perimeter Drive, across from the Palouse Mall.

When going from west to east on the campus trail, signs on the western edge read BIKE ROUTE initially, then later PARADISE PATH. The trail passes by the Student Recreation Center, which houses the University of Idaho Outdoor Program. You can rent cross-country skis or snowshoes here during the winter.

Nearby Attractions:

- Camas Prairie Winery, 110 South Main Street, Moscow, (208) 882–0214 or (800) 616–0214, www.camasprairie winery.com. Lays claim to be Idaho's oldest independent winery.

- The Alehouse, 226 West Sixth Street, Moscow, (208) 882–BREW. A good place to refresh yourself after a trip on the local trails is at the Moscow branch of the Coeur d' Alene Brewing Company.

When you are ready, turn around and return to the Latah Trail and Troy. It is 1.8 miles from the Chipman Trailhead to the Berman Creekside Park Trailhead and another 1.5 miles to the unmarked start of the west end of the Latah Trail.

While you are in the Moscow area, experience the Bill Chipman Palouse Trail (Trail 41), Washington's portion of the Bill Chipman Palouse Trail (Trail 29), and the Ed Corkill Memorial River Trail (Trail 42). Additionally, there are miles of excellent mountain bike single-track trails on Moscow Mountain.

Future Plans

Future plans are to obtain easements to pave the rest of the Latah Trail between mile 2 and mile 3.7, and to reconstruct the trestle over Wallen Road. Also, there are plans to develop the old gravel railbed that travels through a beautiful remote canyon from the town of Troy, near the intersection of Idaho Highway 99 and ID 8, to Kendrick. Once finished, the trail would connect with the Ed Corkill Memorial River Trail, completing an uninterrupted trail system from the border of Idaho and Washington, through Moscow, and to Juliaetta.

41 BILL CHIPMAN PALOUSE TRAIL— MOSCOW, IDAHO

Running from one university town to another, this trail is a well-used urban commuter option featuring detailed interpretive signs about railroad lore and local history.

Activities:

Location: City of Moscow, in Latah County in north-central Idaho, and city of Pullman, in Whitman County in eastern Washington

Length: 1 mile in Idaho and 6 miles in Washington

Surface: Asphalt

Wheelchair access: The wheelchair-accessible trailheads include the terminuses at Moscow, Idaho, and Pullman, Washington.

Difficulty: Easy

Food: Eateries, gas stations, and grocery stores are near the trailheads in Moscow, Idaho, and Pullman, Washington.

Restrooms: Emergency phones and restrooms are located near trail miles 1.5, 4, and 5 as measured from the western terminus in Pullman.

Seasons: The trail can be used year-round.

Access and parking: To start in Moscow at the eastern terminus of the trailhead, take Idaho Highway 8 west from the junction of U.S. Highway 95 and ID 8, which becomes Idaho Highway 270 at Perimeter Drive. (ID 270 is also locally called West Pullman Road). Turn right into the Palouse Mall shopping center at the intersection with Perimeter Drive and ID 270. Park on the eastern edge of the mall and cross ID 270 to get on the trail. The eastern trailhead is clearly marked by a railroad station shelter and kiosk.

There are some parking opportunities on the University of Idaho campus. You can get a free day pass for parking on campus on weekdays. Passes are available at the Parking Office on campus at 645 West Pullman Road, (208) 885–6424. They are also available at the Student Union, 709

Deakin Avenue, (208) 885–6111. Free parking is available on weekends in the Gold, Blue, and Red parking lots on campus.

To start in Washington, take ID-WA 270 west from Moscow to Pullman for about 6 miles. When Washington Highway 270 turns into Main Street in Pullman, continue 2 more miles by following Main Street to the first stoplight and turning left onto Bishop Boulevard. The boulevard veers to the left; in 1 block, turn left into the Quality Inn Hotel parking lot. The designated trailhead location for the western terminus starts at the northeast edge of the parking lot.

Rentals: In Moscow, bicycles can be rented at Paradise Creek Bicycles, 513 South Main Street, (208) 882–0703. Snowshoes and bicycles can be rented at Follett's Mountain Sports, 407 South Washington, (208) 882–6735. Snowshoes and cross-country skis can be rented from the University of Idaho's Outdoor Program at their Outdoor Rental Center in the Student Recreation Center, 1000 Paradise Creek Street, (208) 885–6170, www.campusrec.uidaho.edu/outdoor.

Contact:

- Pullman Civic Trust, www.pullmancivictrust.org/chipman.html
- University of Idaho, Outdoor Program, (208) 885–6810, www.campusrec.uidaho.edu/outdoor

Bus routes: For Moscow routes, contact Valley Transit, (208) 883–7747, users.lewiston.com/valleytransit. For the Moscow-to-Pullman route, contact Wheatland Express, (800) 334–2207 or (509) 334–2200, www.wheatlandexpress.com.

Even though only 1 mile is on the Idaho side, this 7-mile trail is worth a visit for all the rail history you can learn along the way. A jaunt the whole distance into Pullman, Washington, extends the trip. You will be counting trail mile markers from the start at 7 miles, descending to 0 miles at the western terminus in Pullman, Washington.

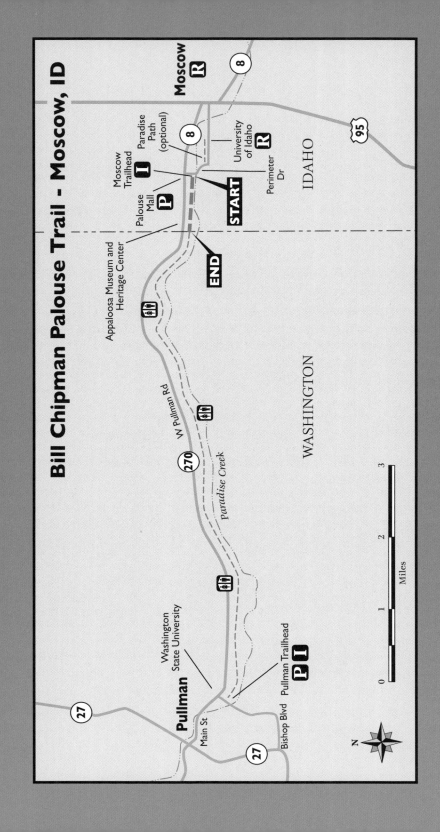

Bill Chipman Palouse Trail - Moscow, ID

The eastern terminus of the Bill Chipman Palouse Trail in Moscow, Idaho. (Courtesy
Natalie Bartley)

Begin your journey on this popular trail by reading the kiosk information at the rail station replica that stands as the eastern terminus. Frequent
benches, portable toilets, and emergency phones smooth the way for visitors. Educational signs along the way inform trail users about railroad lingo
and other Palouse region tidbits. For example, the word "station" is a train
stop, and a "depot" is similar, but always with a smaller building. Another
interesting item is that the area produces the majority of peas and lentils
grown in the United States. This is due to the Palouse region's warm, dry
summers and rich soils.

Dedicated in 1998, the trail is part of the federal rails-to-trails program.
It is jointly managed by the cities of Moscow and Pullman, the University
of Idaho, Washington State University, and Whitman County, Washington.
The trail was named in honor of Bill Chipman, an important community
member who was killed in a vehicle accident in 1996.

In 1885 the first railroad cars arrived in Moscow, having traveled from
the Snake River. Five years later, in 1890, the Northern Pacific Railway
completed a parallel line that linked Moscow to Pullman and Spokane.

Nearby Attractions

Appaloosa Museum and Heritage Center, 2720 West Pullman Road, Moscow, (208) 882–5578, www.appaloosamuseum .org. Live appaloosa horse exhibit in the summer and indoor exhibits year-round.

Between 1919 and the 1950s, the train line carried students to the University of Idaho from all over the state. It was called the Silver and Gold Student Special.

The trail quickly leaves Moscow, traveling alongside ID 270. Within a mile of the start of the trailhead, you cross the border between Idaho and Washington. Your options are to continue on the Bill Chipman Palouse Trail (Trail 29) 6 miles farther into Pullman, Washington, or return to Moscow. Consider visiting the Appaloosa Museum and Heritage Center before you leave Idaho. It is easily accessed off the trail by crossing the highway at the state border.

Future development of the route will consist of spur trails in Moscow and Pullman connecting to the Bill Chipman Palouse Trail.

While you are in Latah County, try the Latah Trail (Trail 40), which starts on the east side of the University of Idaho campus in east Moscow, and the Ed Corkill Memorial River Trail (Trail 42), southeast of Moscow.

42 ED CORKILL MEMORIAL RIVER TRAIL

Rural in nature, this trail winds beside two small towns as it runs along the Potlatch River and amid lush vegetation. It follows the original Northern Pacific/Burlington Northern Moscow–Arrow rail line in west-central Idaho.

Activities:

Location: In the towns of Juliaetta and Kendrick, in Latah County

Length: 5.3 miles

Surface: Asphalt

Wheelchair access: The trail is wheelchair accessible.

Difficulty: Easy

Food: There are gas stations, grocery stores, and restaurants near the trail in the rural towns of Juliaetta and Kendrick.

Restrooms: There are restrooms at the eastern trailhead at the Juliaetta Centennial Park in Juliaetta.

Seasons: The trail can be used year-round.

Access and parking: Take U.S. Highway 95 north from Lewiston, exiting onto U.S. Highway 12. Travel east to Idaho Highway 3. Turn left onto ID 3 and go 8.2 miles to the southern terminus trailhead located on the right at the Juliaetta Centennial Park in Juliaetta.

Or you can continue a total of 13.5 miles from the junction of US 12 and ID 3 to the northern terminus trailhead in Kendrick, passing through Juliaetta on the way. In the town of Kendrick, ID 3 changes into West Main Street, then East Main Street. Continue across the bridge and turn left into the Kendrick High School parking lot to access the Kendrick Trailhead. The trail heading toward Juliaetta starts from the front of the school property. Cross back over the bridge and go across East Main Street. Turn left onto the trail. You can also cross the bridge via the gravel Bear Creek Road just on the edge of the property and then get on the trail by turning left just after the bridge crossing, then crossing over East Main Street and turning left onto the trail.

An alternative parking spot is located in Kendrick 13 miles from the intersection of US 12 and ID 3. Turn right into an RV dumping station in Kendrick. Cross over Railroad Street. The paved trail is just off the gravel lot, putting you 5 miles from Juliaetta via the trail.

Rentals: None in this rural area. See Appendix A for bike rentals in Latah County.

Contact:

• City of Kendrick, (208) 289–5157.

• Kendrick-Juliaetta Community Development Association, www.kendrick juliaetta.org.

Bus routes: None

The Juliaetta grain elevator along the Ed Corkill Memorial River Trail. (Courtesy Natalie Bartley)

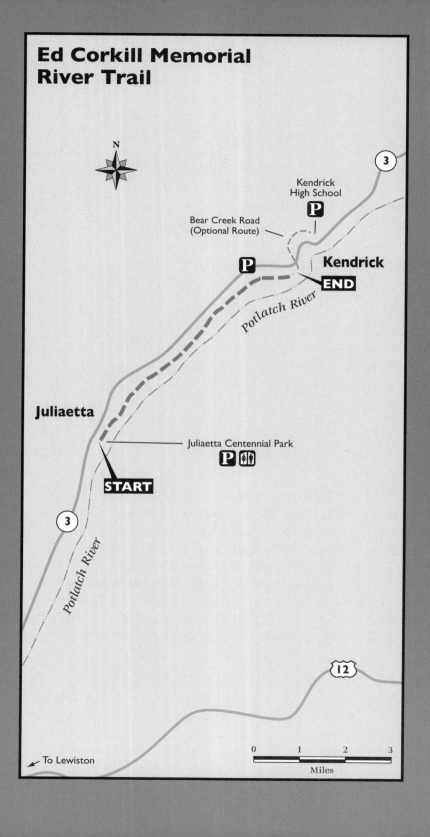

Ed Corkill Memorial River Trail

N

3

Kendrick High School

P

Bear Creek Road (Optional Route)

P

Kendrick

END

Potlatch River

Juliaetta

Juliaetta Centennial Park

P

START

3

Potlatch River

12

To Lewiston

0   1   2   3
Miles

The Ed Corkill Memorial River Trail was dedicated in 2004. The Idaho Department of Transportation awarded more than $336,000 to the Julietta–Kendrick Recreation District as an Enhancement Award to develop the rail trail. On the trail visitors learn about locomotive whistle signals (described on interpretive signs) and pass beside grain elevators towering above the trail near Juliaetta and Kendrick.

Starting at the trailhead at Juliaetta Centennial Park near open canyons of basalt rock and green lawns, the trail heads toward the town of Juliaetta. During the spring and summer, lush berry bushes, white syringe flowers, and cat-o-nine-tails line portions of the trail.

During the first 0.5 mile, the trail passes an old ranch along the river and a telephone pole log manufacturer on the north side of the trail. Soon after, the Juliaetta silo and grain elevator dominates the scenery as you travel between the river and the town of Juliaetta.

From the late 1800s to the late 1950s, the Northern Pacific and Idaho Railroad had tracks between these two towns, which were the end of the branch line from near Spokane. Timber, livestock, fruits, grains, and vegetables were transported on the rails, making the Potlatch River Valley an important trading post. In 1958 the Juliaetta depot was closed.

Interpretive signs along the trail at mile 0.8 describe rail post signage, including mileposts, Flanger markers, speed restrictions, and other signs. Continue along the river, crossing a trestle at 1.2 miles. If you need a rest, settle in on one of the many benches along the way.

Between mile 2 and mile 3.5, you'll travel away from ID 3, with small ranches appearing trailside. Once you reach 3.5 miles, the Kendrick city limits begin and the town's silo and grain elevator come into view. Soon the trail runs behind houses, along the grain elevator and silo, and beside the river. At 4.5 miles you can read about locomotive whistle signals that were used before modern forms of communication were developed. Often the train engineer and the train crew could not see each other, so whistle signals became the standard to indicate train maneuvers when stopping, backing up, and releasing brakes.

At 5 miles, read more about Kendrick's train history. To get to the northern terminus trailhead at 5.3 miles, go to the end of the paved trail, turn right on East Main Street, cross the bridge, then turn left into the Kendrick High School parking lot. There is a small gravel path on the north

The Kendrick grain elevator along the Ed Corkill Memorial River Trail. (Courtesy Natalie Bartley)

side of the bridge, Bear Creek Road, which you can use instead of riding the road across the bridge. Return to Juliaetta the way you came.

If you have the time while you're in the area, visit the Latah Trail (Trail 40) and the Bill Chipman Palouse Trail in Idaho (Trail 41) and Washington (Trail 29).

Future Plans

Near the trailhead at Kendrick High School, you can see the closed portion of the old railbed. Future goals include continuing the trail from Kendrick and up the canyon to Troy, where rail trail enthusiasts can connect with the Latah Trail, then continue to Moscow and connect with the Bill Chipman Palouse Trail at the Idaho/Washington border. In Juliaetta the railbed is gravel and heads south. It is currently used by motorized off-road vehicles and at present is on hold regarding further development.

43 CROWN POINT TRAIL

Views of West Mountain, on the far shore of Lake Cascade, add beauty to this trail. In the winter snow blankets the area, while in the spring and early summer, snow-covered mountains add contrast to the glittering lake.

Activities:

Location: Cascade, in Valley County

Length: 2.8 miles

Surface: Sand and dirt

Wheelchair access: This trail is not wheelchair accessible.

Difficulty: Easy

Food: Restaurants, gas stations, and a grocery store are in the town of Cascade.

Restrooms: Restrooms are available at the free public parking lot on Vista Point Boulevard and at the day-use and camping fee areas at Crown Point Lake Cascade State Park.

Seasons: The trail can be used year-round. Skiers, snowshoers, and snowmobilers are allowed to travel on the trail when the snow is at least 6 inches deep.

Access and parking: Take Idaho Highway 55 north out of the town of Cascade. Cross the bridge over the north fork of the Payette River. From the north side of the bridge, drive 0.5 mile to Vista Point Boulevard and turn left. Stay on the dirt road for 1 mile to the intersection with Crown Point Parkway. Turn left at the intersection, then immediately left into a free public paved parking lot. Or go straight through the intersection and into the Crown Point Lake Cascade State Park and pay the day-use fee of $4 per vehicle. Access the trailhead just as you enter the state park.

Rentals: The town of Donnelly, 15 miles to the north, offers rentals in several locations. Bicycles and snowshoes are available at Pro Peak Sports on 412 West Roseberry, (208) 325–3323, or visit www.propeaksports.com. Bikes, snowshoes, and cross-country skis can be rented at West Mountain Gear and Grind, 270 North Main Street, (208) 325–8191, www.gearandgrind .com. See Appendix A for more rental options in Valley County.

Contact:

- Idaho Department of Parks and Recreation, Lake Cascade State Park, (208) 382–6544, www.parksandrecreation.idaho.gov

- Valley County Pathways, www.valleycountypathways.org

- Cascade Chamber of Commerce, (208) 382–3833, www.cascadechamber .com

Bus routes: None

Interpretive signs add interest to a visit to the Crown Point Trail along Lake Cascade.
(Courtesy Natalie Bartley)

Pine trees, sagebrush, and a combination of basalt rocks and decomposing granite line the Crown Point Trail. Strategically placed benches afford stunning views of Lake Cascade. When full of snowmelt water in the spring, the lake sits at 4,828 feet in elevation. It is the fourth-largest lake in Idaho. As water is released for irrigation purposes downstream, 86 miles of shoreline are exposed.

Fishing for rainbow trout, perch, and bass are popular pursuits. During the winter cross-country skiers, snowshoers, skijorers, and dogsledders use the trail.

The town of Cascade served as a depot for the railroads when the rails were built in Long Valley between 1912 and 1914. The Oregon Short Line Railroad (Union Pacific) placed tracks from Smith's Ferry to McCall to move supplies up and down the mountainous valley.

During the late 1940s a reservoir was built next to the town of Cascade, and the train tracks along the north fork of the Payette River had to be rerouted. The tracks were moved from their original location near the waterfalls on the north end of Cascade to the eastern shoreline of Lake Cascade. Crown Point Trail is on the rerouted railbed.

Railroad use in the area continued for decades after the 1940s, until the Boise Cascade lumber mill shut down in McCall. Rail tracks were removed in 1980, with the land reverting to the adjacent owners.

You can follow the sandy railbed, which runs for a mile along the lake with easy access to the shoreline. It then shifts slightly inland away from the lake among the ponderosa pine trees.

The squawks of ospreys and the "tap-tap-tap" of woodpeckers can be heard. Foxes also live in the area, and you might be treated to their calls. Soft sand on the trail serves as a perfect medium for local wildlife to imprint their paw prints. Wolves, cougars, deer, raccoons, badgers, and black bears travel this rail trail. Interpretive signs along the trail describe the flora and fauna in the area.

Intermittently the trail returns to the lake, where wide-open views of the long valley are possible. At 0.9 mile it enters a small basalt canyon. Then at 1.3 and 1.7 miles from the trailhead, you enter small canyons of decomposing granite rocks. It's easy to imagine the train chugging through these narrow passageways.

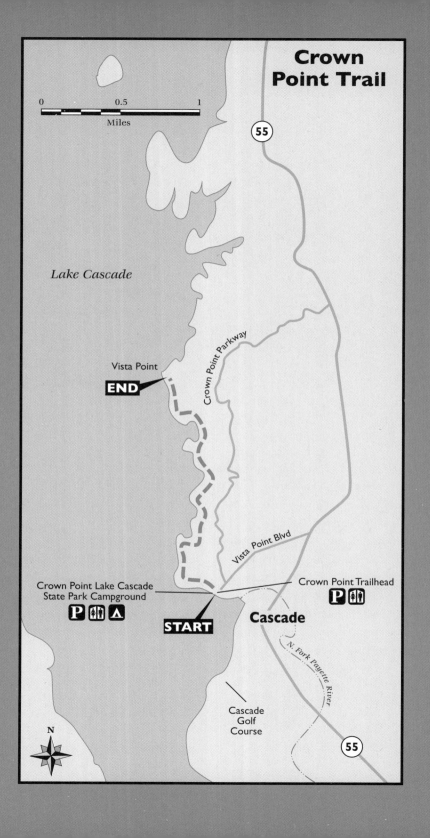

White, sandy beaches emerge along Lake Cascade at lower water levels. (Courtesy Natalie Bartley)

On the latter half of the trail, many small bays appear and the grade gently increases. During the early spring and late summer, coarse-sand beaches and boulder gardens emerge due to the lowering of reservoir water levels for irrigation purposes downstream.

Continue on the trail past some homes to 2.8 miles, where the trail currently ends at the privately owned Vista Point off Four Seasons Drive.

When you are ready, return the way you came and enjoy the scenery. West Mountain dominates the landscape on the west side of the lake. Sweeping views of the Cascade Golf Course and other Lake Cascade campgrounds come into view at 0.25 mile from the border of the Crown Point campground and the trailhead.

Nearby Attractions

Ride Thunder Mountain Line Cabarton Flyer along the north fork of the Payette River from Cascade to Smiths Ferry. Trains run from late May to end of September on Saturdays and Sundays from the Ashley Inn on the north side of Cascade on ID 55. For more information, call (877) 432–7245, or visit www.thundermountainline.com.

Future Plans

A small trailhead is being added on the north end of the trail, on the south side near Vista Point off Four Seasons Drive. Additionally, Valley County Pathways's long-range plan includes developing the rail line between Cascade and McCall as land negotiations are achieved.

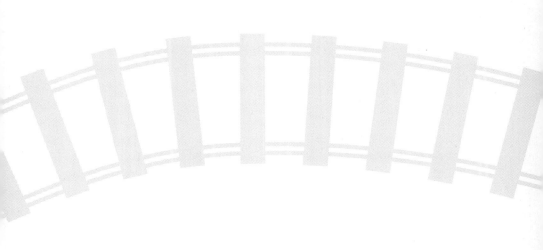

44 WEISER RIVER TRAIL

At 85.7 continuous miles, the Weiser River Trail is the longest non-motorized multiuse rail trail in Idaho. It travels on the original railbed beside the Weiser River and through rural towns of southwestern Idaho. Along the way it passes by farmland, basalt canyons, riparian zones, and the alpine setting of the Payette National Forest.

Activities:

Location: Weiser, Midvale, Cambridge, Council, and Rubicon near New Meadows, in Washington and Adams Counties

Length: 85.7 miles

Surface: Primarily original ballast material that has been graded and rolled. There are also dirt and gravel sections and short paved segments in the towns of Weiser, Cambridge, and Council.

Wheelchair access: The trailheads at Weiser, Cambridge, and Council are wheelchair accessible.

Difficulty: Easy on the paved sections; intermediate on the remote segments

Food: Restaurants, grocery stores, and gas stations can be found in Weiser, Midvale, Cambridge, Council, and New Meadows.

Restrooms: Portable toilets are available April 1 to October 31 at the Weiser, Midvale, Cambridge, Council, and Starkey Trailheads. The vault toilet at Presley Trailhead is open seasonally, and there are vault toilets at the Evergreen Campground.

Seasons: The trail can be used year-round. The southern segment is free of snow by March; the northern section is generally free of snow from May to October.

Access and parking: There are several established trailheads and a number of small roadside spots that you can use to access this long trail. The following trailheads reflect the larger, more easily accessed locations.

- Weiser Trailhead: From Interstate 84, take U.S. Highway 95 north to Weiser. After crossing the Weiser River and entering the town of Weiser, continue a few blocks and turn right on East Main Street. Go 0.6 mile to the trailhead parking lot on the left. The trail goes southwest for 0.2 mile to US 95 and stops. Take the trail going east to access the full length of the trail.

- Rebecca Trailhead: Access this small parking area on Unity Road, just before the bridge. From Weiser, head north on US 95. Turn east on Park Street, which becomes Weiser River Road. Drive east 5.3 miles. Turn right on Unity Road at the fork in the road. The trail crosses Unity Road before the bridge. Park on the east side of the road at the small site of an old siding named Rebecca.

- Presley Trailhead: Take US 95 into Weiser. Go 0.3 mile and turn right at the stoplight onto Park Street. Park Street changes to Weiser River Road about a mile from the stoplight. Continue for a few miles to the intersection of Mann Creek Road. Presley Trailhead is 5.6 miles beyond on Weiser River Road. Drive past the Galloway Dam and up the hill into the canyon. Soon the road turns to gravel. The trailhead is on the right, and the trail runs in front of the trailhead.

- Midvale Trailhead: Take US 95 north from Weiser 20 miles to Midvale. The trailhead is near highway mile marker 104 on the east side of the road in a large gravel lot next to the Midvale Community Park.

- Cambridge Trailhead: From Weiser, take US 95 north about 41 miles into Cambridge. US 95 turns sharply east at an intersection. Continue east to the trailhead kiosk on the east side of the highway by the Washington County Fairgrounds.

- Mesa Siding access point: From Council, drive 3.4 miles south on US 95. Park on the west side of the highway, where the trail heads west away from the road.

- Council Trailhead: From the Mesa Siding access point, follow US 95 north 3.4 miles into Council. US 95 becomes Michigan Avenue. Turn left at Moser Road and wind through a residential area for 0.3 mile to the trailhead at the small paved parking lot. The trail is beside the lot.

- Starkey Trailhead: Take US 95 north 5.2 miles from the Council Trailhead. When US 95 swings right, take Fruitvale–Glendale Road, which appears directly in front of you and slightly to the left of US 95. Drive 5.5 miles past Fruitvale and the Starkey Hot Springs. You will find trailhead parking to the right just before the road and the trail cross the Weiser River.

- Evergreen U.S. Forest Service campground: Take US 95 north 13.8 miles from the Council Trailhead. Turn east into the campground. Day-use parking is available at the lot to the south. When staying in the campground, parking is also available. Access the trail from the day-use area by crossing the bridge, going to the middle of the tent camping area, and moving up a gentle path that connects with the trail.

- West Pine Trailhead: This is the current northern terminus. Take US 95 north from the Evergreen Campground to highway mile marker 157. Turn east onto Old Highway 95. Drive 0.4 mile on Old Highway 95 to a small gravel lot. Access the trail by taking the spur on the left, which leads to the main trail in 0.4 mile. Or park on the east side of US 95 at mile marker 157. Access the trail beside US 95.

Rentals: Mountain bikes, cross-country skis, and snowshoes can be rented near the northern terminus in New Meadows at Mud Creek Outdoor Gear, 202 Virginia Street, (208) 347–2025, www.mudcreekoutdoorgear.com. Or see Appendix A for rentals in nearby Valley County.

Contact: For information on current trail conditions, or to purchase the comprehensive trail guidebook, *The Weiser River Trail,* written by Margaret Fuller and Anita Van Grunsven, call Friends of the Weiser River Trail, (888) MY–TRAIL, or visit www.weiserrivertrail.org.

To arrange shuttles, contact Colonial Motel in Weiser, (208) 549–0150, www.colonialmotel.us; or Mud Creek Outdoor Gear in New Meadows, (208) 347–2025, www.mudcreekoutdoorgear.com.

Bus routes: None

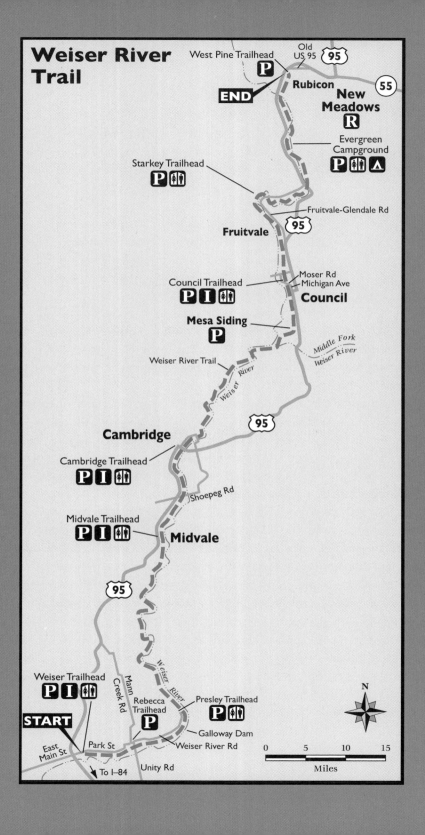

Weiser River Trail

West Pine Trailhead **P**

Old US 95 **95**

Rubicon

END

New Meadows R

55

Evergreen Campground **P** 🚻 △

Starkey Trailhead **P** 🚻

Fruitvale-Glendale Rd

95

Fruitvale

Council Trailhead **P I** 🚻

Moser Rd
Michigan Ave

Council

Mesa Siding P

Middle Fork Weiser River

Weiser River Trail

Weiser River

95

Cambridge

Cambridge Trailhead **P I** 🚻

Shoepeg Rd

Midvale Trailhead **P I** 🚻

Midvale

95

N

Weiser Trailhead **P I** 🚻

Mann Creek Rd

Rebecca Trailhead **P**

Presley Trailhead **P** 🚻

START

East Main St

Park St

Galloway Dam

Weiser River Rd

To I–84

Unity Rd

0   5   10   15

Miles

Weiser, Midvale, and Cambridge form the southern portion of the Weiser River Trail. Cambridge, Council, and Rubicon, near New Meadows, form the northern portion. Both segments are on the original railbed almost the entire length. The mileage begins at mile 0.5 in Weiser, west of where US 95 crosses the Weiser River. It is near the terminus of the original railbed.

In 2007 the Weiser River Trail celebrated its tenth anniversary with long-distance bicycle rides, traditional wagon train journeys, and nature walks. Since the trail passes through four rural communities and two counties, there wasn't one single organization able to oversee the vast miles of the trail. The Friends of the Weiser River Trail, a nonprofit volunteer group, was formed in 1996 to coordinate trail efforts.

By 1997 the former railbed was converted into a recreational multiuse trail, and now the Friends of the Weiser River Trail preserves and improves the rail corridor. The Weiser River Trail is unique in that very few rail trails in the country are owned and managed by a volunteer organization and its members.

Historically, the Weiser-to-New Meadows rail system was in operation under various owners from as early as 1895 until 1995, when the rails were abandoned. The Oregon Short Line, the Pacific & Northern Railway, and, more recently, the Union Pacific were involved over the years. Rails moved timber, livestock, and farming supplies. They also transported passengers as the populations of Adams and Washington Counties grew.

From its humble start as an abandoned Union Pacific Railroad corridor that was first converted to 7 miles of nonmotorized rail trail, the trail is a labor of love in constant motion. Thanks to the Friends of the Weiser River Trail, the trail distance and quality have steadily improved over the years.

When renovation began, rails were removed and the surface smoothed. Grants were awarded to pave small segments near the towns. During a few weeks each year, goats were brought onto the trail for invasive weed control. They swiftly destroyed the weeds by devouring them. Trestles were improved by adding side rails for safety and planking to the surface for smooth crossings. In 2006 and 2007, 7 blocks of the trail were paved from US 95 to the Weiser city limits. An information kiosk, a small paved parking lot, and a trailhead were constructed at Weiser's city limits, serving as an ideal launching spot for northward travel on the trail. Users can now travel the entire trail.

The Weiser Trailhead at the southern end of the Weiser River Trail. (Courtesy Natalie Bartley)

Bicyclers, hikers, and horseback riders traverse various segments of the route. Other outdoor activities near the trail include canoeing and fishing on the Weiser River. Bird-watching and wildlife photography opportunities also abound.

Weiser to Midvale, 31.3 miles

There are a number of access points in and near Weiser. Visitors can travel short segments of the trail and then head into town to enjoy the history and amenities that this town of 5,000 offers. Check out Weiser's historic buildings, including a train station, courthouse, church, and various homes.

Spring is the best time of year to experience this section. Green fields, chirping birds, cool weather, and the absence of weeds that puncture bicycle tires make for ideal traveling on the trail. However, the trail can be wet and muddy in the spring, so contact the Friends of the Weiser River Trail for current conditions.

Trail miles are indicated by old rail spikes, such as the one at mile 10 on the Weiser River Trail. (Courtesy Natalie Bartley)

If beginning at the Weiser Trailhead, you will be starting near mile 0.7, on a paved section of the trail. The trail mile markers indicate the distance from the Weiser Depot, west of US 95 in Weiser. For a brief jaunt on the paved portion, you can head west for 0.2 mile to the US 95 bridge at the actual end of the trail, then return to the trailhead.

Shortly after leaving the Weiser Trailhead heading east, the pavement turns to dirt and gravel, and it will remain so until Cambridge. The farther you go from Weiser, the more rural the trail becomes. Along the way you cross trestles near 2.5 miles and after 5 miles. Just before 6 miles you cross Unity Road.

From here the trail continues through agriculture fields. Though you cannot see the river yet, you will meet up with it soon. Notice the mile markers as you travel the trail. They are made of old railroad spikes and ascend in number as you head east.

When you arrive at mile 10, you will see Galloway Dam. This is a good boating and fishing access spot, though boaters should consider a portage around the low head dam. After leaving the dam you enter a remote canyon. Just ahead is the Presley Trailhead and restroom at mile 11.4.

The trail from Weiser to beyond Galloway Dam has noticeably shifted from a small rural town to ranch lands and into a canyon where you may even see a herd of deer. Ring-necked pheasants, killdeers, hawks, chukars, and ospreys are but a few of the birds that trail users can see or hear. Bring a flower book if visiting in the spring or summer; the wildflowers are prolific along the trail.

There is hardly any shade on the trail from Weiser to Midvale, so use sunscreen and protective clothing. During the summer, consider traveling in the early morning before it gets hot.

After leaving Presley Trailhead you enter a remote area, cross over a trestle, view trailside cliffs, and travel through an area without any signs

Remote canyons are common along the Weiser River Trail. This one is between Galloway Dam and Midvale. (Courtesy Natalie Bartley)

of residents. At 14.5 miles you can see a concrete structure on the hill that was used to load grain into railroad cars.

You will be traveling near the Weiser River and crossing another trestle over a creek after 18 miles. From here you enter a narrow canyon and pass a rocky slope at 21 miles. Just ahead is a lengthy high trestle at Thousand Springs Creek before 22 miles. Another trestle is at 23.5 miles at Sheep Creek.

Continue on the trail, where you interact frequently with the river and small creeks. Basalt rocks are visible in the surrounding canyons, and the environment is a mix of desert grasses, sagebrush, and river vegetation such as poison ivy.

Eventually trail adventurers heading east and then north from Weiser see the upcoming mountains, which appear at about 28 miles when the scenery opens and affords views of the valley. The trail crosses Sage Creek trestle at 30 miles. Farm fields and the town of Midvale materialize shortly after. Midvale is a small town consisting of several hundred residents. It was known as the wool capital of the United States in the 1900s. The Pacific & Idaho Northern Railway reached the town in 1899. There is a grocery store, a coffeehouse, a bed-and-breakfast, and a park with an outdoor swimming pool. All amenities are within a block or two of the trailhead in Midvale.

Midvale to Cambridge, 8.7 miles

From the Midvale Trailhead there are about 8 miles of trail that pass intermittently along the Weiser River and US 95. The dirt gravel trail is generally level, with slight inclines and declines.

Seeds from noxious weeds called goat heads have been known to puncture bicycle tires. If riding a mountain bike, it helps to buy tire tubes that are internally coated with a gel that helps to keep the air from escaping in case you puncture your tire with a goat head seed. Due to the rugged nature of the trail, a mountain bike with shock absorbers will make the journey more pleasant. Many stretches of the trail are desolate, so carry drinking water, snacks, and perhaps a cell phone, although there will be sections of the trail where cell phones won't work.

A walker approaches the Midvale Trailhead on the Midvale to Cambridge section of the Weiser River Trail. (Courtesy Natalie Bartley)

Many views of the river, and in the spring of the distant snowcapped mountains, are available on the Midvale-to-Cambridge section. The scent of green alfalfa fields, the tweet of meadowlarks, and glimpses of red-winged blackbirds are but a few of the many experiences along the trail.

You will come to the Shoepeg Road Bridge over the Weiser River at about 36 miles. There is parking for a few vehicles near the bridge. Enjoy a view of Cuddy Mountain before continuing north on the trail along the river, entering a canyon along US 95. At about 39 miles you can see the dirt road that once served as the old highway and crossed the river. In 1997 Silver Bridge was swept away in high water. Now the site serves as a fishing access and has limited parking.

Head on to the town of Cambridge. At 40.5 miles you will enter the Cambridge Trailhead, passing the Washington County Fairgrounds along the way. Within 2 blocks of the trail, you will encounter a grocery store, motels, and restaurants.

Cambridge to Council, 19.7 miles

Late spring, summer, and autumn are fine times to travel the cooler alpine northern section that passes through ponderosa pine trees and along the Weiser River from its source in the mountains north of Council.

From riparian areas along the Weiser River to the mountainous terrain in the Payette National Forest, the northern segment of the Weiser River Trail offers a variety of ecosystems. Going north from Cambridge, a slight uphill grade runs on packed dirt and gravel.

The trail is paved a short distance in Cambridge. After the pavement ends, the trail moves through fields and into another canyon. Vegetation increases as you reconnect with the river. At about 46 miles the trail crosses over a trestle at Grizzly Creek. Continue through this secluded segment, along the river and hills. Sunflowers, willows, and cottonwoods grow along the trail. Deer, yellow warblers, and wild turkeys dart in and out of view.

Ranching and farming occur along sections of the Weiser River Trail. A cow stands on the trail south of Mesa Siding on the Cambridge-to-Council section. (Courtesy Natalie Bartley)

Travel over the trestles that cross Cottonwood Creek and Goodrich Creek. Pass over Cow Creek on a small trestle at 47.5 miles, then the Goodrich Creek trestle at 49.5 miles. Goodrich Road reaches the trail before 50 miles. It serves as an access point with limited parking. Goodrich was once a small town on the rail line.

At 51.5 miles you cross a bridge over the river, and at about 54 miles you travel over a trestle that crosses the middle fork of the Weiser River. Near 56.5 miles the trail returns to the highway 4 miles south of Council near Mesa Siding. Fruit-growing was popular in this area in the early 1900s.

Between Mesa Siding and Council, the trail runs beside US 95 in the open area of the valley from 56.5 miles to 60 miles. The trail is paved in Council from Cool Creek, near 58 miles, to Airport Road, which is north of town. Take a break at the Council Trailhead at 60.2 miles and read local history at the railroad-themed kiosk shelter.

Council to West Pine Trailhead, 26 miles

In this section the trail leaves the drier climate and enters a lush forest containing Douglas fir and ponderosa pine. Much of the trail can be viewed from Fruitvale–Glendale Road and, later, US 95. There are a few small access sites along the way.

As the trail flows north from Council, it merges into a mixture of meadows and timbered areas near the highway bypass between Council and Fruitvale. You will encounter the old town of Fruitvale at 66 miles. Fruitvale had a depot building until 1915, when it was removed and taken to Council to serve as the depot there. Continue on the trail as it passes along Fruitvale–Glendale Road and continues near residences in the forest and on to a narrow bridge crossing beyond 67 miles. Near 69.5 miles is the Starkey Trailhead and a restroom.

From this point the trail travels through the deep forest and out to an open valley. You will cruise by the old rail line town of Glendale at 72 miles.

Bicyclists make their way south toward Council on the Weiser River Trail. (Courtesy Natalie Bartley)

Continue to 73 miles, where you can see a narrow canyon and US 95. Get ready to cross the river on a trestle as it passes under the US 95 bridge, at about 74 miles. Two more trestle crossings are ahead, followed by some homes and a long trestle near 76 miles.

Continue on the trail as it travels above the river. Near 76.5 miles the small settlement of Evergreen existed near the tracks in the early 1900s.

Trestle crossings are frequent on the northern reaches of the Weiser River Trail. (*Courtesy Natalie Bartley*)

Continue toward mile 77 where a footpath accesses the rail trail from the Evergreen Campground. The U.S. Forest Service campground was built in the early 1920s and now serves as the only designated campsite on the trail until future sites are developed. This is a good place to hop off the trail and use the restrooms and refill your water containers. The lush green forest may entice you to camp overnight in this pleasant spot.

Follow the trail as it goes uphill and through the forest to the flats of the upper valley, exiting the timbered area and traveling next to US 95 at about 78.5 miles. The trail crosses a trestle at about 79 miles. Near 81 miles you can see the road to Lost Valley Reservoir as it departs from US 95; you can also see a restaurant at the intersection.

The next few miles run along US 95 and include a short bypass off the original railbed. The present-day Evergreen Forest Products sawmill sits atop the original railbed. Take the gravel road between mile 81 and mile 82.5 that detours you around the mill. It heads uphill and includes

---

Nearby Attractions

Annual events in the area include:

- Cambridge's Hells Canyon Days, first week in June, www
.cambridgeidaho.com

- Weiser River Wagon Train Event, first weekend in June,
(888) My-Trail, www.weiserrivertrail.org

---

a sharp turn to the left, then downhill to rejoin the original railbed. Near mile 83 you'll encounter the Wye, a potential future camping site. The Y in the tracks was originally used to turn trains around. Rubicon, which is now just a name on the map, is located at 84.5 miles. It was the end of the tracks after the rails were abandoned. Continue north on the trail to near mile 85.7 to access the current northern terminus at Old Highway 95 and present-day US 95.

Consider taking advantage of the gentle downhill gradient by traveling the trail from north to south. Between Rubicon and Council the trail loses more than 1,200 feet of elevation. Another 275 feet of elevation are lost from Council to Cambridge, and 527 feet of elevation between Cambridge and Weiser.

Future Plans

The Friends of the Weiser River Trail has many plans for improvements along the trail. A small equestrian campground will be built near the northern terminus at the future Wye Trailhead. At the town of Midvale, the trail will have a paved section. Trailheads, parking, access points, and interpretive signs will be improved as funds become available. Ultimately the trail is to extend from the present northern West Pine Trailhead to the town of New Meadows and to New Meadows's old train depot, built in 1911.

45 NAMPA RAILS TO TRAILS

For a reprieve from the hustle and bustle of suburban life, this trail offers a restful path along grasslands and trees, through a neighborhood park, and among open fields. It serves as a reminder of Nampa's rural personality.

Activities:

Location: City of Nampa, in Canyon County

Length: 2 miles

Surface: Asphalt

Wheelchair access: The trail is easily wheelchair accessible.

Difficulty: Easy

Food: There are nearby convenience stores and plenty of eateries in Nampa.

Restrooms: None

Seasons: The trail can be used year-round.

Access and parking: Head west on Interstate 84 from Boise. Take exit 38. Turn left on Garrity Boulevard. Go 1.3 miles and turn left on Kings Road. Drive 1.8 miles and cross Amity Road. At this point Kings Road changes to Southside Boulevard. Continue 1 mile more and turn right onto East Greenhurst Road. Go 0.4 mile to trailhead on the right across from Maple Wood Park.

Rentals: None in Nampa. See Appendix A for Treasure Valley rentals.

Contact: City of Nampa Parks Department, (208) 468–5890, www.nampa parksandrecreation.org.

Bus routes: None

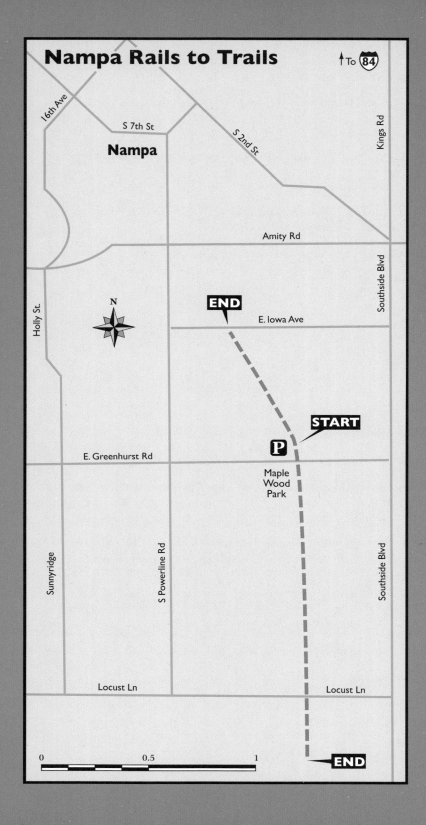

City trails are becoming more important and increasingly available as population growth continues in the Treasure Valley. Nampa offers citizens and visitors this rail trail for escaping and spending time with nature.

Originally the rail tracks ran from Nampa to Melba, and on to Silver City in the Owyhee Mountains. When the railroad closed the rails in this area, the city agreed to take them over as a trail. During the mid-1990s the trail was an undeveloped dirt path, which the city of Nampa re-created as a paved multiuse rails-to-trails conversion trail.

From the established paved trailhead across from Maple Wood Park, the smooth paved trail heads north 0.5 mile to East Iowa Avenue, passing through a grass- and tree-studded corridor between homes. The City of Nampa Forestry Department planted trees in 2004. There are interpretive signs describing the purple catalpa, Australian pine, and other trees in the area. At the end of this stretch, you can view the original railbed with metal tracks intact. To visit the rest of the trail, return the way you came to get back to the trailhead across from Maple Wood Park.

The southern section of the Nampa Rails to Trails passes between farmland and residential areas. (Courtesy Natalie Bartley)

There are 1.5 miles of paved trail on the southern segment, accessed by leaving the trailhead, crossing over East Greenhurst Road, and entering the Maple Wood neighborhood park. The trail passes through the edge of the park, then runs by homes and to open fields, giving a rural flavor. It currently ends at a closed trestle that crosses an irrigation ditch just past Locust Lane. Retrace the trail you just traveled on, ending back at the trailhead across from Maple Wood Park.

Original plans were to develop the trail to Melba, but the landowners along the rails declined. Long-range plans are to continue the trail northward and loop it back to Lakeview Park off 16th Avenue and Garrity Boulevard.

While you are in the area, consider visiting the Indian Creek Greenbelt (Trail 46).

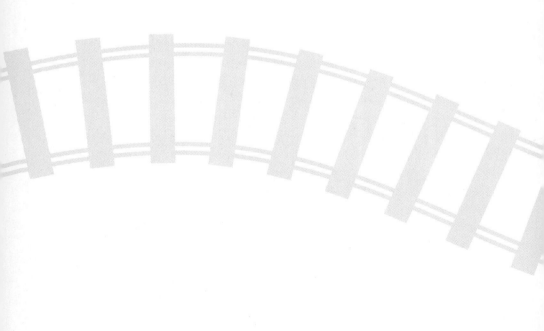

46 INDIAN CREEK GREENBELT

Classified as a trail-by-rail, this short greenbelt offers variety. During the irrigation season, typically April through September, the creek along the trail glitters in the sunshine and expands activity options to include fishing, tubing, canoeing, and kayaking. After a jaunt on the trail, you can readily access a restaurant for a quick bite to eat.

Activities:

Location: Kuna, in Ada County

Length: 1.4 miles

Surface: Asphalt for the first 0.5 mile, followed by basalt rock single-track trail, a paved road bike path detour, and dirt road shared by occasional vehicles.

Wheelchair access: Wheelchair accessible from the parking lot at the trailhead onto the paved portion of the trail

Difficulty: Easy on the paved portion, then changes to difficult on basalt rock single-track

Food: There are eateries along the trail and a few short blocks into the town of Kuna.

Restrooms: You can find restrooms at the Indian Creek Greenbelt Park Trailhead, a Kuna city park.

Seasons: The trail can be used year-round.

Access and parking: From Meridian, or exit 44 off Interstate 84, take Idaho Highway 69 south for 8 miles, then turn right onto Kuna Road. Kuna Road becomes East Avalon Avenue; follow it to Swan Falls Road, where the trailhead starts next to the Kuna Chamber of Commerce Visitor Center in the Indian Creek Greenbelt Park.

Rentals: None in Kuna. See Appendix A for rentals in the Treasure Valley.

Contact: Kuna Chamber of Commerce, (208) 922–9254, www.kunachamber
.com

Bus routes: None

||||||||||||||||||||||||||||||||||||||||||||||||||||||||||||||||||||||||||||||||||||||

Kuna, pronounced *Q-nuh,* is a small rural town of 14,261. It hosts the
Indian Creek Greenbelt and is the place to head if you want to admire
the sparkling Indian Creek when it runs during irrigation season or to par-
take in the variety of other recreation activities available year-round.

Visitors and residents enjoy walking, biking, fishing, picnicking, and
bird-watching. There is a BMX bicycle park along the paved portion of the
trail. An active Union Pacific rail track is on the other side of the creek,
lending atmosphere.

The best access point is at the parking lot, with heated restrooms and
wheelchair accessibility to the trail. Start at the Indian Creek Greenbelt
Park, next to the Chamber of Commerce Visitor Center.

*The paved portion of the Indian Creek Greenbelt passes through a Kuna city park. (Cour-
tesy Natalie Bartley)*

Indian Creek Greenbelt

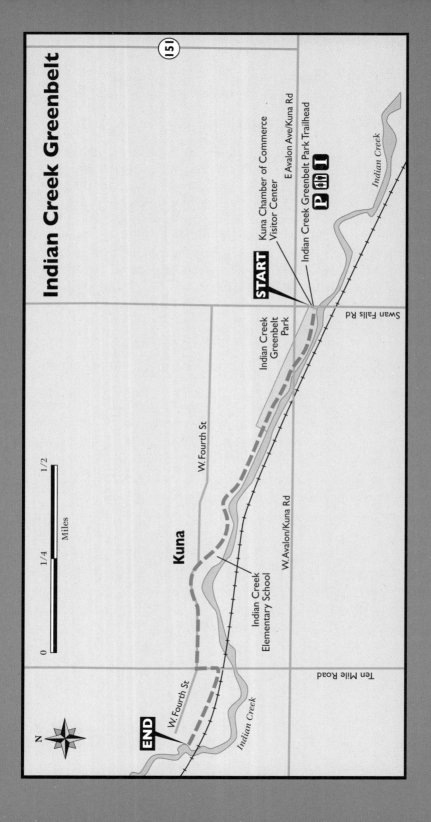

151

Kuna Chamber of Commerce
Visitor Center

E Avalon Ave/Kuna Rd

Indian Creek Greenbelt Park Trailhead

START

Swan Falls Rd

Indian Creek

Indian Creek
Greenbelt
Park

W. Fourth St

Kuna

W. Avalon/Kuna Rd

Indian Creek
Elementary School

Ten Mile Road

0   1/4   1/2

Miles

N

W. Fourth St

END

Indian Creek

Nearby Attractions

Kuna is considered the gateway to the Snake River Birds of Prey National Conservation Area (NCA) and the 30-mile Western Heritage Historic Byway. Stock up on food and gas before heading off into the desert to explore these areas, as you travel through undeveloped countryside. Be sure to stop at the Kuna Chamber of Commerce Visitor Center and pick up a scenic highway map, the raptor identification guide, and other brochures to get you started.

• Snake River Birds of Prey National Conservation Area, www.birdsofprey.blm.gov

• Western Heritage Historic Byway, www.byways.org

Indian Creek Greenbelt consists of paved asphalt for a little over 0.5 mile, then changes to a dirt and basalt rock trail behind the school. If you continue for about 0.3 mile, you leave the dirt trail and hit a street bike path that detours you for approximately 0.3 mile through a residential area and back onto a dirt trail. Another 0.3 mile takes you to the end of the trail beside a small basalt rock canyon of Indian Creek near a residential area.

Return the way you came, perhaps taking a break trailside to enjoy a hamburger and salad at the Peregrine Steak House. Other trailside options include a Pizza Hut, plus a number of restaurants in town just off the trail.

While you are in the area, consider visiting the Nampa Rails to Trails (Trail 45) and the Boise River Greenbelt (Trail 47).

Future Plans

At present the railroad right-of-way crosses private property; this limits further development for the time being.

47 BOISE RIVER GREENBELT

Each visit to the Greenbelt along the Boise River brings new discoveries about this wonderful resource that runs through the heart of Boise and westward through the Treasure Valley. Encounters with nature are common. On any given trip you might see great blue herons, mallards, Canada geese, or even deer. Plus, there are numerous stops along the trail that can add variety to any outing. This description covers a section of the trail that serves as the heart of the culture- and nature-based activities on the north side of the river, from downtown Boise to Lucky Peak Reservoir.

Activities:

Location: City of Boise, in Ada County

Length: 10.8-mile northeast segment

Surface: Asphalt

Wheelchair access: All trailheads are wheelchair accessible except for the dirt lot near the Idaho Highway 21 bridge.

Difficulty: Easy

Food: Numerous eateries are located just off the trail in Boise.

Restrooms: You will find restrooms in Julia Davis Park, Municipal Park, Warm Springs Golf Course, Barber Park, at the trailside near the Idaho Department of Parks and Recreation headquarters, in Lucky Peak State Park–Discovery Unit, and in Lucky Peak State Park–Sandy Point Unit.

Seasons: The trail can be used year-round.

Access and parking: A number of Boise city parks, street intersections, and roadside pullouts serve as access points for the Greenbelt. This description covers the trail on the north side of the Boise River, from Capital Boulevard east to Lucky Peak State Park.

- Julia Davis Park: From Interstate 84 take exit 53 (Vista Avenue), turning north onto Vista Avenue. From the north side of the I-84 overpass, head toward the mountains, traveling 2 miles to the stoplight where

The Boise River Greenbelt travels through many lush parks, including the Julia Davis Park in Boise. (Courtesy Natalie Bartley)

Vista Avenue turns into Capital Boulevard (near the intersection with Federal Way). Continue on Capital Boulevard past the Boise Depot and Boise State University. Cross the bridge over the Boise River, and at 0.7 mile (at the stoplight), turn right into Julia Davis Park, passing under the entry arch. Turn immediately right and park anywhere you can find space. Parking is free, though signs indicate there is a two-hour limit on weekdays. The Greenbelt is next to the Boise River on the south side of the park.

- Municipal Park: Leave Julia Davis Park, turning right onto Capital Boulevard. Go 2 blocks and turn right onto Myrtle Street. Continue 0.7 mile on Myrtle Street to Broadway Avenue, getting into a left lane. At the stoplight, turn left onto Broadway Avenue, continuing 0.3 mile to the intersection of Warm Springs Avenue. Turn right and follow Warm Springs Avenue another 0.5 mile to Walnut Street and turn right. Go 0.2 mile and turn left into Municipal Park. Parking is free. The Greenbelt runs along the south edge of the park, and there is a spur on the north side heading east to connect to the Greenbelt. You can easily visit the Morrison–Knudsen Nature Center on the southwest edge of the park by the river.

- Warm Springs Golf Course: Return to the intersection of Warm Springs Avenue and Walnut Street. Turn right onto Warm Springs Avenue and drive 1.5 miles, turning right into the golf course parking lot. Park for free here. The Greenbelt is on the south side of the parking lot. Access some of the Foothills Trails in the Ridge to Rivers Trail System by crossing over Warm Springs Avenue on the north side of the parking lot.

- Barber Park: This park serves as the launching spot for floating in the Boise River. From the golf course parking lot, turn right. Continue on Warm Springs Avenue, passing by a large dirt parking lot for Greenbelt access at 2.5 miles. At 2.8 miles, turn right onto South Eckert Road and go 0.7 mile, crossing a bridge over the Boise River and turning right into Barber Park. There are a few free parking spots on the northeast side of the bridge; otherwise pay the day-use fee if leaving your vehicle at the park. To access the Greenbelt heading to Lucky Peak, retrace the route on South Eckert Road back to Warm Springs Avenue and turn right onto the trail.

- Idaho Department of Parks and Recreation Headquarters: From South Eckert Road, turn right onto Warm Springs Avenue and go 0.5 mile, turning right into the state park headquarters. Park for free and pick up the trail, which runs along Warm Springs Avenue. The entry gate is locked at 6:00 p.m., so make sure you remove your vehicle in time.

- Junction of Warm Springs Avenue and ID 21: Turn right on Warm Springs from the state park headquarters. Go 1.7 miles and turn right into the unmarked free dirt parking lot before the ID 21 bridge over the Boise River.

- Lucky Peak State Park–Discovery Unit: From the dirt lot before the bridge, go 0.1 mile to the intersection of Warm Springs Avenue and ID 21. Turn left at the stop sign, onto ID 21 heading upstream along the river. Drive 2 miles and turn right into the park; pay the day-use fee if leaving your vehicle.

- Lucky Peak State Park–Sandy Point Unit: Turn right out of the Discovery Unit and go 0.1 mile into the free parking lot by the sign LUCKY PEAK LAKE. You can pick up the Greenbelt off the end of the lot adjacent to the Discovery Unit and head into Discovery Park, or go in the opposite direction to get to the end of the path at Sandy Point Beach. To drive to Sandy Point Beach, follow the road that starts in the parking lot for another 0.7 mile to the park's toll booth and pay the day-use fee.

Friendship Bridge affords an open view of rafts and tubes floating the Boise River in the summer. (Courtesy Natalie Bartley)

Rentals: In Boise bicycles, cross-country skis, and snowshoes can be rented at Idaho Mountain Touring, 1310 West Main Street, (208) 336–3854, www.idahomountaintouring.com. Bicycles and snowshoes can be rented at Bikes 2 Boards, 3525 West State Street, (208) 343–0208, www.bikes 2boards.com.

Contact:

• Boise Parks and Recreation Department, (208) 384–4486, www.cityof boise.org/Departments/Parks/

• Check the Boise Parks and Recreation Department's Web site for up-to-date information on Greenbelt access and potential closures due to high water on the Boise River. For the Ada County segment, contact Ada County Parks and Waterways, (208) 577–4575, www.adaweb.net.

Bus routes: Contact Valley Regional Transit (208) 345–7433, www.valley ride.org.

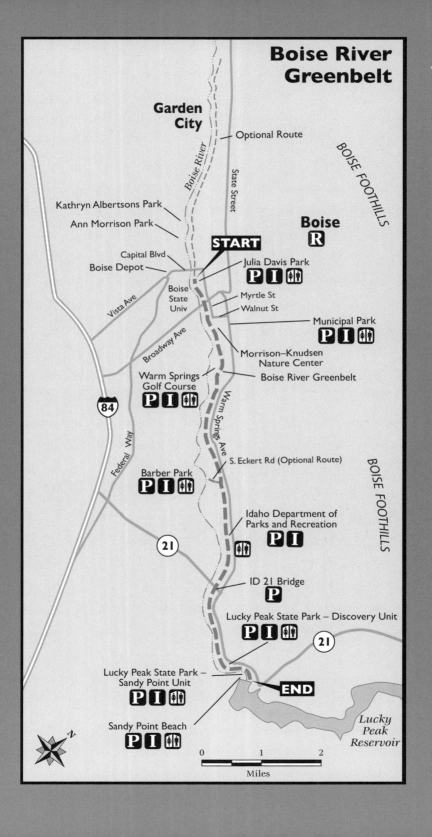

Comprised of approximately 21 miles of trails in Boise that pass through twelve parks, the Boise River Greenbelt runs on both sides of the Boise River. The longest segment goes along the river from Lucky Peak Reservoir downstream for more than 16 miles, until it meets up with the Garden City Greenbelt. A segment of the Boise River Greenbelt also runs for 7 miles on the south side of the Boise River, from Barber Park to Ann Morrison Park, with spurs near Kathryn Albertson Park. There are additional paved trails along the southern portion of the river through Garden City and also through the city of Eagle west of Boise.

The Boise River Greenbelt got its start back in 1964, when it was first suggested that a greenbelt along the river would be an asset to the city of Boise. Initially, a regulation was established stating that structures and parking areas had to be at least 70 feet from the river, resulting in a buffer zone between the river and the encroaching city.

Gradually land was acquired and protected. The Boise River Greenbelt grew into the lovely refuge that it is today. The Boise Parks and Recreation Department maintains more than 21 miles of the beltway, while the areas

Table Rock, a famous Boise Foothills landmark, looms large near the Warm Springs Golf Course on the Boise River Greenbelt. (Courtesy Natalie Bartley)

beyond the city limits are taken care of by Ada County Parks and Water-ways and by Garden City.

There are many places to access the Greenbelt's path on both the north and south sides of the river. The following describes the segment on the north side of the river, from Capital Boulevard southeast to Lucky Peak Dam.

You can learn about local history along the Greenbelt, thanks to the Ada County Centennial Committee and the Idaho Historical Society. Inter-pretive signs dot the beltway.

Electric streetcars ran on tracks through the valley in the early 1890s, passing on streets near what would later become the Boise River Green-belt. In 1907 the electric interurban streetcar line was completed. By the late 1920s the streetcar routes were dismantled as motorized buses came into use.

Other rail activity in the area included the Oregon Short Line Railroad. It traversed southern Idaho and was extended to Boise in 1887, moving fruit and other wares. The Union Pacific Railroad constructed a spur into Boise along Front Street, which was finished by 1903. In 1925 the depot and rail were rerouted to the present location of the Boise Depot on the hill south of the Boise River. Rails also ran to the Barber Park area.

Though the tracks never went along the river, they crossed it in a few places. You can see an old railroad bridge crossing at the Eighth Street Bridge on the northwest side of Boise State University. Built in 1911, it is now a pedestrian bridge crossing over the Boise River.

To get on the Boise River Greenbelt from Julia Davis Park, head to the southern edge of the park. Mile 0 starts nearby on the west side of Capi-tal Boulevard in the middle of the paved trail beneath the Eighth Street pedestrian bridge underpass. Mileage numbers ascend toward Lucky Peak Reservoir. There are mile marker posts along the trail spaced at 0.5-mile intervals in the city of Boise segment. Also look for frequent mileage markers painted on the asphalt path displaying N.E. and the mileage.

Go east on the trail by turning left onto the paved path along the river through Julia Davis Park. Known for its cultural and recreational opportu-nities, the park is a good place to spend time exploring as part of your visit to the Boise River Greenbelt. At mile 0.3 you could turn right and cross the Friendship Bridge that leads to the Boise State University campus

The Diversion Dam Power Plant on the Boise River along the Boise River Greenbelt is a popular trailside stop. It is located across from the Black Cliffs climbing area, 8.7 miles from the trail's start at Julia Davis Park. (Courtesy Natalie Bartley)

and a south bank section of the Greenbelt. The bridge is a good vantage point from which to watch rafters and tubers floating on the river on a hot, sunny day.

Continue on the north side of the river through Julia Davis Park. At mile 0.9 you pass under Broadway Avenue and then pass the Ram Restaurant and Brewery. By 1.5 miles you are next to the Morrison–Knudson Nature Center. It's worth a stop to explore the self-paced nature trail. Interpretive signs lead visitors to points of interest. Learn about the plants, fish, and animals that live there. Immediately adjacent to the nature center is the Municipal Park. Large, old trees provide shade and a cool contrast to the upcoming stretch that heads out into the sunshine.

The trail departs from the river, and by 2.1 miles the Warm Springs Golf Course comes into sight, as does a broad view of Table Rock. Stay to the left side of the path to continue to Lucky Peak. On the far side of the golf course, you'll see the trailhead parking lot shared with the golfers.

This is a convenient place to access the trails in the Foothills that are in the Ridge to Rivers Trail System. Go across Warm Springs Avenue to get on a dirt footpath that passes the site of an old sandstone rock quarry.

Just beyond 3 miles the trail opens up and returns to the river. Ada County takes over jurisdiction of the trail. Beyond 3.4 miles you can watch kayakers playing on a wave at the weir at the old Goodwin Dam site. As you travel upstream, the road is on your left and the river on your right. Popular with in-line skaters, this segment is less congested and moves through a more rural setting. At 5.7 miles you come to a closed road and a dirt parking lot. There is a spur trail to the right that takes you to Barber Park. Or go to 5.9 miles, to the newer South Eckert Road and Warm Springs Avenue intersection, to use the road's bike path to travel 0.7 mile to Barber Park. The park serves as the official launch site for tubers and rafters floating the Boise River.

Beyond South Eckert Road heading toward the reservoir, you come to the Idaho Department of Parks and Recreation headquarters at about 6.5 miles. On weekdays you can drop in to the lobby of the headquarters and pick up tourist brochures. The Shakespeare Festival is located next to the headquarters. There is a restroom trailside.

A potential food stop along the trail is Ben's Crow Inn, near 7.4 miles. Here you can have a seafood or burger meal. After passing Ben's and the Southside Ada County Habitat Area, where bald eagles winter, you'll see the river. Soon, at 8.2 miles, the trail passes under the ID 21 bridge. At the bridge is the Barber Pool Conservation Area, which protects 200 species, including deer, otters, raccoons, and foxes. It is off-limits to visitors.

Next, at 8.6 miles, is the Diversion Dam Power Plant on the right side of the trail. The Greenbelt continues beside ID 21. The Black Cliffs rock-climbing area looms to your left. In the distance you can see climbers braving the vertical basalt rocks.

Enjoy the expanse of the river canyon, surrounded by tall cliffs on both sides of the river. At 10.2 miles the route drops into the tree-sheltered Discovery Unit of Lucky Peak State Park, a day-use fee area on the banks of the Boise River. Continue through the park and on to the LUCKY PEAK LAKE sign at 10.5 miles. Sandy Point Beach at Lucky Peak State Park is just ahead. Take a break and a swim in the small lake with a fountain gushing natural water. Above the beach the Lucky Peak Reservoir holds snow-melted water for

Bicyclists depart from the Lucky Peak State Park day-use area at the Discovery Unit along the Boise River Greenbelt. (Courtesy Natalie Bartley)

recreational, domestic, and irrigation use. The reservoir is a popular fishing and motorboating destination.

After enjoying the terminus of this segment of the Boise River Greenbelt, return the way you came. From Julia Davis Park you could also head out on the northeast and southern segments of the trail. Also, the Greenbelt is located near the Boise Foothills and is considered part of the Ridge to Rivers Trail System. Walkers, mountain bikers, and equestrians use the trails in the system to access approximately 75,000 acres of land in the Foothills. While you're in the Treasure Valley area, give a Foothills trail a try or take in the Nampa Rails to Trails (Trail 45), the Indian Creek Greenbelt (Trail 46), or the Old Boise, Nampa, and Owyhee Rail Bed Trail (Trail R).

Future Plans

Plans are in progress to extend the western end of the Boise River Greenbelt, which links to the Garden City Greenbelt, on to the city of Eagle.

Nearby Attractions

The heart of the Boise River Greenbelt originates next to Julia Davis Park. Stop by the cultural institutions at the park, including the Idaho State Historical Museum, Boise Art Museum, Idaho Black History Museum, Discovery Center of Idaho, and Zoo Boise. You can also catch a ride on the Trolley Tour that originates in the]park. It travels through historic city districts. To visit the nearby Log Cabin Literary Center and the Idaho Anne Frank Human Rights Memorial west of Julia Davis Park, go under the Capital Boulevard underpass. For detailed information on Julia Davis Park attractions, view www.cityofboise.org.

If you're not afraid to get wet, you can join the more than 100,000 people who float the Boise River each year. You can rent an inner tube or raft at the launch at Barber Park and float to the takeout at Ann Morrison Park. Shuttles are available from the takeout back to Barber Park. The season is typically June through August, depending on water levels. There is a day-use fee for parking at Barber Park. For current rental rates and shuttle fees, contact Ada County Parks and Waterways, (208) 577–4575, www.adaweb.net.

If hiking is your pleasure, consider the Ridge to Rivers Trail System. Occupying a prominent position in the Treasure Valley landscape is the Boise Front, consisting of the Foothills leading into the Boise National Forest. The Ridge to Rivers Trail System emerged as a cooperative venture between landowners, government agencies, and other associations. Various ecosystems await exploration, ranging from the valley floor at 2,500 feet elevation to the mountaintops at 7,582 feet. Consider exploring the Old Penitentiary to Table Rock trails, located off the eastern portion of the Boise River Greenbelt between downtown and Lucky Peak Dam. An uphill climb, starting from the Old Penitentiary, will take you to the top of the cliffs for a sweeping view of the Treasure Valley. For information, visit the Ridge to Rivers Trail System Web site, www.ridgetorivers.org. See Appendix A for Treasure Valley bicycle rental shops that sell Ridge to Rivers maps.

48 WOOD RIVER TRAIL

Originating close to the rugged Smoky and Boulder Mountains south of the Sawtooth National Recreation Area in central Idaho, this trail passes through the Wood River Valley. Following on or next to the original railbed, the trail goes by the town of Ketchum near the famous Sun Valley Resort. The valley widens as the trail heads south through the towns of Hailey and Bellevue.

Activities:

Location: Towns of Ketchum, Hailey, and Bellevue, in Blaine County

Length: 20 miles

Surface: Asphalt

Wheelchair access: Due to the dirt and gravel parking lots, the path is not accessible from designated parking sites; however, the trail is wheelchair accessible from street access and neighborhood intersections.

Difficulty: Easy, except for a few moderate hills at the beginning of the trail and at the bridges near 9 miles.

Food: Eateries, grocery stores, and gas stations are just a few blocks from the trail in the towns of Ketchum, Hailey, and Bellevue.

Restrooms: You can find restrooms at Sun Peak Picnic Area trailside between mile 0 and mile 1. There is also one restroom trailside near the Gimlet Bridge near trail mile 9, accessed by going by road or trail from the parking area on East Fork Road.

Seasons: The trail can be used year-round. Between the months of November and April, the trails are groomed for cross-country skiing.

Access and parking: There are many small informal options along the trail. The following have been identified by the trail managers as designated parking areas for trail access, starting from the northern terminus at Hulen Meadows and heading south. Currently, many of the parking sites do not have formal names, so titles refer to landmarks and roads in the area.

- Hulen Meadows: Take Idaho Highway 75 north from Bellevue and Hailey into the town of Ketchum, where ID 75 turns into Main Street. Continue north past the turn for Sun Valley. From the stoplight on Main Street/ID 75 and Saddle Road, continue north 1.9 miles to Hulen Meadows Road and turn left, then immediately left again into the large dirt trailhead parking lot. The trail starts on the west side of the lot.

- River Run: From Hulen Meadows Road, head south on ID 75, passing through Ketchum, where ID 75 turns into Main Street. At 3.4 miles from Hulen Meadows Road, turn right at the sign RIVER RUN LIFT AREA. Turn immediately left into trailhead parking. A feeder trail leads you to the main trail in a few hundred yards.

- Broadway Run, near hospital and trail tunnel: From the River Run Lift Area trailhead, take Main Street/ID 75 south for 1.9 miles. Turn left on Broadway Run and immediately right into the parking lot near the trail.

- Box Car Bend Overview: Take ID 75 south from Broadway Run, travel 2.3 miles, and turn left into a roadside dirt lot parallel to ID 75. The trail is on the east side of the parking lot.

- East Fork Road: From the Box Car Bend parking lot, head south on ID 75 for 0.7 mile; turn left at the stoplight onto East Fork Road. Continue for a block, crossing over the trail. Park on the left.

- Ohio Gulch Road: Head 1.7 miles from the stoplight at East Fork Road and ID 75. Turn left onto Ohio Gulch Road, which is also at highway mile marker 121. Then turn immediately right into the dirt lot. Pick up the trail to the west of the lot.

- Buttercup Road: Take ID 75 south to highway mile marker 120 on the fringes of Hailey. Turn left onto Buttercup Road, then immediately left into the dirt parking lot. Pick up the trail next to the lot.

- Myrtle Street: This parking/access area is located in the northern portion of Hailey. To reach it, return to ID 75 and head south from highway mile marker 120, turning left onto Myrtle Street at 3.2 miles from the Buttercup Road and ID 75 intersection. (ID 75 turns to Main Street in Hailey.) Continue on Myrtle Street for 0.3 mile, crossing the trail and arriving at a stop sign. Turn left onto Buttercup Road, then immediately left into a small dirt parking lot. The trail is to the west of the lot.

- Fox Acres Road Trailhead: Officially noted as a trailhead, this is located on the south side of the town of Hailey. Reach it by driving 1.3 miles from the intersection of Myrtle Street and Main Street. Turn left onto Fox Acres Road at the stoplight. Immediately turn left again into the small gravel trailhead lot near the Native Arboretum foot trail. Join the paved Wood River Trail to the east of the lot.

- Spruce Street: This parking/access area is located in the northern portion of Bellevue. To reach it, head south on ID 75 from Fox Acres Road. Drive about 3.5 miles and turn left onto Spruce Street upon entering Bellevue. Go 1 block to Second Street and park. The trail parallels Second Street. If you miss Spruce Street, turn left on Ash Street at the gas station on ID 75. Go 1 block to the trail.

- Gannett Road–Bellevue southern terminus: From ID 75 and Fox Acres Road in south Hailey, head south to Bellevue. Travel 4.5 miles to highway mile marker 111, in the southern part of Bellevue. Turn left onto Gannett Road and find a parking spot along the road in the industrial area. The trail starts to the northeast.

Rentals: In Ketchum, bicycles, cross-country skis, and snowshoes can be rented at Backwoods Mountain Sports, 711 North Main Street, (208) 726–8818, www.backwoodsmountainsports.com; or at The Elephant's Perch, 280 East Avenue, (208) 726–3497, www.elephantsperch.com. Bikes can also be rented in Ketchum at Formula Sports, 460 North Main Street, (208) 726–3194, www.formulasports.com; or at Sturtos, 340 North Main Street, (208) 726–4512, www.sturtos.com. In Hailey, bikes and cross-country skis can be rented at Sturtos, 1 West Carbonate Street, (208) 788–7847, www.sturtos.com.

Contact: Blaine County Recreation District, (208) 788–2117, www.bcrd.org

Bus routes: Contact KART Peak Bus, (208) 726–7576 or (208) 726–4638, or visit www.kart-sunvalley.com.

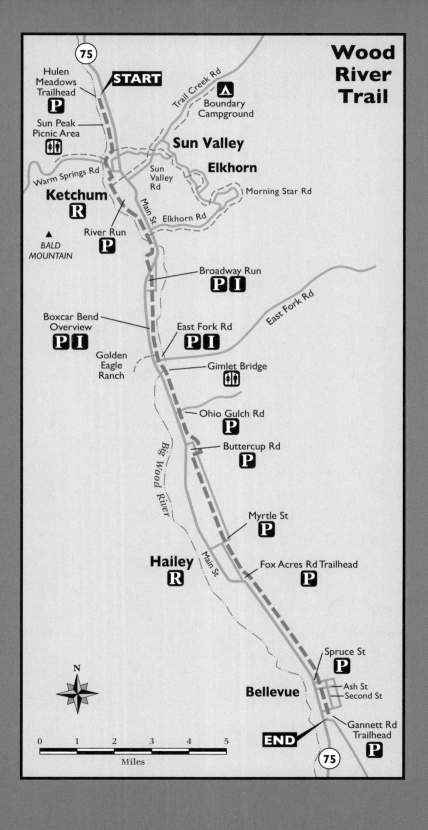

From the trail's start in the upper reaches of the valley with eye-popping views of snowcapped mountains, to the open terrain with feeder canyons at the southern end of the trail, visitors move through a segment of Idaho's rich history. Following the Wood River and ID 75, the trail is dotted with educational signs that identify points of interest and nature-related information on the local wetlands, geology, and plants.

Popular year-round, the trail experiences a steady flow of visitors. During the winter the rail trail is groomed for cross-country skiing, with snow possible between November and April. In spring, summer, and autumn the trail is enjoyed by both local residents and visitors to this popular outdoor recreation destination.

Mining was once integral to this area, beginning with the rush of 1879. The Wood River mining district was once Idaho's major mining area, producing lead and silver. Cattle- and sheep-raising also gained momentum here. The Union Pacific served the mines and livestock industries via a spur line that ran from Shoshone to Ketchum, with the Wood River Branch–Oregon Short Line Railroad reaching the Ketchum Depot in 1884.

The Wood River Trail starts beside the Wood River at the Hulen Meadows Trailhead north of Ketchum. (Courtesy Natalie Bartley)

A fisherman accesses the Wood River near the 208-foot Cold Springs Pegram-style rail-road bridge on the Wood River Trail south of Ketchum. (Courtesy Natalie Bartley)

Further contributing to the growth of the area was the development of the first destination ski resort in the United States. Averell Harriman, a chairman of the Union Pacific, had a strong vision of creating a prominent resort, and he helped to develop the Sun Valley Resort, which still stands as a world-renowned ski and snowboard destination. Railroads played a major role in the resort's success. In the late 1930s the Union Pacific Railroad helped to build the ski slopes and ski lifts. The railroad owned and managed the Sun Valley Resort between 1936 and 1968.

In 1987 the Idaho Department of Transportation bought the spur line, known as the Oregon Short Line, and in turn the Blaine County Recreation District picked it up. The original railroad right-of-way was developed into a multiuse nonmotorized rail trail that is part of an extensive system of trails. This network of trails includes the paved trail on the railbed, known as the Wood River Trail, as well as the Nordic ski trail system in the North Valley Trails. It also includes the pathway called the Harriman Trail, which travels between the Sawtooth National Recreation Area headquarters and Galena

Lodge to the north. As you drive ID 75 between the towns of Ketchum and Bellevue, the Wood River railtrail is visible along the highway.

Starting at the northern terminus at Hulen Meadows at mile 0, the paved trail runs downstream from north to south along the Wood River. Be sure to glance back frequently for stellar views of the mountains up the valley that hold a snowpack on the summits into midsummer.

Shortly, at mile 0.5, you encounter the Sun Peak Picnic Area on your right. This is one of the few trailside restrooms, so consider using it. In addition to the water source here, there are a number of water fountains along the trail. Bald Mountain, with a height of 9,150 feet, pops into view and will remain along your right side for the upper reaches of the trail. It is nicknamed "Baldy" and even looks like a bald head.

As you leave this area, the trail has a few slight hills and bends as it goes by aspen trees and purple lupine wildflowers. At mile 1 the woods open up and you get a full view of Baldy. The Sun Valley Resort, of which Baldy is a part, has the largest snow-making system in the United States.

Continuing south, the Big Wood Public Golf Course appears to the left, on the east side of ID 75, as you pass residences on the west side of the trail. The Ketchum city sign comes into view at about mile 1.8. Between mile 2 and mile 3, the trail crosses over a number of intersections and winds its way through the western edges of Ketchum and back to the Wood River. Watch for the tall wooden trail signs that mark every road crossing, and keep Baldy on your right. Consider a side trip into town for refreshments at one of the many fine eateries located just a few blocks from the trail.

Pass by Big Wood Preschool and Kindergarten School at 2.3 miles. Baldy looms large to your right, then the Ketchum Skate Park. Just before the Rotary Park, turn left at the intersection and cross the road, picking up the trail as it runs on the east side of the road. Shortly you turn right and cross Warm Springs Road and reenter the trail. Next you weave through the parking lots of the Ernest Hemingway Elementary School, then along Hemingway Lane. Turn right on Eighth Street toward Baldy. At 2.8 miles you will see the trail marker at Atkinson Park. Turn left and continue on the marked trail on Second Avenue over the back roads of Ketchum, passing condominiums and arriving at Sixth Avenue. Cross over Sixth Avenue and continue to the right on the trail, then curve left to trail mile marker 3.

At this point the trail returns to the river and becomes peaceful, away from the hustle of Ketchum. Pass by condominiums between mile

Boxcar Bend Overview on the Wood River Trail is used to access the river for fishing.
(Courtesy Natalie Bartley)

3 and mile 3.4. Soon you will come to a trail information sign with water at the site. Continue past a large parking area on the left that serves as ski lift parking in the winter. Shortly after, you cross over a bridge trestle at 3.7 miles. In-line skaters need to be careful on the crossing. The wood is roughly cut and generates a rugged ride.

Built in 1883, this bridge is one of the oldest of its type in Idaho. It is the last link of the Wood River Branch of the Oregon Short Line.

After leaving the bridge, the trail goes along wooded areas near the river, where you might see a red or gray fox or even deer. Take a glance north for views of the distant mountain peaks. After 4 miles the trail moves left off the railbed. You can see the rails of the original line as the trail quickly returns to the railbed.

Just beyond 5 miles is a famous bridge trestle named Cold Springs Bridge. This frequently photographed icon is one of only ten known Pegram bridges still standing in the United States. Idaho is fortunate to have seven of the bridges, with two on the Wood River Trail. This one is a 208-foot single span that was first used by the Oregon Short Line to transport lead and zinc. Between 1936 and 1981 trains crossed this bridge as they shuttled skiers from California to Ketchum.

Rail bridges vary based on their unique truss designs, of which there are over thirty variations. A truss is composed of structural triangles placed together with riveted or pinned connections. The Pegram truss is a blend between the Warren and Parker trusses.

Shortly after passing over the bridge, the trail goes through a tunnel under a road at the Saint Luke's Wood River Medical Center near 5.6 miles. A Healing Garden and water fountain lie trailside. Continue on the trail through another tunnel beneath ID 75.

From this point you will travel between the highway and residential areas, though the route has open views of the widening valley. Many side canyons enter from the east and west as you head toward the town of Hailey and Bellevue beyond. An assortment of neighborhood and road access points present themselves, and you can use them to exit the trail if you choose to. Avoid private roads if using informal parking for your vehicle.

Just past 7 miles you arrive at Gimlet Road. Consider stopping for a visit at the Sawtooth Botanical Garden, located on the west side of the trail. Another bridge crossing is at 7.6 miles. Along the way you will pass cottonwood trees and chokecherry bushes, and large homes set away from the trail. Shortly the Wood River comes into view at 7.7 miles, with the Boxcar Bend Overview just ahead.

Situated above the river, the overlook features interpretive signs describing local fishing regulations and how the area earned the name Boxcar. Old railroad cars, vehicles, and ski gondolas were once used to prevent erosion of the river's bank. Now modern techniques are used. Take the established path to the river's edge to enjoy a closer look at this waterway or try some fishing.

As the trail approaches 8 miles, the valley spreads out as you travel between the river and the highway. To continue toward Hailey, take a left at about 8.5 miles when you come to a Y-intersection in the trail. Go over the East Fork Road, and before you head south, read about the East Fork mines on the information sign.

Near 8.7 miles the trail runs beside a gravel portion of the original railbed and crosses the 217-foot Gimlet Bridge, another Pegram-style trestle bridge, which hikers and horseback riders can use. Wheeled users should stay on the paved trail and cross on the newer bridge. Between the two bridges sits a little park with a shaded picnic table and an old-fashioned

Trail users can cross the Wood River via the 217-foot Gimlet Pegram-style railroad bridge or use the smooth new trail bridge over the Wood River on the Wood River Trail south of East Fork Road. (Courtesy Natalie Bartley)

water pump with potable water. This area is also a fishing access trailhead. There is a toilet trailside.

After crossing the bridge, start up the biggest hill on the trail, which shortly rejoins the railbed after the detour. At about 9.3 miles the route flattens and the trail moves away from the noise of the road. The valley widens, which results in the wind velocity increasing and moving up the valley during the afternoons.

Cross over Ohio Gulch Road after 10 miles. You can see the old railbed to your right. Between 10 and 13 miles the trail alternates between small road crossings, tiny ranches, vegetated areas, large homes, and the Valley Club private golf course.

By 13 miles you begin to enter the outskirts of the town of Hailey, passing a CITY OF HAILEY sign trailside at about 14.2 miles. While passing on the trail through residential areas, you may get whiffs of barbecues or laundry soap as the locals go about their daily lives.

The downtown area is only 4 blocks to your right if you want to stop for food and beverages. International cuisines greet the hungry traveler. Try Mexican, Thai, German, Japanese, or fast food if you desire.

Watch for the tall wooden signs that mark the trail, such as this one on the north side of Bellevue. (Courtesy Natalie Bartley)

An established trailhead comes into view on the south side of Hailey at about 15.4 miles. The corner of Fox Acres Road and ID 75 serve as the location of the Blaine County Native Plant Arboretum. Take time to walk the short path and view native pine trees, fir trees, and berry plants. The site is the results of local students' efforts.

Continue south to Bellevue, passing the Friedman Memorial Airport, which is to the right. Pass by open fields and housing construction projects. The original railbed lies to your right, serving as a buffer between the trail and highway. Mourning doves and other birds can be seen along this rural stretch.

At about 17.7 miles you enter the north edge of Bellevue, and by 18.2 miles you are in Bellevue. If you go 1 block west from the trail, you can get on Main Street and find food and beverages nearby.

Numerous road crossings may slow your travel. No worries; it is a small town with an easy pace. At the south end of town you pass ranches with horses, and at 20 miles the paved trail ends at Gannett Road. You will see the gravel path that is the railroad right-of-way that continues to U.S. Highway 20. It is used by runners, equestrians, motorized vehicles, ranch machinery, and snowmobiles.

Nearby Attractions

Bicycling, hiking, fishing, skiing, and camping are but a few of the outdoor activities that this region is famous for. Spend some additional time enjoying the mountains.

- Sawtooth National Recreation Area
  This recreation area contains 756,000 acres of forested, mountainous terrain. The headquarters is located 8 miles north of Ketchum on ID 75. (208) 727–5013

- Wood River Trail
  Auxiliary to the 20-mile right-of-way paved trail are paved spurs linking to Sun Valley, Elkhorn, and East Fork, adding another 10 miles to the system.

- Harriman Trail
  This trail features an 18-mile pathway between Sawtooth National Recreation Area and the Galena Lodge Trail System.

- North Valley Trails Nordic Ski Trail System
  Comprised of 30 miles of moderate-to-difficult single-track trails, the system includes Galena Lodge Trails and other trails in the Sawtooth National Recreation Area.

- Sun Valley Resort
  A four-season destination with easy access to area attractions. (800) 786–8259, www.sunvalley.com

Future Plans

Additional interpretive signs will be placed along the trail. There is a possibility of extending the trail into emerging communities in the valley.

More Rail Trails

R OLD BOISE, NAMPA, AND OWYHEE RAIL BED TRAIL

Located at the fringe of the Snake River Birds of Prey National Conservation Area, the 500-foot-long Guffey rail bridge at Celebration Park serves as a gateway to 475,000 acres of open sagebrush desert. Start by crossing the renovated rail bridge and continue upstream on dirt trails along the Snake River. The Union Pacific as well as other rail companies once owned the original railbed, known as the Stoddard Line. Abandoned in 1948, Celebration Park purchased the old rail bridge in 1989. The park renovated the bridge for foot traffic. It is a historic icon used by recreationists to access motorized and nonmotorized trails in the conservation area

Activities:

Location: Near Melba, in Canyon County

Length: 500-foot-long rail bridge accesses the trail system in the Snake River Birds of Prey National Conservation Area.

Surface: Wooden boards on bridge, dirt trails in conservation area.

Wheelchair access: The decked bridge is wheelchair accessible.

Difficulty: The bridge crossing is easy. Trails in the conservation area are easy to moderate.

Food: Food services in the town of Melba include a cafe at the supermarket and a bar that serves hot cooked food.

Restrooms: There are restrooms at the main parking lot at Celebration Park.

Seasons: The trail can be used year-round.

Access and parking: To get to the Guffey Bridge at Celebration Park, take Idaho Highway 45 south from Nampa to Ferry Road. Turn left on Ferry Road and drive about a mile to a T-intersection in the road. Turn right at the T onto Hill Road, which becomes Warren Spur Road. From the T, continue for about a mile until you see the cattle feedlot. Turn right on Sinkder Road and drive to the Guffey Bridge. There is a small parking lot at the bridge. To get to the large paved parking lot at Celebration Park, turn left at the bridge and drive on the paved road into the parking lot.

Rentals: See Appendix A for bicycle rentals in the Treasure Valley.

Contact: Celebration Park, (208) 495–2745, www.canyoncounty.org

Bus routes: None

S NORTHERN PACIFIC TRAIL

Traveling through deep forests and up a steady incline to Lookout Pass on the Idaho/Montana border, this trail is known for its remoteness, scenery, and potential wildlife sightings. It is a continuation of the Union Pacific Railroad that served the Silver Valley in Idaho. During the winter it is a popular trail for snowmobiles. The town of Mullan is the start of the multiuse Northern Pacific Trail and the eastern terminus of the nonmotorized Trail of the Coeur d' Alenes.

Activities:

Location: Mullan, in Shoshone County

Length: 11.7 miles

Surface: Asphalt road, dirt, and gravel

Wheelchair access: The trail is wheelchair accessible during the first 3 miles, where it is an asphalt rural road.

Difficulty: Moderate to difficult. There is a steep climb as the trail progresses to Lookout Pass.

Food: There is a restaurant in Mullan.

Restrooms: There are restrooms at the Mullan Trailhead parking area, East Shoshone Park, Stevens Lake Trailhead, and Lookout Pass Trailhead.

Seasons: The trail can be used year-round. Snow may be on the trail from late October to late May. During the winter the trail is heavily used by snowmobiles.

Access and parking: To reach the western terminus in Mullan coming from western Idaho, take exit 68 off Interstate 90. The off-ramp becomes River Street and practically puts you at the trailhead. Travel on River Street, driving toward the town of Mullan, which is visible from the exit. Take a left off River Street onto Second Street, then turn immediately into the trail's western terminus parking lot. The trail begins at the eastern end of the parking area and starts as an asphalt road, which runs for about 3 miles, until just before East Shoshone Park. Follow the signs at each intersection to stay on the road/trail, which turns into a dirt and gravel road.

To reach the eastern terminus, head east on I–90 and take exit 0 at the Idaho/Montana border. Turn right off the ramp and right again into the Lookout Pass Ski and Recreation Area. Park in the large lot. Look for the signs directing you onto the trail.

Rentals: Mountain bikes, cross-country skis, and snowshoes can be rented at the eastern terminus at Lookout Pass Ski and Recreation Area, (208) 744–1301, www.skilookout.com. See Appendix A for additional rental options in northern Idaho.

Contact: For trail information, visit the Friends of the Coeur d'Alene Trails Idaho Panhandle Web site, friendsofcdatrails.org.

Bus routes: None

T YELLOWSTONE BRANCH LINE RAILROAD ROW TRAIL

Known for scenic views of rivers, wildlife, and mountain ranges, this trail runs on a railroad right-of-way through the Caribou-Targhee National Forest. It goes from near the town of Ashton to the Montana border. Visitors travel along 4 miles of the Warm River, cross the Henry's Fork of the Snake River, and pass through a long tunnel. The Teton and Centennial Mountain Ranges are visible from the trail.

Activities:

Location: Ashton and Island Park, in Fremont County

Length: 38 miles, of which 3.2 miles are designated for nonmotorized trail use at the southern end between Warm Springs Campground and the Bear Gulch Trailhead.

Surface: Gravel

Wheelchair access: There is no wheelchair access along this trail.

Difficulty: Easy

Food: Eateries can be found in Ashland and Island Park.

Restrooms: There are restrooms at the Bear Gulch Trailhead and the Warm River Campground.

Seasons: The trail can be used year-round. Beyond the 3.2-mile nonmotorized section, the trail is used by off-road vehicles in the summer and snowmobiles in the winter.

Access and parking: The southern nonmotorized segment is accessed at Warm River Campground by taking Idaho Highway 47, the Mesa Falls Scenic Byway, 10 miles east out of Ashton. Turn right into the campground. To get to the trailhead at Bear Gulch, continue east on ID 47 for about 3 miles to the Bear Gulch pullout on the left side of the highway. This lot is plowed in the winter and serves as the only access point during snow season. Many Forest Service roads pass over the trail. Procure a Forest Service map.

Rentals: None

Contact: Caribou-Targhee National Forest's Ashton Ranger District, (208) 652–7442, Island Park Ranger District, (208) 558–7301; or www.fs.fed.us/r4/caribou-targhee

Bus routes: None

APPENDIX A
RENTAL INFORMATION

IDAHO

Northern Idaho

Bicycles
Great Cycles Touring Company
643 C Street
Plummer 83851
(208) 686–1568

Bicycles
Pedal Pushers Bike Rental & Repair
101 North Coeur d'Alene Avenue
Harrison 83833
(208) 689–3436
www.bikenorthidaho.com

Bicycles
Excelsior Cycle
21 Railroad Avenue
Kellogg 83837
(208) 786-3751

Bicycles, Cross-country Skis, and
    Snowshoes
Lookout Pass Ski and Recreation
    Area
I–90 Exit 0
Mullan 83843
(208) 744–1301
www.skilookout.com

Bicycles
Mountain View Cyclery and Fitness
306 Spokane Street
Post Falls 83854
(208) 457–8439
www.mountainviewcyclery.com

Bicycles, Cross-country Skis, and
    Snowshoes
Vertical Earth
308 Coeur d'Alene Avenue
Coeur d'Alene 83814
(208) 667-5503
www.verticalearth.com

Latah County

Bicycles
Paradise Creek Bicycles
513 South Main Street
Moscow 83843
(208) 882–0703

Snowshoes
Follett's Mountain Sports
407 South Washington Street
Moscow 83843
(208) 882–6735

Bicycles, Cross-country Skis, and
    Snowshoes
University of Idaho Outdoor Pro-
    gram
Outdoor Rental Center
Student Recreation Center
1000 Paradise Creek Street
Moscow 83844–1230
(208) 885–6170
www.campusrec.uidaho.edu
    /outdoor

Valley County

Bicycles and Snowshoes
Pro Peak Sports
412 West Roseberry Road
Donnelly 83615
(208) 325-3323
www.propeaksports.com

Bicycles, Cross-country Skis, and
 Snowshoes
West Mountain Gear and Grind
270 N. Main Street
Donnelly 83615
(208) 325-8191
www.gearandgrind.com

Bicycles, Cross-country Skis, and
 Snowshoes
Alpine Sciences
401 South 3rd Street
McCall 83638
(208) 634-4707
www.alpinesciences.com

Bicycles, Cross-country Skis, and
 Snowshoes
Gravity Sports
503 Pine Street
McCall 83638
(208) 634–8530
www.gravitysportsidaho.com

Bicycles, Cross-country Skis, and
 Snowshoes
Home Town Sports
300 Lenora
McCall 83638
(208) 634–2302
www.home-town-sports.com

New Meadows

Bicycles, Cross-country Skis, and
 Snowshoes
Mud Creek Outdoor Gear
202 Virginia Avenue
New Meadows 83654
(208) 347–2025
www.mudcreekoutdoorgear.com

Treasure Valley

Bicycles and Snowshoes
Bikes 2 Boards
3525 State Street
Boise 83703
(208) 343–0208
www.bikes2boards.com

Bicycles, Cross-country Skis, and
 Snowshoes
Idaho Mountain Touring
1310 West Main Street
Boise 83702
(208) 336–3854
www.idahomountaintouring.com

Blaine County

Bicycles
Sturtos
340 North Main Street
Ketchum 83340
(208) 726–4512
www.sturtos.com

Cross-country Skis
Formula Sports
460 North Main Street
Ketchum 83340
(208) 726–3194
www.formulasports.com

Bicycles and Cross-country Skis
Sturtos
1 West Carbonate Street
Hailey, 83333
(208) 788–7847
www.sturtos.com

Bicycles, Cross-country Skis, and
    Snowshoes
The Elephant's Perch
280 East Avenue
Ketchum 83340
(208) 726–3497
www.elephantsperch.com

Bicycles, Cross-country Skis, and
    Snowshoes
Backwoods Mountain Sports
711 North Main Street
Ketchum 83340
(208) 726–8818
www.backwoodsmountain
    sports.com

APPENDIX B
ORGANIZATIONS FOR ADVOCACY, EDUCATION, AND INFORMATION

Adventure Cycling Association
P.O. Box 83082
Missoula, MT 59807–8308
(800) 755–2453
www.adv-cycling.org

BBTC (Backcountry Bicycle Trails Club)
P.O. Box 21288
Seattle, WA 98111–3288
www.bbtc.org

Bicycle Alliance of Washington
311 3rd Avenue South
Seattle, WA 98111
(206) 224–9252
www.bicyclealliance.org

Bike North Idaho
www.bikenorthidaho.com

Bike Works
3709 S. Ferdinand Street
Seattle, WA 98118
(206) 725–9408
www.bikeworks.org

Cascade Bicycle Club
P.O. Box 15165
Seattle, WA 98115
(206) 522–3222
www.cascade.org

Friends of the Coeur d'Alene Trails
friendsofcdatrails.org

Friends of the Weiser River Trail
3494 Rush Creek Road
Cambridge, ID 83610
(888) MY-TRAIL
www.weiserrivertrail.org

International In-line Skate Association
(IISA)
www.iisa.org

The Latah Trail Foundation
www.latahtrailfoundation.org

League of American Bicyclists
1612 K Street, NW, Suite 800
Washington, D.C. 20006
(202) 822–1333
www.bikeleague.org

Moscow Area Mountain Bike
Association
www.bikemoscow.org

North Idaho Centennial Trail Foundation
www.northidahocentennialtrail.org

Pullman Civic Trust—Bill Chipman
Palouse Trail
www.pullmancivictrust.org/chipman.
html

Ridge to Rivers Trail System
www.ridgetorivers.org

Skate Northwest
www.skatenw.com

Southwest Idaho Mountain
Biking Association
www.swimba.org

Tri–City Bicycle Club
P.O. Box 465
Richmond, WA 99352
www.tricitybicycleclub.org

Valley County Pathways
www.valleycountypathways.org

ABOUT THE AUTHOR

A Pennsylvania native, Natalie L. Bartley moved to Idaho in 1987 to work as an outdoor program manager and has lived there ever since. When she is not working as a freelance writer, she can be found mountain biking, whitewater kayaking, crosscountry skiing, or exploring the outdoors with her yellow Labrador retriever.

She has over 500 articles to her credit in publications including *Paddler, Canoe and Kayak, Ski Patrol, National Ski Areas Association Journal, Women in the Outdoors,* and the *Idaho Statesman.* Natalie is a certified kayak and ski instructor, and a member of the Outdoor Writers Association of America, the North American Snowsport Journalists Association Western Region, and the Northwest Outdoor Writers Association.